A Short Course in Intellectual
Self-Defense

A Short Course in Intellectual Self-Defense

NORMAND BAILLARGEON

Translated by Andréa Schmidt

Illustrations by Charb

SEVEN STORIES PRESS

New York | Toronto | London | Melbourne

Originally published in French under the title *Petit Cours d'autodéfense intellectuelle* in
2005, by Lux Éditeur (Québec)
First English-language edition published by Seven Stories Press, January 2008

The English-language version was translated with the support of the Société de développe-
ment des entreprises culturelles du Québec (SODEC).

Seven Stories Press
140 Watts Street
New York, NY 10013
http://www.sevenstories.com

In Canada: Publishers Group Canada, 559 College Street, Suite 402, Toronto, ON M6G 1A9

In the UK: Turnaround Publisher Services Ltd., Unit 3, Olympia Trading Estate, Coburg
Road, Wood Green, London N22 6TZ

In Australia: Palgrave Macmillan, 627 Chapel Street, South Yarra, VIC 3141

College professors may order examination copies of Seven Stories Press titles for a free six-
month trial period. To order, visit http://www.sevenstories.com/textbook or send a fax on
school letterhead to (212) 226-1411.

Library of Congress Cataloging-in-Publication Data:

Baillargeon, Normand, 1958–
   [Petit cours d'autodéfense intellectuelle. English]
   A short course in intellectual self-defense / Normand Baillargeon ; translated by Andrea
Schmidt. -- Seven Stories Press 1st ed.
   · p. cm.
   ISBN 978-1-58322-765-7 (pbk.)
   1. Critical thinking. 2. Belief and doubt. 3. Reasoning. I. Title.

BF441.B26413 2007
121'.6--dc22

                    2007010176

Book design by Jon Gilbert
Printed in the USA

9 8 7 6 5 4 3 2 1

To Martin Gardner, the polymath,
for everything he has taught me.

CONTENTS

Introduction..II

PART ONE: SOME INDISPENSABLE TOOLS FOR
CRITICAL THINKING

1 Language..19

Introduction 20

1.1 Treacherous Words 24

1.2 The Art of Mental Trickery and Manipulation: Some
    Everyday Fallacies 50

2 Mathematics: Those Who Refuse to Be
  Conned, Count!..87

Introduction 87

2.1 Treating Common Forms of Innumeracy 89

2.2 Probability and Statistics 110

PART TWO: ON THE JUSTIFICATION OF BELIEF

3 Personal Experience..171

Introduction 171

3.1 Perceiving 172

3.2 Remembering 189

3.3 Judging 196

4 Empirical and Experimental Science...............223

Introduction   223

4.1 Science and Experimentation   228

4.2 Science and Epistemology   242

4.3 A Few Questions for the Critical Reading of
    Research Results   261

4.4 The SEARCH Model   263

5 The Media..267

Introduction   268

5.1 Another Kind of Democracy   273

5.2 The Propaganda Model of Media   277

5.3 Thirty-one Strategies for Fostering a
    Critical Approach to the Media   290

Conclusion...307

Appendix: Independent Media Guide.............309

Suggested Readings...............................321

Notes..327

About the Author..................................333

About Seven Stories Press.........................335

I have done everything I can to recognize my debts to all the authors I borrowed ideas from. If I failed to do so in a particular case, please let me know so that I correct this omission in a future edition.

—N. B.

INTRODUCTION

To doubt everything or to believe everything are two equally convenient solutions; both dispense with the necessity of reflection.

—HENRI POINCARÉ

The slumber of reason breeds monsters.

—FRANCISCO DE GOYA

My personal feeling is that citizens of the democratic societies should undertake a course of intellectual self-defense to protect themselves from manipulation and control, and to lay the basis for more meaningful democracy.[1]

—NOAM CHOMSKY

This little book has emerged from the convergence of two of my concerns. They are not mine alone—far from it—but that does not make them any less vivid. Lacking the ability to justify each of them, which would require an entire book of its own and which, in any case, is unnecessary here, permit me simply to state them.

The first of these concerns could be described as epistemological, and includes two series of worries. First, I am concerned about the prevalence of all the beliefs that circulate in our societies under names such as paranormal, esotericism, or New Age, and which include beliefs and practices as diverse as telekinesis; telepathy; past lives; kidnapping by extraterrestrials; the powers of crystals; miracle cures; exercise programs and equipment that produce immediate results with no effort at all; communication with

dead people; a range of applied Asian mysticism; chiroprac-
tic, homeopathic, astrological, and all sorts of so-called alternative medicines; feng shui; Ouija boards; the possibility
of bending spoons by means of thought alone; police re-
sorting to the use of psychics; cartomancy; and . . . I could
go on.[2]

Furthermore, I am concerned—perhaps I should even
say appalled—by what appears to me to be the truly deplorable state of reflection, knowledge, and rationality in large
strata of academic and intellectual life. I will say it as tem-
perately as possible: I am staggered by some of the things
that are done and said in certain sectors of the contemporary university, where a lack of education and charlatanry
are flourishing. And I am not the only one to think so.

My second concern is political, and has to do with the
access of citizens of democracies to an understanding of
the world in which we live—to rich, serious, and plural information that allows us to understand this world and to
change it. I will be frank: like many other people, I worry
about the state of our media, about media concentration
and convergence, and the way it is driven by the market. I
worry about the propagandic role that the media have come
to play in society at a time when each of us is bombarded
with information and discourses trying to obtain our approval and make us act in certain ways.

We know that in a participatory democracy, education is
the other major institution that has a privileged obligation
to contribute to producing a sense of citizenship worthy
of the name. But it is also in bad shape. Recent developments have provided serious cause for worry: for example,
we seem to be blithely giving up the pursuit of the ideal of

a liberal education for each person. This makes me particularly indignant, given that this training is more necessary for future citizens today than ever before. The client-centered mentality and economic reductionism that one finds in too many people these days, and particularly amongst the decision-makers of the education world, constitute, in my view, more serious reasons to be uneasy about the future of participatory democracy.

But if it is true, as I think it is, that each advance of irrationalism, of stupidity, of propaganda and manipulation, can by confronted by means of critical thinking and reflexive assessment, then, without deluding ourselves, we can take a certain comfort in spreading the art of critical thinking. From this point of view, exercising intellectual self-defense is an act of citizenship. It is what has motivated me to write this little book, which offers exactly this: an introduction to critical thinking.

What you will find in the following pages does not purport to be new or original. What I advance here is well-known, at least amongst those who are familiar with scientific literature or writings on critical and skeptical thinking. Nonetheless, I have tried to make it an accessible synthesis by presenting, as simply and clearly as possible, the concepts and skills which seem to me to be necessary for every citizen to master.

Here, then, is what you will find in this book.

In the first part, entitled "Some Indispensable Tools for Critical Thinking," I begin by examining language and studying certain properties of words, before reviewing some useful notions of logic and examining the principal fallacies. The second chapter offers an overview of "citizen mathematics." It deals with common forms of innumeracy, probability, statistics, and forms of data presentation.

The second part of the book, "On the Justification of Belief," deals with this issue in three particular domains: personal experience, science, and the media. In other words, we will try to clarify in what cases, on what conditions, and to what extent we can hold a proposition true when it is justified by our personal experience, by recourse to experimentation, and by the media.

If the study of critical thinking is a new thing for you, I am well aware that this description does not tell you very much, and that you still do not know what exactly is meant by "critical thinking" or "intellectual self-defense." The rest of this book is intended to explain exactly that. In the meantime, and to close this introduction, I would like to suggest a little game that may go some way to satisfying your curiosity, and may even rouse it further.

In the box below, you will find a passage taken from the final work published by the late Carl Sagan (1934–1996) during his lifetime. A reputable astronomer and an exemplary popularizer of science, Sagan also worked hard to make critical thinking known and to encourage its practice. The text I cite is adapted from a passage in which he offers a collection of precepts of critical thinking that he called a "Baloney Detection Kit." Read it carefully. I suspect that some of his entries will seem a little bit obscure. But I am also convinced that, when you have finished reading this book, you will understand perfectly not only what Sagan meant, but also, and above all, why it is so important to practice these precepts. If that is indeed the case, neither you nor I will have wasted our time.

Carl Sagan's Baloney Detection Kit

(Excerpts)

• Wherever possible there must be independent confirmation of the "facts."

• Encourage substantive debate on the evidence by knowledgeable proponents of all points of view.

• Arguments from authority carry little weight—"authorities" have made mistakes in the past. They will do so again in the future. Perhaps a better way to say it is that in science there are no authorities; at most, there are experts.

• Spin more than one hypothesis and don't jump on the first idea that comes to mind.

• Try not to get overly attached to a hypothesis just because it's yours. . . . Ask yourself why you like the idea. Compare it fairly with the alternatives. See if you can find reasons for rejecting it. If you don't, others will.

• Quantify. If whatever it is you're explaining has some measure, some numerical quantity attached to it, you'll be much better able to discriminate among competing hypotheses. What is vague and qualitative is open to many explanations. Of course there are truths to be sought in the many qualitative issues we are obliged to confront, but finding them is more challenging.

• If there's a chain of argument, every link in the chain must work (including the premise)—not just most of them.

• Occam's Razor. This convenient rule-of-thumb urges us when faced with two hypotheses that explain the data *equally well* to choose the simpler.

• Always ask whether the hypothesis can be, at least in principle, falsified.

Propositions that are un-testable, un-falsifiable are not worth much. Consider the grand idea that our Universe and everything in it is just an elementary particle—an electron, say—in a much bigger Cosmos. But if we can never acquire information from outside our Universe, is not the idea incapable of disproof? You must be able to check assertions out. Inveterate skeptics must be given the chance to follow your reasoning, to duplicate your experiments and see if they get the same result.

The reliance on carefully designed and controlled experiments is key. . . . We will not learn much from mere contemplation. . . . If, for example, a new medicine is alleged to cure a disease 20 percent of the time, we must make sure that a control population, taking a dummy sugar pill which as far as the subjects know might be the new drug, does not also experience spontaneous remission of the disease 20 percent of the time.

Variables must be separated. Suppose you're seasick, and given both an acupressure bracelet and 50 milligrams of meclizine. You find the unpleasantness vanishes. What did it—the bracelet or the pill? You can tell only if you take the one without the other, next time you're seasick. . . .

Often the experiment must be done "double-blind." . . .

In addition to teaching us what to do when evaluating a claim to knowledge, any good baloney detection kit must also teach us what not to do. It helps us recognize the most common and perilous fallacies of logic and rhetoric.

Carl Sagan, *The Demon-Haunted World: Science as a Candle in the Dark* (New York: Ballantine Books, 1996).

Part One
SOME INDISPENSABLE TOOLS FOR CRITICAL THINKING

CHAPTER I

LANGUAGE

*It would not be impossible to prove with sufficient
repetition and psychological understanding of the people
concerned that a square is in fact a circle. What after
all are a square and a circle? They are mere words and
words can be molded until they clothe ideas in disguise.*
—JOSEPH GOEBBELS, Nazi Minister for Public
Enlightenment and Propaganda

*When words lose their meaning, people lose their
freedom.*
—CONFUCIUS

How many feet does a pig have?
Four.
*And what if we call its tail "foot," then how many feet
does it have?*
Five.
*No: you can't change a tail into a foot simply by calling
it a foot.*
—ANONYMOUS CHILDREN'S RIDDLE

*Xanthus [his master] commanded [Aesop] to buy the
best there was. He bought only language. The appetizer,
main course, the palate cleanser, all were languages.
And what is there that is better than language? Aesop
carried on: It's the connection to civil life, the key to
science, the organ of truth and reason. Ah, well, said
Xanthus, tomorrow buy me the worst there is. The next
day, Aesop served the same dishes, saying that language
is the worst thing in the world: It's the mother of all
arguments . . . the source of division and of war . . ."*
—LA FONTAINE, *Life of Aesop*

Introduction

Plato claimed, with great finesse, that wonder is a passion proper to philosophy. What does that mean? There is no doubt that the capacity to feel wonder is a privileged starting point for thought in general, and for philosophy in particular. In fact, it presupposes that one is able to rid oneself of preconceived ideas and prejudices, and tear oneself from the immense force of opinion's inertia to the point of being profoundly stunned by what seemed up to that point insignificant and uninteresting. Then wonder arises and opens trajectories for thought.

Language is such an everyday experience that we rarely stop to wonder at it. We are making a mistake: merely a minute of thought allows most people to discover how tremendously stunning and worthy of our wonder human language is.

An image first used by John Serale may help. In the lower part of our face, we all have a cavity that we can open and close as we wish. Somewhere at the back of this cavity, we have cords of a certain kind; by pushing air through them, it is possible for us to produce innumerable modulations of sound. These sounds are projected out through the cavity and, traveling through the air, they make it to people within their reach who, with the help of other complex mechanisms, are able to receive them. Thanks to these sounds, a huge number of things can be achieved. One can, for example:

—transmit information;
—affirm or deny a fact;
—ask a question;
—provide an explanation;

—exhort someone to do something;

—give an order;

—make a promise;

—get married;

—rouse emotion;

—hypothesize;

—suggest a thought experiment.

And those are just a few of thousands of examples. How is all of that possible? How does language have meaning? How to explain, for example, that we can produce original statements—and even produce as many as we want? And furthermore, how is it possible that those statements are generally perfectly understood by those who hear them for the first time?

As soon as we think about what talking means, innumerable fascinating questions and problems arise that linguists, philosophers, and other thinkers have tried to penetrate for a long time. For the time being, language remains full of mystery.

Although these considerations are fascinating, we will not delve further into them. But since language is able to produce the effects we just described (convince, move, exhort, and so on), it seems clear that we should dwell on it for a while if we wish to assure our intellectual self-defense—even if we don't have a definitive and philosophically satisfying answer to all our questions. Such a powerful tool can prove to be a formidable weapon. For those who might have forgotten or never knew, it is worth remembering how language was used to speak of politics during the twentieth century. To refresh our memory, there is nothing better than to reread George Orwell who invented the notion of

"Newspeak," that strange language that allows one to say, for example, that slavery is freedom.

Orwell on Language and Politics

In our time, political speech and writing are largely the defense of the indefensible. Things like the continuance of British rule in India, the Russian purges and deportations, the dropping of the atom bombs on Japan, can indeed be defended, but only by arguments which are too brutal for most people to face, and which do not square with the professed aims of political parties. Thus political language has to consist largely of euphemism, question-begging and sheer cloudy vagueness. Defenseless villages are bombarded from the air, the inhabitants driven out into the countryside, the cattle machine-gunned, the huts set on fire with incendiary bullets: this is called *pacification*. Millions of peasants are robbed of their farms and sent trudging along the roads with no more than they can carry: this is called *transfer of population* or *rectification of frontiers*. People are imprisoned for years without trial, or shot in the back of the neck or sent to die of scurvy in Arctic lumber camps: this is called *elimination of unreliable elements*.

George Orwell, "Politics and the English Language" (1946), *The Orwell Reader: Fiction, Essays and Reportage*, (Orlano, FL: Harcourt & Brace, 1984), 363.

It's an ancient lesson. History teaches us that people who are sensitive to the power of language are quick to take advantage of it. It seems that, at least in the West, all this began in Sicily around the fifth century BCE, when people whose land had been usurped endeavored to take it back from the evil-doers by launching legal proceedings against them. At that point, the oratory techniques that became rhetoric began to develop.

Soon, teachers were going from city to city, selling the art of speech and promising fame and glory for anyone who learned to master it. They came to be known as "sophists," the name derived from the term "sophism," which refers to invalid reasoning that is put forward with the intention of tricking its audience.

History may be unfair to these teachers, portraying them as charlatans concerned only with the efficacy of their practice and social success. Whatever the case, the sophists had become fully aware of the power that language can confer when it is handled by an able rhetorician. Here is the opinion of Gorgias, one of the sophists, on the matter:

> Speech is a powerful lord. . . . [It] can stop fear and banish grief and create joy and nurture pity. . . . Fearful shuddering and tearful pity and grievous longing come upon [its] hearers, and at the actions and physical sufferings of others in good fortunes and in evil fortunes, through the agency of words, the soul is wont to experience a suffering of its own. . . . Sacred incantations sung with words are bearers of pleasure and banishers of pain, . . . substituting opinion for opinion, taking away one but creating another, [rhetors] make what is incredible and unclear seem true to the eyes of opinion; then, second, logically necessary debates in which a single speech, written with art but not spoken with truth, bends a great crowd and persuades. . . . The effect of speech upon the condition of the soul is comparable to the power of drugs. . . . In the case of speeches, some distress, others delight, some cause fear, others

make the hearers bold, and some drug and bewitch
the soul with a kind of evil persuasion.[1]

In the following pages, we will deal with language as it
relates to intellectual self-defense.

Our trajectory will take us through two phases. First we
will consider words, the choice of words, and some deceptive ways of using them with which it is crucial to be familiar in order to guard against them. Then we will arrive
at logic, or the art of combining propositions, and above
all this very particular art called rhetoric, understood as
mental treachery and manipulation. At that point, we will
examine some common fallacies.

1.1 Treacherous Words

Words, words, words.
—WILLIAM SHAKESPEARE

What is well-conceived is easily articulated
And the words to say it come easily.
—French poet and critic
NICOLA BOILEAU,
from his *Art of Poetry, I*

This section invites you to show great vigilance with regard
to words, a vigilance that should equal the attention that
those who know how to use words effectively to convince,
deceive, and indoctrinate shrewdly pay them. I will begin
by introducing an important distinction between the verbs
"denote" and "connote."

1.1.1 To Denote/To Connote

Our spontaneous conception of language is often quite naive. It is based on the idea that words designate objects in the world, objects to which we could otherwise point. One minute of reflection shows that it is far from being that simple. Many words do not have such referents: they are abstract, imprecise, vague, and they change meaning depending on the context. Still others reify, transmit emotions, and so forth.

It is useful to distinguish between what words denote (the objects, people, facts, or properties to which they refer) and their connotations, that is, the emotional reactions that they elicit. Two words can thus denote the same thing but have very different connotations, positive in one case, negative in the other. Knowing this is crucial, because in this way one can glorify, denigrate, or neutralize that of which one speaks, as the case may be, merely by choosing one's words. Thus, it is different to talk about a car, a cruiser, or a beater: each of these terms denotes a motor vehicle designed for individual transport, but each also carries with it connotations and elicits very different emotional reactions. So it is advisable to be attentive to the words used to describe the world—especially in all the polemical and contested categories of social life. Think, for example, about the vocabulary used to speak about abortion. The protagonists in that debate refer to themselves as being pro-life or pro-choice. That is no accident: who would want to be anti-life or anti-choice? Whether an activist is more willing to speak of a fetus or a baby is not accidental either. Think also about Wal-Mart employees, who are referred to as associates. Or again, think about comedian Roseanne Barr's joke: "I've found a fail-proof way of making sure that the kids eat healthily: the health mix. One spoonful of M&Ms and two of Smarties. The kids love it. You know it's good for them: Hey! It's a health mix!"

Look, too, at the use of what are known as euphemisms, which are words used to mask or at least minimize a disagreeable idea by referring to it with a word with less negative connotations. They are a good illustration of how this property of language can be used to mislead an audience.

.Think about the following case, reported and studied by Sheldon Rampton and John Stauber.[2] It shows how groups with specific interests can use language to their advantage. In 1992, the US International Food Information Council (IFIC) was concerned about the public perception of food biotechnology. So they launched a vast research project to determine how to talk to the public about these technologies. Some words were identified as carrying positive baggage, and it was strongly recommended that they be used exclusively. For example: beauty, abundance, children, choice, diversity, earth, organic, heritage, hybrid, farmer, flowers, fruits, future generations, hard work, improve, purity, soil, tradition, and whole. On the other hand, others were absolutely proscribed, notably: biotechnology, DNA, economy, experimentation, industry, laboratory, machine, manipulate, money, pesticides, profit, radiation, security, and researcher.

As one might easily guess, war is another domain particularly propitious to the use of euphemisms, as shown by the following table.[3] In the first column, you will find several examples of vocabulary that have been used to talk about war from Vietnam to our day. The second column suggests a translation of what is likely referred to by each of the words or expressions.

Collateral damage	Civilian deaths
Pacification center	Concentration camp
Caribbean peacekeeping force	The army, marines, and air force that invaded Grenada
US Department of Defense	Ministry of Aggression?
Operation Desert Storm	War on Iraq
Operation Provide Relief/ Operation Restore Hope	Entry of American troops into Somalia
Incursion	Invasion
Surgical strike	Bombing hoped to be precise because of the proximity of civilians
Defensive strike	Bombing
Strategic withdrawal	Retreat (ours)
Tactical redeployment	Retreat (the enemy's)
Advisors	Military officers or CIA agents— before the US admitted to its involvement in Vietnam
Terminate	Kill
Particular explosives	Napalm

The Demonstrations Against the Quebec Summit in Spring 2001, As Seen by Mario Roy

People dressed up as dolphins or sea-turtles—or even cows, as they were at the meeting of the Finance Ministers of the Americas in Toronto. Street musicians and dancers. Placards and posters. Rants and songs. Slogans and flyers. A demonstrator offers a flower to a police officer, as in that photo from the 1960s that was broadcast around the world and became an icon for the same reasons as Che.

A poster that says: Capitalism sucks! Like in 1970.

Everywhere, lanky teenagers and young adults race to the party, for the sole reason that you have to be where the action is, with your friends, whether it is Seattle or Quebec. For them, at night after the demo, once the placards have been stacked along the wall, there will be music and pot, love and wine. . . .

We're not talking here about professional demonstrators, often paid by big unions or "community" organizations, who are leashed to the State, and who are completely uninteresting. Nor about the hooligans, the word we use in these instances for the little bums, who are scarcely less so.

Not at all.

We're talking about the big anonymous crowd of youth brimming with hormones and enthusiasm who go to the WTO or to the Summit of the Americas for the same reasons that other young people went to Woodstock, or to "McGill français," or to the Sorbonne for the big show in May of '68.

It's normal. And it's healthy. Don't you remember being eighteen?

Editorial, *La Presse*, April 14, 2001, A18.

1.1.2 On the Virtues of Imprecision

If words are often used to express precise and clear ideas, they can also be vague and imprecise. This property is sometimes even very useful. Thanks to it, something can be affirmed with such vagueness that there is little chance that an interpretation of the facts can confirm the affirmation. Or, again, a thorny question can be answered with generalities that don't commit to anything specific, precisely because they say nothing specific.

Q: Mr. President, critics of your proposed bill on interrogation rules say there's another important test—these critics include John McCain, who you've mentioned several times this morning—and that test is this: If a CIA officer, paramilitary, or special operations soldier from the United States were captured in Iran or North Korea, and they were roughed up, and those governments said, well, they were interrogated in accordance with our interpretation of the Geneva Conventions, and then they were put on trial and they were convicted based on secret evidence that they were not able to see, how would you react to that, as Commander-in-Chief?

THE PRESIDENT: David, my reaction is, is that if the nations such as those you named, adopted the standards within the Detainee Detention Act, the world would be better. That's my reaction. We're trying to clarify law. We're trying to set high standards, not ambiguous standards.[4]

Nostradamus's Predictions

Michel de Notre-Dame, the doctor and astrologer who came to be known as Nostradamus, was born in Saint-Rémy-de-Provence, France, in 1503.

In 1555, he published his first collection of enigmatic quatrains, entitled *Centuries*, that immediately became immensely popular and are still held by his followers to be extraordinarily accurate predictions. The second edition of *Centuries* appeared in 1558: it was dedicated to King Henry II, to whom Nostradamus wished "a happy life." Henry II died the following year of a wound received in a tournament.

Was the visionary's sight clouded? Not at all, reply his sycophants, who maintain that the prediction of Henry II's death is, on the contrary, one of the clearest of all of Nostradamus's predictions. For Henry II died in a tournament held in Paris (on Saint-Antoine Street), hit by the Count of Montgomery's lance, which shattered and then penetrated his skull.

Nostradamus did indeed write the following:

The young lion will overcome the older one,
On the field of combat in a single battle;
He will pierce his eyes through a golden cage,
Two wounds made one, then he dies a cruel death.

Let us first note that such predictions are always formulated explicitly *after* the fact, which means they are not really predictions. For example, the events of September 11, 2001, could certainly be read into Nostradamus, but only starting on September 12, 2001.

But let's look more closely at this exemplary prediction/postdiction. This is the way James Randi analyzes the quatrain about King Henry II:

1. Speaking of "young" and "old" is questionable here because the two men were only a few years in age apart.

2. "On the field of combat" refers to a battlefield, but that is not how one would refer to the location of a jousting tournament, which is a sports competition.

3. "Golden cage": no piece of armor, and no helmet were made of gold, because it is a soft metal.

4. "He will pierce his eyes": no witness at the time spoke of a pierced eye.

5. The lion was not the emblem of the King of France at the time, nor was it ever before or has it been since.

The moral of the story: use vague words and put together obscure sentences—there will always be someone to read something into them and to exalt your gifts.

James Randi, *The Mask of Nostradamus: The Prophecies of the World's Most Famous Seer* (Buffalo, NY: Prometheus Books, 1993), 170–176.

1.1.3 Sexism and Political Correctness

A language reflects the particular ideologies of the society by which it is spoken. It also reflects the transformations in these ideologies. A number of years ago, we became more sensitive to the sexist dimensions of our spoken language (which discriminate according to gender), but also to its classist, ageist, and ethnocentric dimensions (which discriminate according to social class, age, and society or culture, respectively). We have tried to get rid of them, because language can be a powerful vehicle of more and less subtle forms of exclusion and discrimination.

The story that follows is well-known. A man is traveling

in a car with his son. There is an accident, and he is killed on the spot. The child is brought to the hospital emergency room. In the operating theater, however, the doctor declares: "I can't operate on this child; he's my son." How do you explain this perfectly true affirmation? The answer is obviously that the doctor is his mother.

Below are some examples of non-sexist rewriting.[5]

> ORIGINAL: If the researcher is the principal investigator, he should place an asterisk after his name.
> GENDER-NEUTRAL: Place an asterisk after the name of the principal investigator.

> ORIGINAL: Repeat the question for each subject so that he understands it.
> GENDER-NEUTRAL: Repeat the question for all subjects so that they understand it.

> ORIGINAL: The effect of PCBs has been studied extensively in rats and man.
> GENDER-NEUTRAL: The effect of PCBs has been studied extensively in rats and humans.

> ORIGINAL: The governor signed the workmen's compensation bill.
> GENDER-NEUTRAL: The governor signed the workers' compensation bill.

Let us conclude by noting that some authors argue that these modes of expression sometimes limit us to excessive political correctness, which they decry as irritating, pernicious, and even harmful. Diane Ravitch,[6] for example, denounces what she calls the "language police" on American campuses and sees in them a threat to freedom of expression and the free exploration of all subjects and questions.

Here, for example, are two cases reported by the author. A text dealing with the (true) story of a blind man who successfully climbed to the summit of a mountain was declared offensive, because the story of a mountain discriminates against people who live in flat cities and regions and because the story suggests that being blind is a handicap. Further, an article affirming that there were rich and poor people in ancient Egypt was declared offensive to poor people today.

1.1.4 The Art of Ambiguity: Equivocation and Amphibology

In every language there are many words that are polysemous, which is to say that they have many meanings. It is this use of a word to mean one thing and then to subtly alter its meaning that produces the sort of equivocation considered here.

This property of words can, of course, be used to humorous effect.

For example: Everyone agreed that the actor, who had played a hostage, had given a captivating performance. Or: The dead batteries were given out free of charge.

In both cases, the play is with the equivocal character of a word: a "captive" is a hostage or a prisoner, captivating means something that keeps an audience's attention; charge can refer to both a quantifiable property of electricity and the act of taking money in exchange for something else.

But equivocation is not always easy to detect. Thus, it can be used to muddle people rather than to make them smile. For example: You have no trouble accepting the miracles of science; why do you suddenly become so critical when it comes to those in the Bible? After thinking a little, one will see that the word "miracle" is used in two clearly different ways. But if that goes unnoticed, one might think that the argument deserves a reply.

Let me give a final example. Some pedagogues place the concept of interest at the center of their thinking on education. But this word is an equivocal word that can be understood in at least two different ways: on the one hand, it can mean what does in fact interest the child, and on the other hand, it can mean that which is in the child's interest. It may well be that what interests the child is not in her interest and that that which is in her interest does not interest her.

Not specifying what one means by a pedagogy founded on interest can thus give way to a number of hard-to-detect equivocations. And thus do all those empty pedagogical slogans flourish. The rhetorical construction that enables the production of statements with multiple interpretations is called amphibology. Such statements are sometimes very funny and committed unbeknownst to their authors. Because people are trying to express themselves using a minimal number of words, classified ads are an endless sources of examples.

—Dog to give. Eats everything and adores children.

—Renting superb sailboat twenty meters recent with comfortable sailor, well-equipped.

—Dresser for ladies with curved feet.

Newspaper headlines provide us with others: Red Tape Holds Up New Bridge.

Charlatans have known for a long time how to take full advantage of amphibology. The first known use probably goes back to Greek antiquity. King Croesus consulted the Delphic Oracles to know if he would be victorious in a war against the Persians. The Kingdom of Persia was separated from Croesus's own by the Halys River. The king received this answer: "If Croesus crosses the Halys, he will destroy a great empire." Croesus interpreted this to mean that he would win. But the prediction is ambiguous. Do you see why?

Croesus waged the war, convinced that he would be victorious. He was defeated. Taken prisoner by the king of Persia, he sent messengers to complain to the Oracle about her bad prediction. In Herodotus's account, the Pythia answered him thus:

> Croesus recriminates without reason. Loxias predicted that if he went to war against the Persians, he would destroy a great empire. In light of this answer, he should have asked the god which empire he spoke of, his own or that of Cyrus. He didn't understand what we told him, he didn't ask any further: let him reproach himself.[7]

So the Oracle's prediction was ambiguous and would be confirmed no matter who was defeated, which would be a great kingdom in either case.

A Dangerous, Invisible Killer

The following text was written in 1988 before being posted on the Web a few years later by Eric Lechner, one of its authors. It had more than once been presented as a petition and passed to random people in various public places to sign. Each time, it was signed by many people—which obviously has no scientific value. Be that as it may, it is a good read, as you will see, and an attentive read is an amusing critical thinking exercise.

The Invisible Killer

Dihydrogen monoxide is colorless, odorless, tasteless, and kills uncounted thousands of people every year. Most of these deaths are caused by accidental inhalation of DHMO, but the dangers of dihydrogen monoxide do not end there. Prolonged exposure to its solid form causes severe tissue damage. Symptoms of DHMO ingestion can include excessive sweating and urination, and possibly a bloated feeling, nausea, vomiting, and body electrolyte imbalance. For those who have become dependent, DHMO withdrawal means certain death.

Dihydrogen monoxide

• is also known as hydroxyl acid, and is the major component of acid rain;

• contributes to the "greenhouse effect";

• may cause severe burns;

• contributes to the erosion of our natural landscape;

• accelerates corrosion and rusting of many metals;

• may cause electrical failures and decreased effectiveness of automobile brakes;

• has been found in excised tumors of terminal cancer patients.

Contamination Is Reaching Epidemic Proportions!

Quantities of dihydrogen monoxide have been found in almost every stream, lake, and reservoir in America today. But the pollution is global, and the contaminant has even been found in Antarctic ice. DHMO has caused millions of dollars of property damage in the Midwest, and recently California.

Despite the danger, dihydrogen monoxide is often used
- as an industrial solvent and coolant;
- in nuclear power plants;
- in the production of Styrofoam;
- as a fire retardant;
- in many forms of cruel animal research;
- in the distribution of pesticides—even after washing, produce remains contaminated by this chemical;
- as an additive in certain junk foods and other food products.

Companies dump waste DHMO into rivers and the ocean, and nothing can be done to stop them because this practice is still legal. The impact on wildlife is extreme, and we cannot afford to ignore it any longer!

The Horror Must Be Stopped!

The American government has refused to ban the production, distribution, or use of this damaging chemical due to its "importance to the economic health of this nation." In fact, the navy and other military organizations are conducting experiments with DHMO, and designing multi-billion dollar devices to control and utilize it during warfare situations. Hundreds of military research facilities receive tons of it through a highly sophisticated underground distribution network. Many store large quantities for later use.

The hoax continues on a hilarious site (http://www.dhmo.org) that promotes banning dihydrogen monoxide. Luckily, the effort has so far been completely in vain.

1.1.5 Accentuation

This rhetorical strategy relies on the fact that it is possible to change the meaning of a statement simply by changing the tone with which one pronounces certain words. For example, take the following maxim: "A person should not speak ill of her friends." Its meaning is clear and its interpretation generally unproblematic. But one can say it and mean that one can speak ill of those who are not one's friends, simply by emphasizing the last word: "A person should not speak ill of her *friends*." And one can also say it and make it understood that one can speak ill of others' friends: "A person should not speak ill of *her* friends." In a certain context, one would be able to say in insinuating that, if one cannot speak ill of one's friends, one can nevertheless do them ill: "A person should not *speak* ill of her friends."

There is a written equivalent of this oral strategy that consists of emphasizing certain parts of a message. Advertisements often employ this strategy, announcing in big letters, for example, "PERSONAL COMPUTER FOR $300"—and in very small print stating that the monitor is not included in the price.

A similar yet distinct strategy involves selectively presenting only certain passages from a text, thereby giving the impression that one thing was stated when in fact the original text said, if not the exact opposite, at least something entirely different. I suggest that we call this procedure *eduction*.[8]

To offer a fictitious example, here is what was written in the review of a play by Marvin Miller.

The new play by Marvin Miller is a monumental failure! Presented by the producers as an adventure full of twists and turns and suspense that recounts the events of an arctic expedition, the only suspense, for this writer, was in finding out whether he would manage to stay until the end of the first act of this pitiful show. To tell the truth, the only interesting thing about this play is its musical accompaniment, superb and spellbinding, composed by Pierre Tournier.

And here is what one could extract to advertise the show:

> ... monumental! ... an adventure full of twists and turns and suspense ... superb and spellbinding.

1.1.6 Weasel Words

The weasel, charming animal that it is, attacks eggs in bird nests using a very particular method: it pierces them and sucks them, then leaves them there. The mama bird thinks she sees her egg, but it is only the shell emptied of its precious contents.

Weasel words do the same thing, but with propositions. Thus, one can be under the impression that a statement is full of rich content, but the presence of a little word has emptied it of substance.

Advertising relies on this strategy often; an attentive observer will find a great number of incidences. Who hasn't received an envelope marked, "You could have won $1,000,000"?

Here are a few other examples:

A product *can* produce such and such effect.

A product diminishes or augments something *up to* such and such level.

A product *helps* to . . .

A product *contributes* to . . .

A product is a *component* of . . .

A product makes you feel *like* . . .

A product is *like* . . .

A product is *in some ways* . . .

Some researchers say that . . .

Research *suggests* that . . .

Research *tends* to demonstrate . . .

It is claimed that . . .

A product is *almost* . . .

Advertising, however, is hardly the only domain in which these weasel words are used. A critical thinker has to know how to recognize them right away in order not to misinterpret the message. At the same time, one must remember that, in certain cases, it is important to nuance one's thinking. But that should not be confused with using weasel words in a conscious effort to deceive or mystify.

1.1.7 Jargon and Pseudo-Expertise

It is sometimes necessary and altogether legitimate to use specialized vocabulary to express certain ideas clearly. One cannot, for example, seriously discuss quantum physics or Kant's philosophy without making use of technical words and precise vocabulary that allow one to engage in an exchange about complex ideas. This vocabulary, which a neophyte doesn't understand, serves to raise and clarify genuine problems, and yet one can generally give interested neophytes some idea of the meaning of these concepts and of the issues that they raise. With that glimpse, they can decide if they want to advance and deepen their knowledge. Should this be the case, they will have to acquire both the specialized vocabulary and the totality of knowledge which corresponds to it.

Yet one sometimes gets the impression that, far from revealing real problems, and allowing them to be studied and understood more clearly, vocabulary is used to make rather simple things artificially complicated, or to mask poor thinking. I concede that the dividing line between the first and second categories is not always easy to see—but it exists nonetheless. That which comprises the second category is called jargon.

There is a wide variety of jargon and many terms have been suggested for it. For example, lawyers' jargon would be *legalese*; in fact, in the United States, there are groups that work to counter this juridical obscurantism and offer translations of legal documents into everyday language. Education studies jargon is called *educando*; to my knowledge no one has yet broached the Herculean task of translating those texts into language that is comprehensible to mortals.

Here is an example of academic jargon. It is an excerpt from a sociology Ph.D. thesis defended recently at the Sorbonne by a well-known French astrologer. According to the experts who read it, the thesis was unbelievably vacuous, and was intended to be an attempt to introduce astrology into the university curriculum.

The crux and the heart of astrology, that mirror of the profound unicity of the universe, reminds us of the *unus mundis* of the ancients, in which the cosmos was considered to be a massive indivisible Whole. With the rationalism and its Enlightenment, a schism of the heart, soul, and spirit took place—a schism between reason and feeling. It was a socio-cultural schism that went hand in hand with the duality to which our Western culture is still wedded, despite the apparent paradigm shift of the past few years. . . .

However, a new paradigm is generating a growing interest in the stars, in spite of a residual rejection that endures and is basically linked to the confusion and elision of practices such as clairvoyance, tarot readings, and others. In light of our experience, a fundamental element of the outlook of any comprehensive sociology, whether Weberian or Simmelian, we wanted to privilege the phenomenon of the media, reflective as it is of the social, given our more than twenty years of experience in this area, within and beyond the Hexagon.... We have tried to analyze this de facto ambivalence between attraction and rejection; but also to define, by means of a social survey, what the epistemological situation of astrology is today. . . .

Such a dialogue [between scientists and astrologers] could only ever be established around a complex thought, that which governs the New Scientific Spirit and also the astrological paradigm—think of A. Breton's discussion of the multi-dialectical game that astrology necessitates. We have largely practiced that openness, that flexibility of spirit on an empirical plane, to the point of becoming mono-maniacal—or rather, metanoic (Pareto).[9]

The above passage is a perfect example of jargon and manages to condense into a few lines the worst imaginable contrivances: pseudo-wise terms used for no reason at all, and artificial references to concepts, theories, and prestigious authors.

No doubt such jargon has many functions. Some perceive it as a smokescreen intended to procure prestige for those who use it. Noam Chomsky sees it, at least in part, as a way for intellectuals to hide the vacuity of their work:

Intellectuals have a problem: they have to justify their existence. Now, there are few things about the world that are understood. Most of the things that are understood, except perhaps for in certain areas of physics, can be explained with very simple words and in very short sentences. But if you do that, you don't become famous, you don't get a job, people don't revere your writing. There's a challenge there for intellectuals: to take what is rather simple and make it appear to be something very complicated and very profound. Groups of intellectuals interact that way. They speak amongst each other, and the rest of the world is supposed to admire them, treat them with respect, etc. But translate what they are saying into simple language and you'll often find either nothing at all or truisms, or absurdities.[10]

Learning to draw the line mentioned above, and thus to recognize jargon, is not always easy. In fact, it is a long-term task that requires a great deal of knowledge, rigor, and modesty in the face of one's own ignorance, as well as openness to new ideas.

To conclude, I would like to call to mind the results of an amusing study[11] that sought to demonstrate some of the effects of the recourse to jargon in the academic context. Although it is unique and does not allow for meaningful conclusions to be drawn, I will cite it here nonetheless, because it is one of the rare studies to try to deal with this topic.

At the beginning of the 1970s, Dr. Fox gave a talk on three different occasions, entitled "Mathematical Theory of Games and its Application in the Training of Doctors." He spoke in front of a total of fifty-five people, all highly educated: social workers, educators, administrators, psychologists, and psychiatrists. His exposition lasted an hour and was followed by a half-hour-long discussion. Then a questionnaire was distributed to the audience to find out what those present thought of the doctor's presentation. All the participants found it clear and stimulating; none of them noticed that the talk was a mess of nonsense—which it was.

Dr. Fox was actually an actor. He looked very distinguished and spoke authoritatively and with conviction. But the text he spoke, which he had learned by heart and which had to do with a topic he knew absolutely nothing about, was laden with vague words, contradictions, bogus references, knowledgeable references to concepts that had nothing to do with the topic at hand, empty concepts, and so on. In short, it was nothing but hot air, contradictions, and pompous meaninglessness.

Those who pulled off the hoax—which calls to mind So-kal's[12] a few years ago—formulated what they call the Fox hypothesis, according to which an unintelligible speech, if given by a legitimate source, will tend in spite of everything else to be accepted as intelligible. A corollary of this idea is that using vocabulary that gives even the illusion of profundity and erudition can contribute to increasing the credibility of a message.

1.1.8 Defining

"There's glory for you!"

"I don't know what you mean by 'glory,'" Alice said.

Humpty Dumpty smiled contemptuously. "Of course you don't—till I tell you. I meant 'there's a nice knock-down argument for you!'"

"But 'glory' doesn't mean 'a nice knock-down argument,'" Alice objected.

"When I use a word," Humpty Dumpty said, in rather a scornful tone, "it means just what I choose it to mean—neither more not less."

"The question is," said Alice, "whether you can make words mean so many different things."

"The question is," said Humpty Dumpty, "which is to be master—that's all."

—**LEWIS CARROLL**, Through the Looking Glass

Anyone who has ever been sucked into a discussion that got bogged down this way knows some arguments are actually misunderstandings based on the imprecision of a meaning of a given word, or go on because each interlocutor has a different definition for one or more of the terms being used. Obviously, in such cases, it is necessary to produce a definition on which everyone can agree. But defining is no small task.

The first temptation is to rely on the dictionary. Sometimes this is entirely legitimate. Nevertheless, it must be remembered that the dictionary often provides what are essentially a society's conventions in relation to the use of words—conventions that are clarified through the use of synonyms. This is certainly not without value. For example, if you don't know what your interlocutor means by "quadruped," the dictionary will provide you with a useful synonym which will enlighten you sufficiently to be able to continue the conversation: "a four-footed animal, esp. a four-footed mammal." Another example: if you don't know what an author means by "Dearborn," a nineteenth-century English dictionary will tell you that at that time it was the name of a kind of covered wagon.

This type of definition, however—which is called linguistic—is generally not what is required. Suppose that you were discussing whether a given practice were just: appealing to a dictionary to learn that "just" means "acting or done in accordance with what is morally right or fair" will not help you very much. You would immediately want to know what right or fair means, if that accordance is necessary and why, and a thousand other things. If you were having a conversation with someone about whether the creations of Christo—who wrapped the Reichstag in Berlin, the Pont Neuf in Paris, and Central Park in New York—are art or not, the linguistic definition of art would not help you very much.

These problems are not purely theoretical. On the contrary, they are vital and fraught with all kinds of consequences. For example, it is difficult to define terms like terrorism, life, death, abortion, war, genocide, marriage, poverty, theft, or drugs. Think for just a moment about the repercussions of using of one definition rather than another.

In these cases, what has to be produced is called a conceptual definition. In the West, we can say that philosophy was born, at least in part, of the desire to resolve problems related to conceptual definitions, the immense difficulty of formulating them, and their numerous consequences. Socrates's name is still associated with all of this. He urged his contemporaries to adopt an approach that involved arriving at a conceptual definition of a problematic term by way of induction, that is to say, through the examination of a particular case. This approach is still valuable; it is often advantageous to try to clarify the concepts we use in this way. What are the necessary and sufficient conditions that must be satisfied to be able to talk of terrorism? Are these conditions found in every case that is currently understood to be terrorism? And if not, what needs to be revised, our use or our definition of the term?

One old but useful way of proceeding is to look for the general type (*genus*) and the specific difference (*differentia*) of what we want to define. For example, imagine we want to define "bird." The genus is animal; the specific difference is that by which birds—and they alone—differ from other animals (which we could say is having feathers). Try it with "drug": you'll see that the exercise is not as easy as it seems. Science and specialized knowledge often provide definitions that can be helpful to us.

Undertaking such exercises in definition, some people appeal to etymology, the study of the roots of words. Here again, a warning is necessary: the origin of a word is not necessarily illuminating, since the meaning it had yesterday, in its original form, is not necessarily identical to the meaning it has in its new form. Often it is even very distant, such that etymology tells us almost nothing at all. The word "role," for example, comes from the medieval Latin *rotulus*, which referred to a rolled parchment on which a text was written. That is not exactly a big help.

What could be called an "etymological fallacy" can sometimes be pushed quite a distance. Thus, partisans of a liberal conception of education have claimed that the word "education" comes from "*educere*," etymology that invites a conception of education as an act of leading (*induco*) out of (*ex*) ignorance—which conforms to the liberal notion of education. On the other side are those who favor a notion of education understood as nourishing and, more broadly, furnishing the conditions necessary for a person's development. They invoke a second etymological hypothesis, according to which "education" comes from "*educare*," which means "nourish" or "raise." And still others maintain that education is an indeterminate concept and support their thesis with the very uncertainty of the etymology. You see that etymology, as illuminating as it sometimes is, cannot, in any instance, resolve problems of conceptual definition on its own.

Sometimes, we have to agree to a stipulative definition, that is to say a contextual definition. Concepts like "overweight" and "obese," for example, belong to a continuum of excess weight: the line between normal weight, overweight, and obesity are drawn with the help of a body mass index, which provides a stipulative definition of those concepts.

As for science, it often relies on two sorts of definitions, which are important to know.

First, operational definitions. These show the sequence of stages to follow in order to observe the concept that constitutes the object of study. The recipe for a Black Forest cake is an operational definition of the concept of Black Forest cake. Of course, the operational definitions used in science are much more complex.

Secondly, consider indexes. The approach involves a number of steps.[13] Take concept X. We would begin by making ourselves an image representation of the concept: here in this phase, knowledge, sensitivity, and creativity come into play. The next step is the specification of the concept, in which we would clarify its dimensions. The third phase is when we would choose the indicators of those dimensions, the observable characteristics that make them visible. To finish, we would carry out a weighted synthesis of these dimensions according to a unique scale, which comes to constitute the index. To finish, I would note how easy it is to succumb to the temptation of reification, which grants a reality and an autonomous existence to an index that is nothing more than one possible or hypothetical construction. The Intellectual Quotient (the infamous IQ) is just such an index; everyone knows how easily it can be reified.

1.2 The Art of Mental Trickery and Manipulation: Some Everyday Fallacies[14]

Consider the following propositions:
All men are mortal.
Socrates is a man.
Therefore Socrates is mortal.
Everyone knows this form of reasoning, which is called

syllogism. Indeed, it has been repeated so often that Paul Valéry once said jokingly that it was the syllogism, and not hemlock, that killed Socrates.

Aristotle is generally recognized as the inventor of formal logic, or having drawn attention to this sort of reasoning, giving it a name and having done the first systematic study. Until the end of the nineteenth century, the logic that he developed was held to be the zenith and end point of the discipline. It was only through the work of twentieth-century mathematicians and philosophers (notably Gottlob Frege and Bertrand Russell) that a more powerful (mathematical) logic was developed.

What is logic? To find out, let's go back to Aristotle's treatise on logic (or *Organon*, which is to say, *tool*). In these texts, he studied reasoning with attention only to its form, independent of its content—hence the epithet "formal" given to his logic. Aristotle first codified the "laws of thinking":

—The principle of identity: what is, is; A is A;
—The principle of contradiction: nothing can be both A and not A at the same time;
—The principle of the exclusion of the third: something is either A or not A—there is no third possibility.

Then he developed his theory of syllogism. Consider the following reasoning:

All the officers in the NYPD have billy clubs.
Peter is an officer in the NYPD.
Therefore, Peter has a billy club.

This reasoning—or syllogism, as Aristotle says—has content (it is a matter of the NYPD, of Peter, and of billy clubs), and something is affirmed about this content. This syllogism also has a form, and what's more is it has a form that we can make obvious by making abstractions of the content. You will no doubt already have noticed that this syllogism has exactly the same form as the one that concludes that Socrates is mortal. It is even easier to see if we use letters that function as conventional symbols to represent any content. The reasoning above speaks in terms of general classes: the New York Police Department (A), the ownership of a billy club (B), and of an individual, Peter— let's call him X. It speaks of all the As and all the Bs, and of X, by establishing relationships between these classes and the individual. Its structure is the following:

All As are Bs.

X is an A.

Therefore X is a B.

If we consider the structure of this reasoning independent of its content, we notice that it necessarily "works." Indeed, as soon as all As are Bs and X is an A, X also has to be a B. We can see it perfectly, for that matter, by drawing circles called Venn diagrams, named after their inventor:

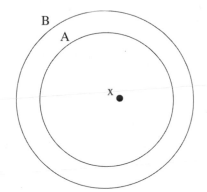

The first and second propositions (all As are Bs, and X is an A) are what Aristotle calls premises. From these premises, we can draw out with certainty a third proposition that follows from the first two: this is the conclusion (X is a B). The premises are the reasons we put forward to support our conclusion. In reasoning like this, the conclusion follows necessarily from the premises: we call this reasoning valid.

A valid syllogism allows us to guarantee that if the premises are true, the conclusion will be also. From there, things get complicated rather quickly. Aristotle described fourteen forms of valid syllogisms, which medieval logicians christened with Latin names: Barbara, Celerant, and so on.

The important distinction between validity and truth has already been mentioned and must now be clarified. As we've seen, certain forms of reasoning guarantee that a *valid* conclusion follows necessarily from its premises. But that does not guarantee that the conclusion is *true*. Let's take up the same form again, but with new reasoning:

All ostriches are elephants.

This green frog is an ostrich.

Therefore this green frog is an elephant.

This syllogism is valid, but the conclusion is not true because the premises are not true.

In thinking a little bit about these categories (validity and truth), you'll see that there are four distinct possibilities:

1. The reasoning is valid and the conclusion is true:

All men are mortal.

Socrates is a man.

Therefore Socrates is mortal.

2. The conclusion is false but the reasoning is valid:
All men are blue.
Socrates is a man.
Therefore Socrates is blue.

3. The conclusion is false and the reasoning is invalid:
Some men are blue.
Socrates is a man.
Therefore Socrates is blue.

4. The conclusion is true, but the reasoning is invalid:
Some men are mortal.
Socrates is a man.
Therefore Socrates is mortal.

If we want to ensure our intellectual self-defense, we gain something by practicing the art of detecting mental trickery and thus by knowing how to spot argumentation that does not stand up to scrutiny and that prompts wrong conclusions. We call an argument employing this sort of reasoning a sophism or fallacy—the difference being that a fallacy is committed in good faith, while a sophism is advanced in order to mislead. (Here, in conformity with common usage, we will refer to all invalid reasoning as fallacy, whether or not it is intentionally misleading.)

We can distinguish between formal and informal fallacies. The former are committed when the reasoning is invalid and so the conclusion does not follow from the premises. We will study those first. But there are also a great number of fallacies we call informal; it is mostly with these that we will be concerned. They rely on the properties of language, on the way in which appeals to facts are made, and more generally, on certain characteristics of the premises invoked. These fallacies are common and it is absolutely necessary to know how to recognize them. But they are also more difficult to classify. Many ways of classifying them have been proposed; it is not surprising, since there are multiple ways to make a mistake, and many of the mistakes could be sorted into more than one category. For these reasons, I will content myself with describing the informal fallacies that I consider to be most common.

1.2.1 Formal Fallacies

To begin with, we will examine three causes of invalid reasoning. In each case, the reasoning does not guarantee, by virtue of its form alone, the preservation of the (eventual) truth of the premises.

INCONSISTENCY

An essential property of any valid argument is that it does not contain a contradiction: it is then called consistent. As soon as you can find a contradiction in an argument, you know it is invalid because it is inconsistent. Here is an example of inconsistent reasoning:

Baltimore is 40 miles from Washington, DC.

New York is 200 miles from Washington, DC.

So Washington, DC, is closer to New York than to Baltimore.

Note that the fact that this argument is invalid does not tell us that the conclusion put forward is false: its truth or falsity is a question for geographers and is of no interest to the logician, who is concerned only with the form of the reasoning, not with its content. A shrewd eye will have little trouble finding inconsistencies in reasoning all over the place. Here are two examples that you have doubtlessly come across before:

People should not be offered social assistance; a market economy requires that each person take care of him or herself. And: Agribusiness companies have to be subsidized, because without subsidies, the companies would not survive.

THE AFFIRMATION OF THE CONSEQUENT

The form of this fallacy is as follows:
If P, then Q.
Q.
Therefore, P.

Here, even if the two premises are true, the conclusion is not necessarily so. This conclusion is called a non-sequitur. Here is an example:
If you are a police officer, you own a billy club.
You own a billy club.
Therefore you are a police officer.

You see that the premises do not guarantee the conclusion. A person could well own a billy club without being a police officer, and the fact of being a police officer does not exhaust the reasons for which one might own a billy club.
Here is another example:
If it rains, the sidewalk is wet.
The sidewalk is wet.
Therefore it is raining.

We know perfectly well that there could be a great number of other explanations for the sidewalk being wet. Therefore, the fact that it is does not guarantee that it is raining. Consider the following example:
If the fundamental structures of a society are just, its citizens do not rebel.
The citizens of our society do not rebel.
Therefore, the fundamental structures of our society are just.

The affirmation of the consequent fallacy is particularly pernicious because it is difficult to detect, for two main reasons. First, it is rarely presented in such a way that its form is explicitly evident, as in the preceding examples. More often, you'll get something like this:

> All impartial observers and all credible theorists hold that when the basic structures of a society are fair, citizens conform to them of their own will. The fact that citizens in our societies do not rebel thus constitutes a powerful and convincing proof of the justice of our basic institutions, and all our so-called revolutionaries would be wise to think about that carefully.

The second reason spotting this fallacy is difficult is that it bears a superficial resemblance to an altogether valid reasoning called *modus ponens*, which has the following form:

If P, then Q.
P.
Therefore Q.

For example:
If the fundamental structures of a society are just, citizens do not rebel.
The fundamental structures of our society are just.
Therefore, the citizens do not rebel.

THE NEGATING ANTECEDENT

This fallacy has the following form:

If P, then Q.
Not P.
So not Q.

Here again, the condition (if P) is wrongly accepted as the necessary and sufficient condition for Q. To get a better understanding of why it does not work, consider the following example:
If I am in London, I am in England.
I am not in London.
Therefore, I am not in England.

It goes without saying that there are many places other than London in which one can find oneself and still be in England. This time, as well, the difficulty of spotting the fallacy has to do with the fact that it resembles another altogether valid form of reasoning called the negating consequent or *modus tollens*. This time we have
If P, then Q.
Not Q.
Therefore not P.

Let's take up the same example:
If I am in London, I am in England.
I am not in England.
Therefore I am not in London.

1.2.2 Informal Fallacies

THE FALSE DILEMMA

One of the most useful strategies in the repertoire of all good magicians is to "force" a choice. The magician invites you to choose something, for example a card from a deck. You do so with the certainty of having freely selected your card. Yet the conditions of this choice, set up by the magician, are such that he knew beforehand which card you would choose; so we can say that your choice was forced. At this stage, you can imagine that there is nothing easier for the magician than to pretend to find or guess your card.

We can say that on the plane of mental trickery, the false dilemma, the fallacy to which we will now turn, is basically the equivalent of a magician's forced choice.

A real dilemma arises when we are faced with an alternative and two choices—only two—are offered us. Because we have as good reasons to want to opt for one as for the other, we are undecided. A false dilemma arises when we allow ourselves to be convinced that we have to choose between two and only two mutually-exclusive options, when that is untrue. Generally, when this rhetorical strategy is used, one of the options is unacceptable and repulsive, while the other is the one the manipulator wants us to choose. Whoever succumbs to this trap has thus made a choice that is forced, and as such, of little value. Placed before a false dilemma, the critical thinker should react by pointing out that between A and Z, there are a great variety of other options (B, C, D, and so forth). Here are a few examples of common false dilemmas:

—Either medicine can explain how Ms. X was cured, or

it is a miracle. Medicine can't explain how she was cured. Therefore, it is a miracle.

—If we don't reduce public spending, our economy will collapse.

—America: Love it or leave it.

—The universe could not have been created from nothing, so it must have been created by an intelligent life force.

Of course it is possible, using the same process, to create trilemmas, quadrilemmas, and so forth. Each time, it is claimed (falsely) that the list of enumerated options is complete, and that one and only one acceptable option is hidden in that list.

The human tendency to prefer simple analyses and descriptions to complex and nuanced ones is widespread. This no doubt explains part of the success of false dilemmas. Whatever it is, no manipulator has failed to notice what can be gotten out of them. It is so much easier to think you have to choose between fighting terrorism by bombing country X or watching Western civilization collapse than it is to consent to the long and complex analyses that require a serious and lucid examination of the many issues at play. Kahane[15] suggested that the false-dilemma strategy combined with the straw-man fallacy (which we will look at further on) is among those that politicians use most frequently. The pattern of argument is as follows: the position of the politician's adversary is caricatured and rendered grotesque; then the politician's own position is presented as the only other possible option. Finally, the conclusion that the proposed policy is the only reasonable one is either stated explicitly or affirmed implicitly.

The moral of all this? If we are presented with a dilemma,

we have to make sure that it is a real dilemma before jumping to a conclusion (or before concluding that it is impossible to choose). To do so, it is crucial to remember that between black and white there are often many shades of gray. In other words, the best antidote to false dilemmas is a bit of imagination, which often suffices to establish that we weren't presented all the available choices in a correct and exhaustive way.

HASTY GENERALIZATION

All generalizations are false,
including this one.

—MARK TWAIN

As its name suggests, this fallacy consists of generalizing too quickly and drawing conclusions about a given group based on a number of cases that is too small. The cases appealed to can be related to the conclusion put forward, but their advocates attempt to propose a rule from an exception. In everyday life, this fallacy often takes the shape of an anecdotal argument, that is to say an argument that invokes a personal experience to support a line of reasoning. "All bosses are unscrupulous. I know; I know a lot of them," is a hasty generalization, just like "Acupuncture works; my brother stopped smoking by seeing an acupuncturist."

All the same, it is necessary and desirable to be able to draw conclusions about a group on the basis of a limited number of subjects from that group. Indeed, we want to be able to support general conclusions even if it is impossible to observe every case, or unfeasible to observe a large number of cases. In fact, we want to be able to draw general conclusions from specific cases by means of deductive reasoning.

The art of drawing such conclusions in a legitimate way

has become a branch of mathematics, and of statistics more precisely, called sampling and statistical inference theory. We will deal with it in the next chapter. Its study is the best antidote to hasty generalization. In any case, the critical thinker remains skeptical when faced with generalizations, and, before accepting them, asks whether or not the sample invoked is sufficient and representative.

THE RED HERRING

They say that in the South, escaping prisoners used to leave red herring behind them to distract the dogs and turn them off their trail. The same principle is applied in this fallacy we are now studying, which owes its name to this old practice. The goal of the strategy is indeed to lead you to deal with a topic other than the one being discussed—to make sure that you start down a new trail, having forgotten the path you were pursuing.

Children can be first-rate at this game:

—Don't play with that sharp stick; you could hurt yourself.

—It's not a stick, Dad. It's a light saber.

Some adults also know how to play red herring very well, too. Imagine a discussion on global warming, where the reality of the phenomenon is being debated. One of the participants speaks: "What you have to worry about is a government that is far too prone to regulating the economy, and those armies of bureaucrats that churn out laws and rules that keep people from being decently employed and being able to support their families." It stinks a lot like fish, don't you think?

Using the red herring is an art form, and practicing it with talent is not something everyone can do. Indeed, to work, the herring must be chosen carefully to present some interest in and of itself, while also giving the impression of really having something to do with the subject from which it is supposed to distract. It is absolutely necessary to satisfy these two conditions if one wants the victims to follow the wrong path for long enough, without noticing that they've been duped. When put into action properly, this strategy is particularly effective at sabotaging a debate for which only a limited and therefore precious period of time has been set aside.

Let's imagine a debate that deals with freedom of expression. An ill-intentioned participant could throw herself into a long digression about the Internet. She could recount its history, explain how it works, describe its characteristics, without ever getting to the issue of freedom of expression. At the point at which the other participants notice, the time left for the rest of the debate will have diminished considerably—if it has not run out altogether.

Critical thinkers guard against the nefarious effects of the red herring by remaining vigilant and by making sure that they don't lose sight of the subject they are discussing, or the questions or problems with which they are dealing.

THE AD HOMINEM ARGUMENT

This Latin expression literally means "argument against the person" and refers to one of the most widespread and most effective fallacies. Happily, it is also one of the easiest to spot, as we will discover.

The *argumentum ad hominem* (or more briefly the *ad hominem*) involves an attack on the person putting forward an idea or an argument rather than on the idea or the argument in and of itself. It is an attempt to divert attention away from the proposal that is up for debate toward specific characteristics of the person who advanced it.

Often, an *ad hominem* insinuates that there is a connection between the character traits of a person and the ideas or arguments that the person is putting forward; it is an attempt to discredit a proposition by discrediting the person who articulates it. It involves pointing out characteristics of the person being attacked that the audience, real or assumed, will tend to perceive negatively, and then concluding that because of these negative traits, the person's arguments and ideas, especially those which were the object of discussion, are also toxic.

You can see that recourse to the *ad hominem* is highly contextual and that sophists' ability lies in their capacity to adjust their aim—that is, their personal attacks—to their audience. In certain contexts, the word "communist" is enough to poison an entire conversation, while in other contexts, it is a mark of purity. Depending on the situation, words describing nationality, sexual orientation, gender, religion, and so on, can all be used to attack (or to praise) a person.

A short example will help to better elucidate the concept. Let's suppose that in the course of a discussion between Leftists, someone puts forward as plausible and pertinent an idea of Milton Friedman's, the monetarist economist. Then suppose that the immediate response is that Friedman is a right- wing economist and that therefore, the idea does not merit any consideration—instead of an attempt to understand and eventually refute the idea in question. That is an *ad hominem*.

It is worth noting that it is sometimes legitimate and reasonable to cast doubt on a proposition, or even to consider it implausible, because of the character traits of the person putting it forward. For example, it is quite understandable for a policeman not to take seriously the complaint of Mr. Glenn when he claims, for the eighth time in three months, to have been kidnapped by extraterrestrials. The same is true of circumstances in which traits having to do with a person's credibility can and must be seriously considered and evaluated. During court testimony, for example, it is very useful to know if the witness who saw the car run the red light is color blind or not, and the lawyer who seeks to find out is not committing an *ad hominem*. But in both these cases, the connection between the person and his or her ideas is pertinent and deserves to be taken into account. When an *ad hominem* is committed, this pertinent link does not exist.

Note, too, that it is necessary to distinguish the *ad hominem* from the accusation of hypocrisy (or *tu quoque*, literally, "you also"). Though an argument is not invalidated by the character traits of the person by whom it is made, it is possible that this person doesn't practice the truth she proclaims. In this case, one could say that the person's practice is inconsistent with her theory or that she is hypocritical.

To spot an *ad hominem* requires that one use one's judgment. The basic principle is as follows: ideas or arguments have value in and of themselves. They can't be refuted simply by attacking the messenger.

THE APPEAL TO AUTHORITY

NAPOLEON: *Giuseppe, what will we do with this soldier?*
Everything he is telling us is ridiculous.
GIUSEPPE: *Your Excellence, make him a General:*
everything he says will be perfectly sensible.

It is impossible for us to be experts at everything. This is understandable and inevitable, given the paucity of time available to us, our tastes, and our individual aptitudes. So we must often consult and rely on authorities with regard to a wide variety of topics. We do this reasonably if

—the authority we consult possesses the expertise necessary to come to a decision;

—we have no reason to think the person will not tell us the truth;

—we don't have the time, the desire, or the ability necessary to find and to understand for ourselves the information or the opinion about which we are consulting the expert.

Even when it is reasonable to rely on expert opinions, it is healthy to preserve at least a small dose of skepticism. After all, experts sometimes contradict each other or have divergent opinions, make mistakes, or reason badly.

There are at least three possible cases, however, in which an appeal to authority is fallacious and demands the greatest suspicion. The first is that in which the presumed expertise proves to be questionable or weak, for example when the domain of knowledge to which an appeal is made either does not exist or else does not authorize the assurance with which the expert states a position. The second is when the expert has vested interests in the topic he or she is addressing. At that point, it is reasonable to think that these interests are orienting or, more radically, driving his or her judgment. Finally, the third arises when the expert speaks on a subject other than that in which he or she has legitimate knowledge.

In all these cases, the appeal to authority is a fallacy and one must be suspicious—while reminding oneself that the expert's opinion might be true all the same. It is very difficult to exercise this legitimate wariness, so much does the attractiveness of expertise confer an aura of respectability on experts' words even when it is unmerited. That's what makes this fallacy so pernicious.

Let's consider the first of the three cases we outlined above: that in which the expert does not have the knowledge to authorize her to speak as she does. Immediately, all the areas in which it is unreasonable to think expertise exists come to mind. It was Socrates who pointed it out first: we would be wary, and with reason, of purported professors of goodness, experts in kindness, schools of generosity, and so on. So think of all those instances in which there simply is no consensus amongst the experts, and in which calling on one of them to decide a debate is fallacious. This is what is happening when, say, one argues that utilitarianism has provided a definitive resolution to a moral dilemma.

The most sensitive cases are always those in which a field of knowledge exists, but where it doesn't allow for the purported conclusion to be drawn. Many economic news commentators who are pervasive in the media provide us with perfect examples. The uncertainty of economic science, on the one hand, and the fact that economic decisions are necessarily value-based political and social decisions, on the other, should prohibit these people from speaking as they sometimes do, committing the fallacy of appeal to authority.

Let's broach the second case. Here, the expert has an interest in the subject about which she is speaking, and this interest—often financial in nature—distorts or determines her conclusion. Alas, there are many examples of this. Tobacco companies suggested to researchers that in return for financial remuneration, they should make public announcements, supported by pseudo-research, that tobacco is not carcinogenic or even bad for your health. These companies found researchers willing to sell their expertise for a song. Public relations firms, businesses, and other interest groups sometimes set up so-called research groups meant to promote their ideas and their interests by giving them the aura of respectability and objectivity that science confers. This category could be expanded to include all forms of appeal to authority; it would then include far more than just knowledge. This is well understood by advertisers who appeal to famous, wealthy, and powerful people to promote their products.

In the third and last case, the expert, perhaps in good faith, makes statements on a subject other than that about which she has legitimate expertise. In spite of the expert's good faith, her audience will tend to attribute an authority to her words that they do not possess. That's what happens when the Nobel Prize winner in medicine makes a public statement about a question of ethics. In a similar sense, Einstein was certainly an important physicist, but that does not mean that his political opinions were necessarily any better than anyone else's.

In this case too, the category can be extended to cover all those instances in which public personalities, stars, and the rich and famous are invited to speak on a range of social, political, or economic questions about which they too often know nothing.

Proverbs and Popular Wisdom

Popular wisdom is often expressed in proverbs, which are short and incisive formulas that justify a decision or a behavior. But you have to be wary of reasoning based on proverbs, which is generally of no value. Moreover, it is amusing to notice how frequently common proverbs contradict one another. If you find one that affirms one thing, you will easily find another that says exactly the opposite. For example: "Absence makes the heart grow fonder." But the same popular wisdom also maintains the reverse: "Out of sight, out of mind." "Look before you leap" is well known, but so is another proverb: "He who hesitates is lost." "Do unto others as you would have others do unto you," of course; but, "Nice guys finish last." In short, depending on the circumstances, the popular wisdom could be used to justify two diametrically opposed situations.

THE CIRCULAR ARGUMENT (OR PETITIO PRINCIPII)

As the name suggests, this is a fallacy of circular reasoning, in which the premise already presumes what the conclusion seeks to establish. This maneuver is also sometimes known as "begging the question."

The following exchange is a simple but widespread example:

—God exists, because the Bible says so.

—And why should we believe the Bible?

—Why, because it is the word of God!

To borrow an image used by Bertrand Russell in a different context, this way of arguing has all the advantages of theft over honest toil. We can guard against this fallacy by distinguishing premises from conclusions.

POST HOC ERGO PROCTER HOC

This Latin expression means "after this, therefore because of this" and once again, it is a very widespread fallacy. It's the one that superstitious people commit. "I won at the casino when I was wearing these clothes," says the gambler, "so I will wear the same clothes every time I go back to the casino." Since the win follows the fact of wearing certain clothes, he falsely designates the clothes as the cause of the win.

Sometimes, the fallacy is subtler and harder to pick out. Science, of course, appeals to causal relationships, but in science an event is not said to cause another simply because it precedes it. Above all, remember that the mere fact that an event precedes (or is correlated with) another does not make it the cause of the second. Correlation and causality should not be confounded; indeed, this is one of the first things statistics teaches, as we'll see in the next chapter. In a hospital, the presence of individuals called doctors is strongly correlated with that of individuals called patients, but this doesn't mean that doctors are the cause of illness.

Establishing legitimate causal relationships is one of the major aims of empirical and experimental science, which deploys many methods in order to guard against the *post hoc ergo procter hoc* fallacy. We'll come back to this difficult but important question later.

AD POPULUM

Everybody else is doing it,
so why can't we?

—THE CRANBERRIES

And if everyone else went
and jumped in the lake,
would you do it too?

—ANONYMOUS PARENT

The Latin name for this fallacy simply means "(to appeal) to the crowd," because it consists of an appeal to its authority. Of course, the fact that everyone thinks something, does something, or believes something isn't in and of itself sufficient to argue that it is right, good, or true. Nonetheless, the *ad populum* remains one of advertisers' favorite fallacies: they affirm that something is just, good, pretty, desirable, etc., because that's everyone's opinion.

—Drink X, the bestselling beer in the US!

—Car Y: N millions of drivers can't be wrong.

—The Pepsi Generation.

A well-known variation appeals to tradition to conclude (wrongly) that, since it has always been done in such and such a way, that it must be the right way to do it.

—No society has ever legalized same-sex marriage, so ours should not.

—In every society, astrology has been practiced, and people of all classes have relied on it.

Obviously, everyone can be mistaken, including the tradition. So the tradition and its teachings have to be evaluated on their own merit, and we have to ask if they remain valid and true today, given our knowledge, our values, and so forth.

The appeal to the crowd and to tradition are efficient strategies and for that reason they are valued by manipulators. Indeed, they have the advantage of flattering the most conformist—and therefore the most common—of convictions, and can therefore be used without much risk in the majority of places. In its most extreme—and dangerous—form, this sort of fallacy becomes a call to populist passion, and as such, can even be used to evoke hatred and fanaticism.

FALLACY OF COMPOSITION AND FALLACY OF DIVISION

Why do the white sheep eat more than the black sheep?
Because there are more of them.

—CHILDREN'S RIDDLE

The fallacies of composition and division are usually studied together because they are both erroneous ways of reasoning about parts and the whole.

The fallacy of composition affirms of a whole what is true of one of its parts, without offering any justification other than that the part belongs to the whole. The fallacy of division does just the opposite: it affirms that what is true of the whole must necessarily be true of the parts, again without offering any justification except that the parts are part of the whole. In both cases, the problem is that the reason is insufficient because the whole possesses properties that the parts do not necessarily.

Here again, this fallacy is misleading because it resembles a legitimate form of reasoning, where the conclusion that the whole must resemble its parts and vice versa is based on good reasons. So it is important to pay careful attention each time we reason from the part to the whole and the whole to the part. We have to examine the merit of the arguments and remember that the simple fact that a part belongs to a whole does not guarantee that what is true of one will be true of the other.

Here are some examples:

—1 and 3 are odd; the outcome of adding them will therefore be an odd number.

—Consuming sodium and consuming chloride is dangerous for humans. Therefore, consuming sodium chloride is dangerous.

—A horse drinks much more water each day than a human being. Horses must therefore consume much more water than humans.

—Each of these different flowers is fabulous; by assembling them we'll create a marvelous bouquet.

—This rose is red. The atoms which constitute the rose are therefore red.

—Atoms are colorless. This rose is therefore colorless.

—Here are the twenty best hockey players; together they will form the best team.

—The first violin of the best symphony orchestra in the world is the best first violin in the world.

—"How can one love one's country without loving its people?" (Ronald Reagan)

—"As is the case within the general framework of globalization, it's Mexico, the poorest of the three countries united by NAFTA, that most desires to solidify North American ties. Indeed, living in the southern part of the continent there are 100 million human beings whose standard of living is five times less than that of Canadians, and six times less than that of US Americans, and who hold on with all their might to the dream that they will one day rise to their northern neighbors' level of prosperity.[16]

THE APPEAL TO IGNORANCE (OR ARGUMENTUM AD IGNORANTIAM)

When, in spite of all our efforts to get them, we do not have all the pertinent facts and the good reasons that would allow us to judge a proposition, the most rational solution is not to draw a conclusion.

We commit the *argumentum ad ignorantiam* when, in the absence of pertinent facts and good reasons, we nevertheless decide whether the proposition up for examination is true or false.

This fallacy can take two forms. The first involves concluding that an affirmation must be true since it can't be demonstrated that it is wrong. The second leads us to conclude that because we can't prove that it is true, an affirmation must be wrong.

A medieval legend provides us with an amusing example.[17] A religious sect possessed a statue with a strange property. Once a year, on a specific date, the members of the sect would meet and, eyes lowered, pray before it. The statue would then fall to its knees and weep. If a single member of the sect looked at it, however, the statue would remain immobile. When the obvious objection was raised by non-believers, the members of the sect responded with a superb and exemplary *ad ignorantiam*: the fact that the statue is immobile when it is being looked at does not prove that it does not kneel and cry when no one is looking.

Here is another example. It would have greatly undermined the glory and the divinity of the Pharaoh to put into writing or keep alive the memory of the fact that Jewish slaves managed to flee Egypt. That is why only the Bible talks about it and why there is no other trace of the event, whether archaeological, historical, or otherwise.

We don't always recognize these fallacies easily, however, maybe especially when we are the ones committing them. It is as if we have a greater epistemological tolerance when we are considering our own favorite beliefs. Then we are tempted to say that the fact that they cannot be determined to be wrong is proof of their worth—or vice versa. For example, someone who believes in extraterrestrials will say sententiously: "After all, no one has ever proved that they don't exist. So there must be something true about it." In the sphere of parapsychology, these fallacies are legion. "No one has been able to demonstrate that X cheated during the clairvoyance sessions—so he must have a gift." During the infamous McCarthy hearings, it was blithely maintained that if the FBI did not have any data indicating that a person was *not* a communist, the person must indeed be one.

Another reason that explains why it is so hard to detect the *ad ignorantiam* is that there are a good number of cases where it is perfectly legitimate to draw conclusions on the basis of a thing's absence. For example, if the results of reliable tests show that there is no cholesterol in your blood, it is reasonable to conclude that there is none. It is worth noting that the absence of cholesterol during such a test provides the relevant facts and good reasons to support this conclusion.

THE SLIPPERY SLOPE

For want of the nail the shoe was lost.
For want of a shoe the horse was lost.
For want of a horse the rider was lost.
For want of a rider the battle was lost.
For want of a battle the kingdom was lost.
And all for the want of a horseshoe nail.

—NURSERY RHYME

As soon as Tongking falls, all the barriers from here to the Suez fall.
—FRENCH GENERAL JEAN DE LATTRE DE TASSIGUY, 1951

The slippery slope is known as fallacy of diversion, because it distracts our attention from the subject under discussion and leads us to a consideration of something else—in this instance, a whole series of undesirable effects said to ensue from a starting point that our interlocutor in the exchange is defending. The fallacious reasoning here is that if we accept A, the point of departure advocated by our interlocutor, B will follow, then C, then D, and so forth, from undesirable consequence to undesirable consequence, until something particularly terrible happens. The argument, of course, aims to prove that we should not accept A. It can also be formulated by starting with an undesirable consequence instead of by finishing with one, and tracing it back to the point of departure advocated by the interlocutor. For example, in the United States, some say that if people accept gun control laws, then laws regulating something else will be implemented, and then something else, and soon Americans will find themselves living under a totalitarian regime. In doing so they are enjoying a little ride down the slippery slope.

The slippery slope draws a substantial part of its effect from the fact that the victims don't notice the weakness of each link in the chain, and that it is unreasonable to conclude that one leads to the other. Thus, since nothing guarantees the reliability of any link in the chain, neither is there anything to guarantee that if we accept A, all the rest will follow. So there are far from being any guarantees that the loss of the nail will result in the loss the kingdom.

Nonetheless, a form of the slippery slope fallacy called the domino effect was the basis of a part of US foreign policy during the second half of the twentieth century. It was held that if a Left government took power in a given country, all the surrounding countries would go Left also.

THE SMOKE SCREEN

Incomprehensible jargon is the hallmark of a profession.
—KINGMAN BREWSTER, JR.

Are you losing a debate? Is your adversary getting the better of you? Are her facts relevant, solid, well established? Are her arguments valid? Don't worry; all is not lost. There is still one trick to use: launch a smoke screen. Deploy it properly and all of your inconvenient adversary's beautiful arguments will disappear with her precious facts and all your troubles. To do so, nothing is as valuable as the use of the jargon discussed above; the example cited there could be cited here, too.

THE STRAW MAN

If you can't beat a given argument, it may be possible to achieve victory with a weaker version of the same reasoning. It will be even easier if we create the weakened version ourselves in such a way to guarantee that it will be demolished. Such is, in essence, the strategy at work in the fallacy known as the straw man. It takes its name from the ancient soldier's custom of training for combat against a dummy made of straw.

Here is an example in which the second interlocutor erects a straw man argument:

> —Abortion is morally condemnable, because it means the death of a human being. A fetus has the right to life, as much as a child who has already been born has the right to life. Well before birth, the fetus actually possesses most of the properties that make him an entire human being; very early, he even kicks his mother.
> —The cow also kicks and that does not make it a human being. If we follow your argument, we would have to stop eating beef. The fetus is no more human than a cow and abortion is morally permissible.

The soldier's dummy is easily recognized as made of straw. But when we resort to the straw man in the course of arguing, we often believe it to be our true adversary and we convince ourselves that in beating the straw figure we have defeated our adversary. In such cases, the ruse is turned back on the person who committed it. We have to be as vigilant against having it committed against us as committing it ourselves. To do so, we have to keep in mind the principle of charity according to which we must present the ideas we are contesting in the most favorable light. Victories won in debate lose their value and their importance in proportion to the lack of respect demonstrated for this fundamental principle.

THE APPEAL TO PITY
(OR ARGUMENTUM AD MISERICORDIAM)

This fallacy consists of appealing to particular circumstances that will elicit sympathy for a cause or a person, and insinuating that because of these circumstances, the usual criteria of evaluation do not apply—or at least do not apply with their usual rigor.

Here are some examples:

—The pressure that X endured was such that you can understand why he finally did such a thing.

—Before criticizing the President, think about how difficult his job is: he has to . . .

Of course, it is sometimes legitimate to appeal to particular circumstances and sometimes these inevitably evoke sympathy. The fallacy of the appeal to pity arises when we invoke these circumstances illegitimately, in such a way as to provoke a sympathy that should not factor into our judgment.

THE APPEAL TO FEAR

This fallacy is committed when we create fear, whether with threats or by other means, in order to put forward a position. Instead of taking the subject under discussion into consideration and weighing the arguments put forward, we instead steer the discussion toward the consequences of adopting such a position, and make people think that for one reason or another, they would be disastrous for the interlocutor holding the position.

The threat does not have to be explicit; it can even be imperceptible to all but the parties involved. That is exactly what makes this fallacy hard to detect. We all have fears, and sometimes they are deeply rooted in us. The demagogues know it, and they profit from it by using the fallacy of appeal to fear. Here are some examples of this fallacy:

—Infidel! You will wind up in hell!

—These activists threaten our way of life, our values, and our security.

—You are opposed to the death penalty, but you will change your mind the day that you or your children are victims of one of the criminals you saved from the electric chair.

—Professor, if you fail me on this exam, I will have to retake it in the summer. I don't think that my father, your dean, would like that very much.

—You should not say such things in public; if the rector were to hear of it, it could be costly for you.

—Mr. Director, I am convinced that your journalists know that this story about defective tires that caused a few peoples' deaths does not deserve to be dwelt on any longer. By the way, we have to find time to meet soon to discuss our annual promotion campaign; we always buy so much advertising space in your paper.

—You are a reasonable person and you will agree that you do not have the money to face an interminable trial.

THE FALSE ANALOGY

We often think with the assistance of analogies, that is, by comparing two things—most often one that is known and another that is less so. This sort of reasoning is often useful and illuminating. For example, at the beginning of the research on atoms, these new objects in physics were represented as mini-solar systems. The analogy is certainly imperfect, but it nonetheless permitted us to understand certain properties of that which was less known (the atom) on the basis of something that was much better understood (the solar system).

But there are cases in which a false analogy can lead us to think erroneously about the very thing we want it to help us understand. Because thinking by analogy is both common and useful, it is sometimes difficult to uncover false analogies. We become able to do so by asking if the similarities and differences between the two objects up for comparison are important or if, on the contrary, they are insignificant. The fallacious or non-fallacious character of the analogy then jumps out at us. Here are some examples that will allow you to exercise your judiciousness. Ask yourself, for each of these examples, if the suggested analogy is legitimate or not.

> —"How can we maintain that fixing prices is a crime when business people do it, but a public good when the government does it?" (Ayn Rand)
> —Nature itself teaches us that the strongest survive: that's why we should legalize and systematically practice euthanasia.
> —Rain and erosion end up overcoming even the

highest mountain peaks, and time and patience will overcome all our problems.

—A school is a small business where the salaries are the marks given to the students.

—Being against the Free Trade Area of the Americas is like being against the weather.

—The Republicans have undertaken important reforms. Re-elect them; you don't switch horses in the middle of the race.

—You can no more force a child to learn than force a horse to drink. You can only bring him water.

—It is time to be finished with this social cancer.

THE SUPPRESSION OF RELEVANT DATA

He who knows only his own side of the case,
knows little of that. His reasons may be good,
and no one may have been able to refute them.
But if he is equally unable to refute the reasons on
the opposite side; if he does not so much as know
what they are, he has no ground for
preferring either opinion.

—JOHN STUART MILL

This fallacy is one of the most difficult to detect, because, by definition, it involves the obfuscation of data related to the conclusion being defended in an argument. Reasoning is always stronger when all the relevant facts have been taken into account. But whether voluntarily or not, it sometimes happens that certain pertinent facts are forgotten.

This fallacy can be intentional: for example, advertisements don't specify that competing products are just as effective as the products they are praising when they tell us that no product is *more* effective. But it can also be unintentional and linked to our propensity not to seek, see, or remember examples other than those that confirm our preferred hypotheses. This sort of selective thinking is certainly at work in all sorts of beliefs, notably in the domain of the paranormal, and in some sense it involves hiding the pertinent facts from oneself.

We will return to this question in Chapter 3.

The Rules of Argumentative Decorum

Here are ten rules of argumentation suggested by Dutch scholars van Eemeren and Grootendorst. Each time a rule is broken, a fallacy is committed that constitutes a "mistake."

RULE 1: Participants must not prevent each other from supporting or challenging the theses up for debate.

Fallacies: The out of hand rejection of any thesis or the affirmation of the sanctity of any thesis; pressuring one's interlocutor; personal attacks.

RULE 2: If you go along with a thesis, you must defend it if you are if asked.

Fallacies: Avoiding the burden of proof; displacing the burden of proof.

RULE 3: When you criticize a thesis, the critique must be made of the thesis that was actually put forward.

Fallacies: Attributing a fictitious or distorted position to an interlocutor by oversimplifying or exaggerating.

RULE 4: You can only defend a thesis with arguments that are related to it.

Fallacies: Argumentation that is unrelated to the thesis being debated; theses defended by means of rhetorical tricks (for example, the *ad populum* or *ad verecundiam*).

RULE 5: You can be called on to defend the premises implicit in your argument.

Fallacies: The exaggeration of an unexpressed premise is a particular case of the straw man fallacy.

RULE 6: You have defended a thesis conclusively if you defended it by means of arguments that share a common starting point.

Fallacies: The misuse of a statement as a common starting point or the inappropriate denial of a common starting point.

RULE 7: You have defended a thesis conclusively if you defended it by means of arguments for which a commonly held framework for argument is properly applied.

Fallacies: The application of an inadequate framework for argument . . . by applying an argumentation framework inadequately. ("The American system doesn't care what happens to the sick. I know a man who died after being turned away from a hospital." "You don't need a computer; your father and I didn't have computers when we were young.")

RULE 8: Arguments used in a discursive text must be valid or subject to validation through the explanation of one or many unexpressed premises.

Fallacies: Confusing necessary and sufficient conditions; confusing properties of the parts with those of the whole.

RULE 9: The failure of a defense must lead the protagonist to withdraw her thesis, and a successful defense must lead the antagonist to retract his doubts about the thesis in question.

RULE 10: Statements must be neither vague and incomprehensible, nor confused and ambiguous; they must facilitate an interpretation that is as precise as possible.

Frans van Eemeren and Rob Grotendorst in A. Lempereur, ed., *L'Argumentation* (Liège: Mardaga), 173–193.

CHAPTER 2

MATHEMATICS: THOSE WHO REFUSE TO BE CONNED, COUNT!

Don't worry too much about your math problems; I can assure you that mine are much worse.
—ALBERT EINSTEIN

The essence of mathematics is its freedom.
—GEORG CANTOR

Sir, there is no royal road.
—EUCLID (addressing his student, King Ptolemy, who was finding his lessons difficult and asked if there wasn't an easier way of making progress)

Introduction

One day, back in the eighteenth century, a teacher who had to absent himself from his classroom gave his seven-year-old students one of those routine exercises for which some teachers seem to have a special knack even now. It involved adding all the numbers from 1 to 100: 1 + 2 + 3 and so forth.

The teacher thought this would keep his students busy for a good period of time. But less than a minute had gone by before one of them was twiddling his thumbs. When the teacher asked him why he wasn't working, the student replied that he'd finished his work. It was true, and he proved it by giving the correct answer: 5,050.

The student's name was Johann Carl Friedrich Gauss (1777–1855) and he would become one of history's most productive and most important mathematicians. Here is what Gauss did. Rather then put his head down and go at it, he first thought about the problem and tried to find out what sort of challenge it presented. Then came the stroke of genius. Gauss noticed an astonishing property, one that could also be generalized; the first term of the series (1) added to the last (100) gives a total (101) that is the same as that of the second term (2) added to the second last (99), the third term (3) added to the third-last (98), and so on. To get the answer that was asked for, this operation had to be repeated 50 times (the last operation in the series is 50 + 51). The final sum is thus the outcome of 50 times 101, which makes 5,050.

You don't need to have taken advanced mathematics to appreciate little Gauss's thinking. It is tidy, it is sound, it is quick—and it is irrefutable. These are the qualities that make mathematics such a powerful and indispensable tool of intellectual self-defense. Alas, math also terrifies a lot of people to the point that a word has been coined to describe those who are frightened and flee it: they are, we now say, mathophobes (or mathphobes).

All the same, we cannot allow ourselves to ignore mathematics completely, if only because we are constantly bombarded with numerical data that we have to understand and evaluate. Besides, as we will see, the consequences of running away from mathematics are often disastrous. The tragedy is precisely that too many people suffer from what a contemporary mathematician, John Allen Paulos, has baptized innumeracy—the equivalent of illiteracy with regard to numbers. Nevertheless, there is good news for mathophobes: to a great extent, the essential mathematical concepts are not very complex.

This chapter makes a wager that with patience, a twinge of humor, and a bit of care, mathophobia can be cured quite successfully. Obviously, I don't pretend to pass on all the mathematical concepts that each person should ideally master. There is too much material, and I have not mastered it all myself—far from it. We will nonetheless undertake a broad overview of citizen mathematics, especially as everyone already has a number of very efficient intellectual self-defense tools, due to the elementary concepts we learned in school. It is to these elementary concepts that we will turn first, in order to show how anyone can make use of their mathematical baggage, however modest, to avoid being conned. Then we will deal with two slightly more difficult, but equally indispensable, questions in the mathematics of intellectual self-defense: probability and statistics. I think I can assure you that if you throw yourself right into it, you will understand the basic ideas that are laid out in this section without any difficulty. At the end of this chapter, I hope that you will agree with me that mathematics amply repay the effort one invests in understanding them.

2.1 Treating Common Forms of Innumeracy

There are three types of people: those who know how to count, and those who don't.
—BENJAMIN DERECA

Numbers govern the world.
—PYTHAGORAS

THE PROBLEM: You suffer from indigestion of numbers that make absolutely no sense.

THE SOLUTION: Count carefully before deciding to consume them.

When the numbers are high, it is vital to ask yourself if they are plausible. To do so, you have to know the topic you are discussing, which sometimes requires specialized knowledge. If you don't have such knowledge, you can't evaluate the affirmation. For example, if I don't have the required knowledge in physics, I will be unable to evaluate numerical affirmations concerning the speed of sound (Mach 1, that is 331.4 meters per second at 0°C.) But often, notably in discussions about social and political issues, it is relatively easy to acquire the necessary knowledge if you don't already have it. In general, elementary arithmetic operations will suffice to demonstrate whether what is put forward is plausible or not, whether it makes sense or doesn't. So it is extremely useful to remain critically vigilant when faced with numerical data. Here are two examples of the enormous benefits that you can hope to gain by adhering to this simple maxim of intellectual self-defense: "Wait a moment while I perform the calculations."

One day, a university student proclaimed to me and to an auditorium of intellectuals that two thousand Iraqi children had died every hour for the past ten years because of the US/UK sanctions against the country. You may have heard the same thing before; it was repeated frequently. Let's leave aside, for now, the question of whether or not the sanctions were justified, and let us look at the affirmation made. Let us simply use arithmetic to do so. If two thousand children die each hour, that makes 17,520,000 children a year. Is it possible for this to go on for ten years in a country of 20 million people?

Let's just say that these sorts of "facts" don't help any cause.

Here is another example, this time about the number of young Americans killed by firearms in 1995. Joel Best relates the following anecdote in his excellent work on statistical lies.[1] In 1995, Best attended a thesis defense during which the candidate maintained that since 1950, the number of young people killed or wounded by firearms had doubled each year. He cited a scholarly article to support this fact. Everyone knows that the issue of firearms is quite explosive in the US. But once again, let us leave aside the debates that cause passions to rise. Now with only arithmetic as our tool, let us think a little about what is being said.

Let's posit, generously, that only one child was killed by a firearm in 1950. Thus, according to the statement advanced above, two children died because of firearms in 1951, four in 1952, eight in 1953, and so on. If you pursue these calculations, 32,768 kids died in 1965, which is definitely far greater than the total number of homicides (children and adults) that were committed in the US in that year. In 1980, there would have been a billion children killed, which is to say four times the population of the entire country. In 1987, the number of children killed by firearms in the US would have surpassed the total number of human beings who have lived on Earth since our species appeared (according to the best available estimates). The number you would hit in 1995 is so enormous that only in astronomy and economics do you normally encounter such figures.

This calculation represents a geometric progression: a sequence in which each outcome, or term, is equal to the preceding term multiplied by a constant. In our example, we had a geometric progression (2, 4, 8, 16 . . .), the common ratio of which is 2:1. In the same way, the ratio of the sequence 3, 15, 75, 375, 1,875, 9,375, 46,875 . . . is 5:1.

A simple formula allows us to quickly calculate any term of a geometric progression. Let U be our sequence; U_r, the Nth term for which we are trying to find a value; let R be the constant (or ratio) of the sequence. To calculate the Nth term, multiply the first term (U_r) by the constant R to the exponent $(n - 1)$. The formula is written thus:

$$U_n = U_r \times R^{(n-1)}$$

THE PROBLEM: You are the victim of mathematical "terrorism."

THE SOLUTIONS: Learn math; count; remain critical; don't be scared of asking for explanations.

The following might be an urban myth, but it doesn't really matter for our purposes here. It seems that in the eighteenth century, there was an attempt to set up a meeting between Leonhard Euler (1707–1783), generally recognized as one of the greatest mathematicians of all time, and Denis Diderot (1713–1783), the leading encyclopedist of the era. Euler was a devoted Christian, while Diderot was famous for his materialist and atheist positions.

They say that Euler finally agreed to the meeting with Diderot while the latter was visiting the tsar of Russia's court. There was feverish speculation as to how the face-to-face meeting of the two intellectual titans would unfold. People feared the worst. The story goes that when he arrived in court, the mathematician went straight for Diderot and said, "Sir, $\dfrac{(a + bn)}{n} = x$, so God exists. How do you respond?"

Up until then, Diderot had attacked and shredded a number of philosophical and theological arguments for the existence of God. This time, however, the philosopher was incapable of answering anything at all, for the excellent reason that he didn't understand what Euler had said, and, we can assume, probably because he felt humiliated to have to admit it.

This little story may be apocryphal, but it provides a perfect example of what I call mathematical terrorism. It involves using the prestige of mathematics in order to confound, deceive, or otherwise confuse people to whom one is speaking.

You can suspect mathematical terrorism is at work if you notice that the author himself does not have a handle on the math he is using or if the mathematical formulation of an idea is at best metaphorical and doesn't really add anything to what could have been expressed with common or specialized language.

It is useful to dwell on this phenomenon a little, because, as deplorable as it is, you will encounter it often, even in places where you shouldn't, like scholarly and university publications. A sociologist named Andreski devoted space in a work on the social sciences to show how these academic tricks work, and ironically instructs readers:

> To attain author-quality in this sort of undertaking, the recipe is as simple as it is rewarding: take a math textbook and copy the least complicated parts, adding a few references to the literature on one or two areas of social science, without worrying too much about whether the formulas you took down

have any relationship whatsoever with actual human actions, and give your final product a grand title that suggests that you have discovered the key to an exact science of collective behavior.[2]

I will leave it to you to find examples—unfortunately, it isn't very hard—and will content myself with concluding by reminding you that Austrian mathematician Kurt Gödel's incompleteness theorem—a mathematical outcome that is as significant as it is subtle and complex—has always been a favorite of mathematical terrorists.

THE PROBLEM: You are unable to deal with large numbers.

THE SOLUTIONS: Use scientific notation and practice.

We frequently encounter gigantic numbers in economics, astronomy, and other fields. For example, take the section of the 2004 US budget that was devoted to the so-called Department of Defense. According to the Associated Press (March 15, 2004), it was 402 billion dollars.

Now take the actual cost of the war in Iraq. According to credible calculations, the details of which I will spare you here, the war will have cost 378 billion dollars as of March 2007.[3] Of course, we should try to understand what this means politically and verify what is really being done under these budget headings. But let's dwell for a moment on the numbers themselves.

What is striking is how extremely limited most people's ability to understand and imagine enormous numbers seems to be. Indeed, what does 402 or 378 billion dollars mean? If we have no clear idea, we're left open to believing (and repeating) almost anything when very big numbers are involved. So it is crucial to look clearly and learn to picture them because after we reach a few thousand, we have a lot of trouble doing so. So here are three little tricks to help us, suggested by mathematician J. A. Paulos.[4]

First, it is helpful to take the main big numbers we're likely to encounter and match them with sets we understand. For example, a thousand could be the number of seats in your favorite stadium; ten thousand the number of bricks in the façade of a building you know. A million? A billion? Here's a suggestion: imagine that someone sends you on a luxury vacation for as long as you want, but the condition is that you have to spend one thousand dollars a day. Including the costs of hotel, restaurant, etc., we can imagine this. After a thousand days, that is, almost three years (two years and nine months) you will have spent a million dollars. But to spend a billion, your trip will have to last more than 27,000 years. Now it is your turn. Try to find ways to imagine the big numbers, all the way up to a quintillion.

The second trick is that it is better to write big numbers in scientific notation. It is simpler, and once you're used to it, it is a lot clearer. Besides, it's easy: 10^n (10 to the exponent n) is 1 followed by n zeros. 10^4 is thus 10,000.

The third trick is to make a game of counting things that force you to make use of big numbers. You will see how unreliable our intuition often is. Here are a few examples of calculations, again thanks to Paulos. How many cigarettes are smoked each year in the United States? (Answer: 5×10^{11}). How many people on the planet die each day? (Answer: 2.5×10^5). And do not fear to tackle immensely *small* numbers either. How fast does human hair grow, in kilometers per hour? (Answer: 1.6 x 10^{-8}). Your turn. Let's say that there are 15 x 10^3 grains of sand per cubic inch. How many grains of sand would it take to fill your entire bedroom?

Getting used to this sort of exercise makes us more self-confident when people throw big numbers at us, and often allows us to evaluate them correctly, and even to know, in certain cases, that what we're being told is implausible.

Let's return to the war in Iraq. Those who have tried to calculate its cost have tried to express the cost in ways that are easier to understand. To find the equivalent of an estimated 345 billion dollars, you can say that it is the same as the cost of registering 45,717,246 kids in the Head Start program, a pre-school education program for poor children. It is also the cost of hiring 5,981,755 public school teachers for a year. It is the cost of a year's worth of health insurance for 206,685,828 children; 16,732,988 four-year college scholarships; and 3,107,890 public housing units. Or you can think of it in this way: on the day these numbers were cited, every US household had spent $3,375 on the war. Every US citizen had spent $1,275.

THE PROBLEM: Figures are overblown through multiple countings.

THE SOLUTION: Limit counting in a major way.

The phenomenon to which I am drawing your attention occurs when you count one or several units more than once, thus arriving at a much higher total than in reality. Of course the risk of this happening increases when you are not clear on what you want to count or not quite sure how to determine what it is. For example, multiple counting happens when the media or the public service misevaluate the number of victims of a disaster because they added the data from various sources: hospitals, police, morgue, paramedics, and so on, with all the risks of duplication that entails. Thus, in 1998, the number of victims of the Quebec ice storm was first estimated as fifty-five, before progressively decreasing and settling at twenty-two.

THE PROBLEM: You hallucinate (supposedly) meaningful numerical coincidences.

THE SOLUTION: Learn to soothe the spirit with a better understanding of the astonishing properties of big numbers.

If we dare to define it, given the jumble of ideas and practices that it entails, numerology is the study of the allegedly mystical powers of numbers as well as their influence on and meaning for humans.

Most often, numerology purports to be able to determine the number that corresponds to a person's name and its meaning. To do so, it uses a system that matches each of the letters in the name to a number. Then the numbers are added and the outcome of this operation is deconstructed into a set of numbers that are added until a unique number (from one to nine) is obtained. This is called calculating the residual of a number. The number is associated with certain character traits that the person in question is presumed to have. Numerology is presented as a science by its followers, who claim to be practicing the same trade as Galileo. (Please, try not to laugh.)

A form of numerology is at work in the search for what

we might call "meaningful coincidences"—a search that some people pursue quite frenetically. In various instances, the numerologist tracks and displays numerical data from a collection of facts related to one or several events—in this last case, as you will see, he compares them. If that was all, it might just be amusing. The problem is that then the numerologist argues that chance cannot explain what he presents as remarkable coincidences, and attributes them instead to some sort of occult force, like a conspiracy, destiny, or a mystical power. The following two examples will allow you to better understand.

In the first, numerical aspects of 9/11 are enumerated. The day after the events of September 11, 2001, Uri Geller, a magician who became famous in the 1970s by attributing his capacity to perform a couple of banal conjuring tricks to paranormal powers,[5] asserted that the event had to be understood and interpreted with reference to the number 11. The number "represents a positive connection and a gateway to the mysteries of the universe and beyond,"[6] he maintained. In support of this "theory," Geller provided the following evidence:

—The date of the attack, 9/11: $9 + 1 + 1 = 11$;
—September 11th is the 254th day of the year: $2 + 5 + 4 = 11$;
—After September 11th there are 111 days left to the end of the year;
—119 is the area code to Iraq/Iran. $1 + 1 + 9 = 11$ (Reverse the numbers and you have the date);
—The Twin Towers, standing side by side, look like the number 11;

—The first plane to hit the towers was Flight 11 by American Airlines or AA. A is the first letter in the alphabet so we have again 11:11;

—State of New York: the eleventh state added to the Union;

—New York City: spelled with 11 letters;

—The *USS Enterprise* is in the Gulf during the attack; its ship number is 65N: $6 + 5 = 11$;

—Afghanistan: spelled with 11 letters;

—The Pentagon: spelled with 11 letters;

—Ramzi Yousef (convicted of orchestrating the attack on the WTC in 1993) is spelled with 11 letters;

—Flight 11: 92 passengers on board—$9 + 2 = 11$;

—Flight 77: 65 passengers on board—$6 + 5 = 11$;

—The house number where they were believed to have lived:#10001 (again, don't count the zeros);

—Names that have eleven letters: Air Force One, George W. Bush, Bill Clinton, Saudi Arabia, ww terrorism, Colin Powell (then US Secretary of State), Mohamed Atta (the pilot that crashed into the World Trade Center).

Concluding the message in which he outlined these "discoveries," Geller asked everyone to pray for—you guessed it—eleven minutes.

Our second example shows the similarities between a range of numerical data related to two events, the presidencies of Abraham Lincoln and John F. Kennedy:

—Lincoln was elected to Congress in 1846, Kennedy in 1946;

—Lincoln was elected president in 1860, Kennedy in 1960;

—Their last names are each seven letters long;

—The names of their assassins—John Wilkes Booth (for Lincoln) and Lee Harvey Oswald (for Kennedy)—each have three parts and both add up to fifteen letters in total;

—Both were killed on the fifth day of the week;

—Lincoln's successor, Andrew Johnson, was born in 1808; Lyndon B. Johnson, Kennedy's successor, was born on 1908;

—John Wilkes Booth was born in 1839; Lee Harvey Oswald in 1939.

What is going on here is very simple and easy to explain. The phenomenon is produced by the events in question, and particularly by the vague way in which they are defined. Indeed, there is a virtually infinite number of things related to these events that can be expressed numerically; so it is not very hard to find the same number in as many places as we want. We can assign an explanation and a precise mathematical formulation for this phenomenon by calculating probabilities (see the following section), which allows us to demonstrate how phenomena that seem like extraordinary coincidences are in fact absolutely ordinary and very likely to occur as long as you take into account the laws of very big numbers by which they are governed. The mistake is to arbitrarily choose ordinary numerical recurrences and attribute meaning to them.

Let me add that it is worth remaining skeptical not just of the interpretations offered by researchers in such pseudo-sciences, but also of their supposed facts. For example, in the lists above, the actual country code for Iraq is not 119 but 964, and Iran's is 98. As well, Booth was actually born in 1838.

THE PROBLEM: There is an illusion of extreme precision.

THE SOLUTION: Remind oneself how that supposed precision was achieved.

For a long time, normal human body temperature was recorded as 98.6°F, but was then reviewed and corrected by compiling the results of millions of temperatures taken. Thus, normal body temperature was redefined as 98.2°F— a very precise and reliable datum. How had they arrived at the first measurement, which was equally precise but not very accurate? The answer is amusing. Normal body temperature had been established rather roughly in degrees Celsius at a rounded average of 37°C. This measurement was converted into Fahrenheit as a very precise 98.6°F. This little story teaches a valuable lesson; when the data you are working with is approximated, extremely precise calculations are ridiculous and the precision of the results obtained is illusory.

Imagine that I measure the length of my six cats, from their noses to the ends of their tails. The results I get are obviously approximations. Say I get the following results, expressed in centimeters: 98, 101, 87, 89, 76, 76. Stating that the average length of cats in the house in 87.83333 makes no sense. This sort of precision is illusory and confers an aura of scientific rigor on my work that it simply does not deserve.

THE PROBLEM: You are a victim of arbitrary definitions intended to promote a biased presentation of the situation.

THE SOLUTION: Ask who counted and how what was counted is defined.

Here we devote ourselves to a little accounting exercise, meant to show that when we are faced with numerical data, it is always relevant to ask who produced it, with what aim, and according to what method and definition. It may well be the case that the data we are given obscures a part of reality. So let's not consider numbers to be sacrosanct, and let's remember that they are the result of sometimes arbitrary choices and decisions.

Maybe you know this joke that makes the rounds in accounting circles. A company wants to hire an accountant. The first candidate is asked what two and two make. Four, he answers. The second candidate is invited into the interview room. Same question, same answer. Then a third candidate is ushered in. When he hears the question, he stands up, carefully closes the curtains, and asks in a low voice: "How much do you want it to make?" He is hired on the spot.

The following fictitious example, also adapted from a classic little book by Darrell Huff,[7] deals with accounting procedures.

Consider the financial information for two companies:

Company A
    Average employee salary: $22,000
    Average owners' salary and profits: $260,000

Company B
    Average salary: $28,065
    Average owners' profits: $50,000

Which of the two companies would you prefer to work for? Which would you prefer to own? Your answer doesn't really matter all that much because they are both the same company. How is that possible? It's very simple.

Let's say that three people own a business that employs ninety people. At the end of the year, the owners have paid $1,980,000 in salary to their employees. The three owners each took a salary of $110,000. That leaves $450,000 in profits to be divided amongst the owners.

You can explain this by saying that the average annual salary of the employees is $1,980,000 divided by 90, or $22,000. The income of each owner can be calculated by adding his or her salary and portion of the profits, which makes $110,000 + ($45,000 ÷ 3) = $260,000. That is company A. Its business figures look great, and if you were one of the company's owners, you could show them off to your advantage in a number of business contexts.

Now suppose that the owners want to highlight their deep humanism and sense of justice.

If the numbers above don't seem like the best ones to use in this case, you can take $300,000 from the profits and spread the amount between the three owners as a bonus. Then calculate the average salary, this time including the three owners in the calculations. This time the average salary is ($1,980,000 + $330,000 + $300,000) ÷ 93 = $28,065. And the owners' profits are now $150,000 ÷ 3 = $50,000 each. That is company B.

This example is doubtless extremely oversimplified. Any accountant will tell you that in reality, you can do much better—or worse—than this!

THE PROBLEM: You find detached or semidetached data.

THE SOLUTION: Attach it to something!

Data is called detached or semidetached when it doesn't refer to anything or when its referents are vague and don't really provide a sense of what is being discussed. If we don't know what a number is supposed to quantify, we don't really know what we're talking about or what is being claimed.

Take for example the statement, "More than 80 percent of people prefer Talou chocolate." What conclusions can we draw from this? The makers of Talou chocolate would like us to conclude that there is also a strong chance that we will prefer their chocolate. But there are excellent reasons not to give into the temptation, because this data is detached, and nothing about the claim allows us to draw that conclusion.

Of course, first of all, what counts is your taste, not that of 80 percent of people. Secondly, how many people were surveyed? What sort of sample was used? And how many times was the test done before these results were obtained? This 80 percent—does that mean 800 people out of 1,000, 80 out of 100, or 8 in 10, or even 4 out of 5, or something other still? Finally, to what exactly did these people prefer Talou chocolate? To an inedible brand? To all the others? To a few? Which ones? As you can see, 80 percent is a detached datum.

"Two times less carbohydrates!" says the sliced bread package in an attempt to appeal to diabetics. That's all well and good, but before anyone rejoices, they would have to know what is being compared. If that is not specified, the datum is detached and doesn't mean a thing other than what the swindler wants you to hear, "Buy me! I'm what you need!" What is the reference point for the comparison? If it is a very carbohydrate-rich bread, bread that contains two times less might still be very high in sugar. If it is an average, which one was chosen and to what sort of sample was it applied? What is a slice of bread, anyway? Are comparable slices being compared? As I write, I have before me a bread slice purported to contain seven grams of carbohydrates instead of the fifteen that a regular slice of the same brand usually contains. But anyone who looks closely enough would immediately see that the new slices are much smaller and thinner than the others. Looking at it I would even say that they appear to be about . . . twice as small.

THE PROBLEM: The patient cannot define what is being discussed, or the definition changes as we go along.

THE SOLUTION: Always ask what is being discussed and ensure that the definition has not been changed surreptitiously.

Particularly in human affairs, the definitions we use to talk about things are conventional constructions. Change a definition and you can make people think that something real has changed. Economic, political, and social data must therefore be examined with great care in order to ensure that the definition of what is being measured is clear, relevant, and constant. If it is not, some sort of justification is absolutely required.

According to a *San Francisco Chronicle* columnist writing in 1996, millions of Americans suddenly became obese without gaining a single pound. How is that possible? The columnist[8] had just learned that obesity is defined according to a Body Mass Index (BMI). According to the World Health Organization, the definition of obesity is a BMI of 25 or more, while in the United States, you have to have a BMI of 27.6 or more to be considered obese.

Here is another example. In 1998, the unemployment rate in Britain grew prodigiously. The number of unemployed grew by 500,000 all at once, causing the unemployment rate to rise from 5 to 7 percent. What sort of calamity had hit the country? None. They had simply changed the definition of unemployed—as had been done thirty-two times in eighteen years in that same country. Each time before, it had been done to diminish the number of people without work; this time, the effect was to raise the number.

A critical thinker demonstrates good judgment by remembering that a good definition is a convention, but not completely arbitrary. Not being tied to the usual, agreed-upon definitions for things can sometimes lead to surprising and even interesting outcomes. Ivan Illich's work demonstrates this well. He developed a critique of advanced industrial societies, notably centered on notions of progress and growth, and emphasizing the way in which citizens are reduced to consumers by monopolistic bureaucracies at the service of productivism.

Illich's analysis had ramifications for medicine, work and unemployment, education, transportation, and energy. Let's take a look at this last topic. According to Illich, the individual car is the solution par excellence that our civilization produced to answer the question of how to move from one place to another most efficiently. Beyond the immediately obvious advantages of this method, the solution has many drawbacks, and is even a genuine danger to health, the environment, and so on. Yet we don't see these at first, and sometimes we even prefer to ignore them out of enthusiasm for the speed and efficiency of the car. But little by little, the tool has become counterproductive and problems have arisen. Now the ideological and bureaucratic system that has been installed in the meantime, and which holds a "radical monopoly" over it, is incapable of coming up with a solution to these problems except by upping the ante. In so doing, it only exacerbates the cause of the problems it is trying to eliminate. The car has to allow us to go quickly from point A to point B. When everyone owns one, they cause traffic jams that slow the speed of travel considerably. We respond by building more highways, more bridges, and so forth. And thus, says Illich, we are faced with the productivist trap, and its close relation, what he calls the tool's counterproductivity.

According to Illich, we have to try to rethink the question in an entirely different way. To do so, he proposes a new definition of speed, one that requires that we consider the social cost of the car. In articulating this new definition, all the hours of immobility and work to which each of us consents to pay for a car, the gas it uses, its upkeep, and the insurance must be taken into account. So must all the hours necessary to pay the collective cost of car use: roads, highways, hospitals, and so on. Illich carries out the calculations and finds that the real social speed of the car is not substantially greater than that of the horse and buggy.

THE PROBLEM: The patient seems incapable of estimating percentages and data calculated per resident.

THE SOLUTION: Try some warm-up exercises.

Last year, fifty homicides were committed in Port-of-Call and fifty in Sleepsville.[9] What should you do if you want to move to the city in which the fewest crimes are committed? You will want to ask what that number means in relation to the past—to keep things simple, say five years ago. That will give you an estimate of the way the crime variable for the two cities has changed over time.

Five years ago, there were forty-two murders committed in Port-of-Call and twenty-nine in Sleepsville. To determine what that represents, we subtract this value from the newer one (fifty, in both cases), and divide the outcome by the old value, then multiply the outcome by one hundred. Thus, we obtain the percentage of the rise in homicides in both cities. It looks like this:

Port-of-Call
$$(50 - 42) = 8$$
$$8 \div 42 = 0.19$$
$$0.19 \times 100 = 19\%$$

Sleepsville
$$(50 - 29) = 21$$
$$21 \div 29 = 0.72$$
$$0.72 \times 100 = 72\%$$

Is that all? I would guess that you wouldn't stop there, knowing perfectly well that this percentage is a semi-detached datum: 72 percent and 19 percent of what? You need to know before comparing and drawing conclusions.

Let's say that the population of Port-of-Call is 600,000 people this year, and was 550,000 five years ago. And let's say that Sleepsville has a population of 800,000 this year, while five years ago it was 450,000. Thus, the two cities have not grown at the same rate and our numbers have to take that into account. We want to express the rate of homicides per resident, that is to say, as a function of the population. To do so, we simply divide the number of homicides by the total population. Then, because the miniscule number we end up with is not very convenient, we multiply it by 100,000 to have a datum valid for every section of 100,000 residents. Let's see how it works with this year's data:

Port-of-Call

$50 \div 600,000 = 8.33 \times 10^{-5}$
$8.33 \times 10^{-5} \times 100,000 = 8.33$ per 100,000

Sleepsville

$50 \div 800,000 = 6.25 \times 10^{-5}$
$6.25 \times 10^{-5} \times 100,000 = 6.25$ per 100,000

Five years ago, the situation in the two cities was the following:

Port-of-Call

$42 \div 550,000 = 7.64$ per 100,000 residents

Sleepsville

$29 \div 450,000 = 6.44$ per 100,000 residents

Expressed in percentages, overall homicides had risen 72 percent in Sleepsville and 19 percent in Port-of-Call. But if we take into account, as we must, the populations of the two cities, what are their homicide rates then? The per capita homicide rate in Sleepville actually dropped, while that in Port-of-Call rose.

2.2 Probability and Statistics

All generalizations are dangerous, including this one.
—ALEXANDRE DUMAS, FILS

It is probable that improbable things will occur.
—ARISTOTLE

There are three kinds of lies: ordinary lies, sacred lies, and statistics.
—BENJAMIN DISRAELI

Thou shall not sit with a statistician,
Nor commit a social science.
—W. H. AUDEN

H. G. Wells, the science fiction writer, predicted in the first half of the twentieth century that knowing statistics would one day become as necessary for exercising citizenship as knowing how to read and write. I think that his prediction has come true and that statistics—and probability, their inseparable companion—are now indispensable citizens' tools. That is why I offer in the coming pages an overview of the basic notions of statistics and probability.

We will begin our journey by playing dice. We'll start by studying probability, which was inspired by games of chance. These origins, perhaps not the noblest in kind, should not make us forget this theory's great seriousness and its immense usefulness in all sectors of life and scientific research. Should I buy insurance or not? What are my chances of winning the lottery? What is the probability that I will get sick if I smoke a pack of cigarettes a day? What is my life expectancy? You can answer all these questions and thousands of others thanks to the calculation of probabilities.

2.2.1 Probability

Probability theory developed out of questions that the Knight of Méré asked his friend Blaise. So let me introduce them.[10]

A RIDDLE FOR PASCAL

Let's go back to seventeenth-century France. The Knight of Méré (Antoine Gombaud, circa 1607–1684) was something of a libertine, a great lover of wine, women, and gambling. Blaise was Blaise Pascal, a brilliant philosopher, physician, and mathematician, who, while he was hanging out with Méré, was still in the rather worldly phase of his life—a phase he would soon end to devote himself exclusively to religion, leaving everything else, including mathematics, behind.

Méré mostly played dice games. He was a scrupulous player who studied the game carefully and took notes on his matches. He developed some basic rules and applied them methodically. First, he always checked the dice before playing. A wary player, Méré had noticed that some cheaters used crooked dice, loaded with a weight that made them more likely to roll a given number. You can imagine the advantage given to the person who knew this. So Méré only played with fair dice, that is to say dice that really did roll randomly and with the same likelihood of turning up each of its six sides.

When you throw a fair die, you obviously can't know what number it will turn up. But Méré knew that each of the faces of a fair die tends to turn up once out of every six rolls.

Of course, Méré knew that sometimes he would roll the same number, six for example, two, three, or even four times in a row. Suppose I want to roll a six and suppose also that I roll the die four times in a row. Well, thought Méré, I have four times one chance in six of rolling a six. It is easy to calculate what that represents: $4 \times 1/6 = 2/3$. Thus, concluded Méré, I have two chances in three of rolling a six if I roll the die four times in a row.

Méré, however, almost always played games that required not one die but two dice of different colors—let's say, one black and one white. So he asked himself what the likelihood of rolling two sixes would be. To find out, he reasoned as follows.

When I throw two dice, the first die can turn up a one, and the second a one, a two, a three, a four, a five, or a six. This makes six possibilities with a one on the first die. But that first die can also turn up a two, and the second a one, a two, a three, a four, a five, or a six. Now there are twelve possibilities. The first die can also turn up a three, while the second die—and so on. In total, there are thirty-six possibilities. You can check it for yourself.

The outcome of Méré's thought process can be represented like this:

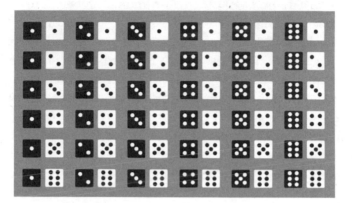

The Knight was only interested in one of these thirty-six possibilities: that in which the first die turns up a six and the second also turns up a six. That possibility is only one of the thirty-six combinations on our table. What is my chance of rolling a double six on the first roll of two dice? One in thirty-six. But suppose for a moment that I roll the two dice twenty-four times. Méré went through the same thought process and concluded that he had twenty-four times one chance in thirty-six of rolling a double six. The calculation looks like this: 24 x 1/36 = 2/3.

That means, our Knight concluded, that we have exactly the same likelihood (2/3) of rolling a six by rolling a die four times as we do of rolling a double six by rolling the two dice twenty-four times. The Knight was very proud of himself; his reasoning, he thought, was impeccable. Yet when he gambled on the basis of this unassailable reasoning, the traitorous diced refused to behave as his reasoning had predicated: our Knight lost more often with two dice than when he played with only one. This upset him. He lost money. The problem obsessed him and he began to have trouble sleeping.

Unable to think himself out of the problem, Méré went to see his friend Blaise, and presented it to him (along with another one that we will not deal with here). Pascal's reflection on these problems and his ensuing correspondence with Pierre de Fermat (1601–1665) gave rise to probability theory. What Pascal found and explained to Méré is something we can also understand. It will open the door to being able to calculate probabilities and statistics, and is extremely valuable.

SOME CONCEPTS OF PROBABILITY

Let's go back to the table that represents the collection of thirty-six possible outcomes of a chancy experiment (throwing two different colored dice). We'll suppose that each outcome has the same chance of appearing as any of the rest. So let's take one at random: draw a one on the black die and a one on the white die. What is its probability? This outcome occurs only once in the thirty-six possible outcomes available to us. So it has one chance in thirty-six of occurring. Probability is often expressed in this way, that is, as a fraction in which the numerator is the favored outcome and the denominator is the ensemble of possible outcomes.

Here the probability of an event defined as "getting one on the white die and one on the black die" is $1/36$. The probability of an event is also understood to lie between zero (in which case the event is impossible and we are certain that it cannot occur) and one (the event is certain to occur). The probability that the sum of the two upward-looking faces of the dice is thirteen is zero; that of rolling two numbers the sum of which is between two and twelve is one (or 36/36). You'll have guessed that each of the thirty-six outcomes in our drawing has a probability of 1/36 and that their sum is one, since 36 x 1/36 = 1.

Let's go a little further. Let's say that this time what we are calling an event can be obtained in a number of dif-

ferent possible outcomes. For example, consider rolling a total of three. That's an event. What is its probability? To find out, you would have to ask how many possible outcomes produce the event. Let's look at the table. The sum of three can be obtained when the black die rolls a one and the white die rolls a two, but also when the white die rolls a one and the black die a two. So two outcomes produce the event. The probability of each outcome is one in thirty-six.

This event thus has two chances in thirty-six of occurring.

Let's write that a little more clearly.

Let there be an event A; we will write its probability $P(A)$. For event A, the total of the rolled dice is three, so we'll have $P(A) = 2/36$.

It is also possible to combine events, and that is precisely what probability allows to be calculated. Take events E and F. We can combine them in a number of ways to get new events. We can try to determine the probability of getting them both, or in other words, the probability of E and F. Or we can find the probability of obtaining E or F; finally we can try to find not E (or not F), that is, the probability of not getting E (or F). Let's test ourselves at this new game.

Let's say that event E is that the white die rolls one and event F is that the black die rolls one. Let's say that we want to calculate the probability of obtaining either one or the other, that is to say, the probability of rolling one with one of the dice. Let's return once more to our table in order to think about this. There are six outcomes in which E occurs and there are also six in which F occurs. Let's black out all these outcomes. Have you noticed? We have twice blacked out the outcome in which both dice roll one. Why? Because the two events share an element and we have to be careful not to count them twice. That gives us the rule for the "or" operation when events are not mutually exclusive. It's our addition rule. Here it is (for an E and F that are not mutually exclusive):

$$P(E \text{ or } F) = P(E) + P(F) - P(E \text{ and } F)$$

In the case of our example, we will get:

$$\frac{6}{36} + \frac{6}{36} - \frac{1}{36} = \frac{11}{36}$$

The probability of rolling one with one of the dice is 11/36.

If the events *are* mutually exclusive, we must simply add the probabilities of each one, without having to subtract. That provides us with our second rule:

$P(E \text{ or } F) = P(E) + P(F)$

Let's introduce another rule. Let there be an event E. By definition, we have:

$P(E) = 1 - P(\text{not } E)$

Let there be an event D, that consists of rolling a double one and of which the probability is 1/36. We can find it by saying that it has a probability of $1 - P(\text{not } D)$, that is, $1 - 35/36$. We will find that this rule will be very useful in solving Méré's problem.

Now we simply have to understand the rules related to $P(E \text{ and } F)$, that is to say the probability that the two outcomes occur. Here, we must introduce a small subtlety: the events we want to combine can be dependent or independent.

Let's again take up our event $P(A)$ = rolling a total of three. There is a probability of 2/36. Now suppose that we first roll the white die; we observe the outcome and then roll the other. Suppose the white die rolls a one. Does $P(A)$ still have a probability of 1/36? Of course not. If the first die turns up a one, the probability of having a three has obviously increased: it is now 1/6. In this case, the outcome of the first roll of the (white) die has an influence on the probability we are trying to determine. Let's call the event of rolling one on the first die B. The probability of B influences the probability of A. This is called conditional probability and it is written like this: $P(A|B)$

If the two events are combined with "and" and they are dependent in this sense, then:

$$P(A \text{ and } B) = P(A|B) \times P(B)$$

If they are independent—which means that the fact that one occurs has no impact on the probability of the other—we will have:

$$P(A \text{ and } B) = P(A) \times P(B)$$

These rules are the only ones that it is absolutely necessary to know in order to begin playing with probability, which I suggest we do right now.

As we've seen, the probability of an event is expressed by the relation of the number of ways an event can occur to the total number of possible outcomes. When we know or have reason to believe that there are X equally possible outcomes, we can determine the probability of an event in advance. This is so with dice rolling, as long as the dice aren't loaded, of course. In the other cases, we have to experiment, run trials, and gather data to determine the probability of an event in retrospect. The probability that a baseball player will hit a home run, that it will rain tomorrow, that you will get a given sort of cancer by smoking

X number of cigarettes a day must all be determined in retrospect. They are estimates that are more or less reliable depending on various factors, particularly the number of cases that have been observed.

LOTTO 6/49

Lotto 6/49 is one of Canada's nationwide lotteries. In Lotto 6/49, the winner is the person who chose six numbers (of forty-nine possible choices) that correspond to the six numbers chosen at random by a mechanism on the day of the draw. What is the probability of winning this game? Combination and permutation rules are required to determine this ahead of time.

Let's take a group of three letters: A, B, and C. We want to know how many ways these letters can be arranged in groups of two without repeating a letter, and if AC is considered to be different from CA. What we're looking for are arrangements of two out of a set of three. You will find six:

AB BC BA CB AC CA

But when the groups are bigger, it gets very hard to count permutations in this way. You'll have guessed already that there is a formula for calculating this. We write A_k^n, where n is the number of elements in the set, A is the permutation operation and k is the number of elements grouped in a set. The formula is:

$$A_k^n = \frac{n!}{(n-k)!}$$

The $n!$ is read "factorial of n" and is the product of all positive integers less than or equal to n. In our example:

$$A_2^3 = \frac{3!}{1!} = \frac{3 \times 2 \times 1}{1} = 6$$

Let's return to the 6/49. We will get:

$$A_6^{49} = \frac{49!}{43!} = 10{,}068{,}347{,}520$$

This gives us roughly one chance in 10 billion of winning with any one ticket. There is, however, a little wrinkle. Remember how the order of the elements is important—in other words, that AC and CA are considered two different permutations. This is not the case in a lottery, since if you chose six numbers—for example, one, two, three, four, five, forty-nine—you would win even if the numbers were drawn in a different order. So what we want to find this time are the combinations. The formula is then:

$$C_k^n = \frac{n!}{k!\,(n-k)!}$$

For the 6/49, we get:

$$C_6^{49} = \frac{49!}{6! \times 43!} = 13{,}983{,}816$$

Our probability of winning has greatly improved. But what is it really worth? Let us round it to one in 14 million chances. If 7 million Canadians each bought a different ticket, there would still be one chance in two that no one would win the prize. We can get some idea of what such a probability really means by trying to represent "one chance in a million" in a more familiar way. Here are a few examples suggested by McGervey.[11] You have one chance in a million of dying if you drive without wearing your seat belt for sixty miles; ride a motorcycle without a helmet for five minutes; fly on a commercial airplane for ten minutes; smoke two cigarettes. So if you drive from downtown Montreal to the nearest US border crossing without wearing a seat belt you have roughly fourteen times more chance of dying than you have chances of winning the 6/49.

The following table replicates Paulos's data[12] and also helps to picture what is meant by "a chance at winning the 6/49."

Death by car accident	1 in 5,300
Death by drowning	1 in 20,000
Death by suffocation	1 in 68,000
Death by bike accident	1 in 75,000
Death in a terrorist attack while in a foreign country	1 in 600,000
Death by lightning	1 in 2 million
Death caused by a bee sting	1 in 6 million

To finish, would you say that the fictitious series of Lotto numbers I made up earlier (one, two, three, four, five, forty-nine) is more, less, or equally probable than that which won this week?

PASCAL'S TRIANGLE

The difficulties we run into when dealing with probability often have to do with the fact that we have trouble defining and thinking about the outcomes we can expect, and deciding whether or not they are exclusive or independent. Pascal's triangle—yes, the same Pascal—can be helpful for certain calculations.

The famous triangle looks like this:

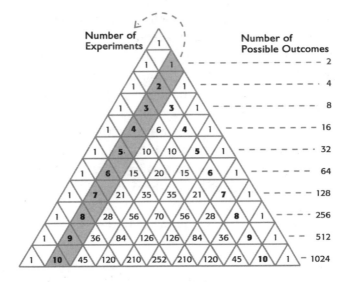

It is very easy to build a Pascal's Triangle. Start by writing the number one in the first cell. The next line down is line one and it is made up of two cells: in each one, write the sum of the numbers that appear immediately above them. As there is only one in this instance, write down the number one twice.

The next line, the second line of the triangle, is made up of three cells with the numbers 1, 2, and 1. And so on. The tenth line reads: 1, 10, 45, etc. Take any line and call it N. It gives us the distribution of N experiments made up of two outcomes. Line ten, for example, indicates the probabilities of ten coin tosses (of which there are two possible outcomes: heads or tails), or of ten births (of which there are two possible outcomes: boy or girl), etc. Let's take a closer look at this line. The total of the numbers therein is: 1 + 10 + 45 + 120 + 210 + 252 + 210 + 120 + 45 + 10 + 1 = 1,024. If we flip a coin ten times, there is one chance (that's the first number in the line) in 1,024 (the total of all the numbers) that heads will turn up every time. There are 10 chances in 1,024 of getting a distribution of 1 head and 9 tails; 45 chances in 1,024 of getting 2 heads and 8 tails, and so on.

What is the probability that there will be 5 heads and 5 tails? Using Pascal's Triangle, the answer jumps right out at you: 252/1,024. Note too that the distribution 6-4 or 4-6 (that is, 6 heads and 4 tails or 6 tails and 4 heads) is the most probable (with 420 chances in 1,024), although that might not have been what we assumed intuitively.

It's your turn now.

In a family with ten kids, what is the probability that three are girls and seven are boys?

We'll conclude this section by examining two other very valuable tools that our study of probability will allow us to store in our critical thinking kit.

THE GAMBLER'S FALLACY

This error of judgment is also called the Monte Carlo fallacy, because it is so very common amongst gamers. It is committed when the person betting is persuaded that a series of a given kind of result indicates that another kind should be expected in the next draw. For example, having turned up four tails in a row, the player believes that the next flip of the coin has to turn up heads. He is wrong, for the simple reason that the events (the coin tosses) are independent: the coins have no memory of the side on which they have landed, and previous results do not have any influence on those to come. The probability of flipping heads is the same each time, or 50 percent.

EXTRAORDINARY? NOT SO FAST . . .

Another very significant repercussion of mastering probability is that it keeps us from persuading ourselves that events we knew were going to happen by chance are in any way extraordinary. So we don't have to appeal to the intervention of any extrinsic power to account for their occurrence.

I will give two examples:

Example 1: The Eldest Sons

A survey showed that most of the famous mediums are eldest sons. Supporters of parapsychology were very perturbed by this fact and they put forward all sorts of daring hypotheses to explain it. Were they right to be so perturbed? Some simple reasoning shows that they were not.

In any given population, especially when the number of children per family is quite low (two, three, or four), there are always more eldest sons.[13] So the majority of just about anyone you want are eldest sons. Consider a fictitious population of one hundred families, each with two children. There will be equal proportions of the following combinations (where G means girl and B means boy):

B, B
B, G
G, B
G, G

In three cases out of four, a son is an eldest son. You'll find that this is also true of families of three: eldest sons (and daughters too) form the majority. In short, there is no mystery to illuminate here, and to paraphrase Marcel Duchamp, there is no solution, because there is no problem!

Example 2: Premonition?
Mr. Paul is excited. He was thinking about an acquaintance, Ms. Jay, and five minutes later, the phone rang; the caller informed him that Ms. Jay had passed away. You have to admit that there is something to the belief in premonitions.

We often hear this sort of reasoning, particularly in support of the paranormal. Here again, our new tool will be very useful because it will show us that there is no mystery to explain.

Suppose—and we'll be very modest—that Mr. Paul knows one thousand people (in the broadest sense of the term, the way he might know Al Gore) whose deaths he will learn of over the next thirty years. Now let's also suppose, again very modestly, that Mr. Paul thinks about each of those thousand people only once in thirty years. The question is the following: what is the probability that he will think about one of these people and learn of their death in the five minutes that follow? Calculating the probability allows us to determine the probability taking all the conventions into account. And the probability is low: a little more than three chances in ten thousand. But Mr. Paul lives in a country of 50 million people. Amongst this population there will be 16,000 "mysterious premonitions" over the next thirty years. That makes 530 cases a year, and more than one a day. In short, as Henri Broch (from whom I have borrowed this example) writes: "Simple chance thus allows for much to be written about the 'fantastic parapsychic premonitions in France' in numerous works that will sell very well."

And now, before moving on to the statistical notions I would like to present to you, let us return to Méré's riddle.

HOW PASCAL SOLVED MÉRÉ'S RIDDLE

The Knight's calculations weren't worth a thing, as you now understand. Let's call what we're looking for (getting a six in four rolls of the dice) E. Méré's problem is more easily resolved by searching for the inverse, that is to say by trying to calculate $1 - P(\text{not } E)$.

The calculation is a little complicated. The rolls of the dice are independent and $P(\text{not } E) = (5/6)^4$ for a die thrown four times, which makes 0.482. Thus,

$$P(E) = 1 - P(\text{not } E) = 1 - 0.482 = 0.518$$

For two dice thrown twenty-four times,

$$P(\text{not } E) = (35/36)^{24} = 0.509$$

$$P(E) = 0.491$$

Notice how instructive these results are. Certainly, we now understand why the Knight was winning with one die but losing with two dice. But the differences are so minimal that it *also* means that our brave Knight was playing a lot and keeping very careful track of each match.

2.2.2 Statistical Notions

The word statistic is used in two ways. On the one hand, it refers to quantifiable data—for example, statistics about the divorce rate in California. On the other, it refers to a branch of mathematics that uses and develops methods for gathering, presenting, and analyzing data. This branch is what we will deal with here, though mostly we will be looking at one smaller branch of statistics, known as descriptive statistics. As the name indicates, descriptive statistics allow us to describe observations about anything—people, objects, or events. (In statistics these are called "populations.")

THE BELL CURVE

Let's go back to our dice rolling, using two different dice. We can represent the theoretical results of our rolls with the help of a graphic. On the (vertical) Y axis, we can express in percentage form the probability of obtaining the sums from two to twelve, which we will have marked on the (horizontal) X axis. Then we will draw rectangles called histograms to represent the probability of each total.

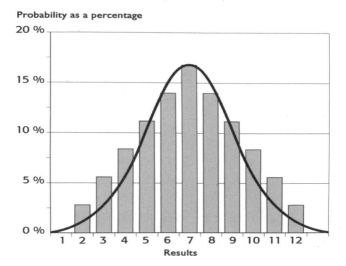

The histogram is an approximate representation of Gaussian distribution—named after the same Gauss featured in the introduction to this chapter. It is also known as the bell curve and as the normal distribution. It represents the distribution of many random human or natural phenomena. It is important to become familiar with it and be able to recognize it.

MEAN, MEDIAN, AND MODE

There are many ways of reducing a collection of data to a single value, which allow you to grasp what is characteristic of your data and so to preserve a sort of snapshot of those characteristics. The measures of central tendency allow you to do this, as they show the typical or central tendencies of the data. Measures of central tendency are widely used, and very useful, so we must learn them, all the more because these three measures of central tendency do not necessarily give the same value. That being the case, they can be used to deceive: all you have to do is choose from among them the measure that you want to see appear, which might not be truly representative of the data.

The measures of central tendency are the average or arithmetic mean, the median, and the mode.

The arithmetic mean or average is simply the average of all the data included in the sample. You get it by adding all the values of all the data and then dividing by the number of entries in the sample. It is written as follows:

$$\overline{X} = \frac{\Sigma x_i}{n}$$

where $\overline{X}$ is the conventional mathematical symbol of the mean value of x_i;

x is the observed value;

$\Sigma\, x_i$ is the sum of all the values of x observed;

and n is the number of observations that make up the collection of data.

If you order your data from the lowest to the highest value, you will easily find the median: it is simply the value that divides the top half of the data from the bottom half of the data. If there is an even number of observations in the sample, you get the median by averaging the two central observations.

Finally, the mode is the value that occurs most frequently within a sample.

Here is an example that will help us understand all of this. Below are the prices of the Bang Bang billy club, according to eight different suppliers of the New York Police Department:

$109	$139
$129	$149
$129	$159
$135	$179

The average is easy to calculate:

$$109 + 129 + 129 + 135 + 139 + 149 + 159 + 179 = 1,128$$

$$\frac{1,128}{8} = 141$$

To find the median, simply order the data as follows:

$$109, 129, 129, 135, 139, 149, 159, 179$$

As there is an even number of data (8), we take the two middle ones ($135 and $139), add them, divide by two, and we have our median: $137.

Finally, the mode can be determined at a glance: $129 occurs most frequently.

You'll have noticed that the three measures of central tendency in this example produce values that are not substantially different. That is what usually happens in a normal distribution, where the mean, the median, and the mode have almost identical values. You can verify this by calculating them for the thirty-six outcomes of the dice rolls presented above. But be careful: this is not always the case. Sometimes relying on one of these measures of central tendency is deceptive, in the sense that the measure chosen does not give an accurate idea of what is typical of a data set. Yet that is precisely what we want to use these measures to express.

Imagine, for example, a university creative writing department that proudly announces that the mean annual income of its graduates is $242,000. That's a very impressive result—too impressive, in fact. When this sort of figure is thrown at you, you should ask to see the data. Suppose one of the graduates also plays hockey and was hired at the end of his studies to play for a professional team. His 4 million dollars a year salary distorts the results. Indeed, the mean is a measure of central tendency that is sensitive to extreme data. In cases like these, it is better to rely on a different measure of central tendency. Which one, and why? Some answers to this question are summarized in the following table.

Summary: Measures of Central Tendency

The mean is the most frequently used measure of central tendency. There is always a mean, and it takes the value of all the data into account, but it is sensitive to extreme values.

The median is also commonly used, but less so than the mean. There is always a median, but it does not take all the values into account (except to count how many there are). It is not sensitive to extreme values. Thus, when such values are present, it can be more representative of what is typical than the mean.

The mode is used most rarely, most often to describe nominal or discrete variables. (Nominal variables are described by a name, and discrete variables can only take on a limited number of real values.) There can be one mode or several, or even no mode at all. It does not take the values of all the data into account.

To illustrate the importance of understanding these measures of central tendency and how to use them well, here is a simple example, adapted from Martin Gardner.[14]

Company ZZZ makes Whackos. The management is made up of a boss, his brother, and six relatives; the personnel includes five supervisors and ten workers. Business is going well, and management is hiring another employee. Paul is a candidate for the job. The boss explains that the average salary in the company is $6,000 a month. He adds that at first, during the probationary period, Paul will receive $1,500 a month. Then his salary will rise rapidly.

Paul is hired. But after a few days, he goes to see the boss, outraged. "You lied to me!" he complains. "None of the ZZZ workers makes more than $2,000 a month." "That's not true," counters the boss, handing him a sheet on which all the salaries that ZZZ pays each month are listed:

The boss: $48,000
His brother: $20,000
Each of the six relatives: $5,000
Each of the supervisors: $4,000
Each of the ten workers: $2,000

"ZZZ pays $138,000 in salaries to twenty-three people each month. The average salary is thus $138,000 ÷ 23 = $6,000," says the boss. "You see, I didn't lie to you."

Monthly salary per person

But Paul is an informed critical thinker. So he retorts: "The average you are using is one measure of central tendency. But there are others. It would have been more honest for you to tell me the median. For that, you would have listed all the salaries in descending order; the one right in the middle is the median. At ZZZ, the median salary is $4,000. That would have been a much more valuable indicator for me. But if you wanted to be really honest, you should have given me the mode. The mode is the number that appears most frequently in a group. At ZZZ, the modal salary is $2,000 a month. That is what you should have told me."

So you have to be careful when measures of central tendency are used, and always ask if the choice can be justified.

STANDARD DEVIATION

In addition to these measures of central tendency, a critical thinker must know the dispersion of a sample, in other words, how spread out the values are. The most important of these measures is the standard deviation. To give you an idea of what it is, imagine the following scenario.

You go fishing in a river that is said to be polluted, which makes some of the fish inedible. But some of the fish, you are told, are okay. Suppose that the toxicity of the fish is distributed on a normal curve. They say that starting at 7 mg of Gunk—a toxic product that the Whacko factory once secretly drained into the river before the factory was transformed into a self-managed workers' cooperative—the fish become dangerous to eat. The average quantity of Gunk found in the fish in this stream of water is 4 mg. Will you eat any?

Before saying anything, you should find out what the standard deviation is; it will tell you how much the values of toxicity vary around this average. If the variation is huge, you will be taking a big risk by eating the fish; on the other hand, if it is small, meaning that the values of toxicity will tend to be gathered around the average, then you run a much lower risk.

In more precise terminology, the standard deviation is a measure of the dispersion of data in relation to the mean. Technically, it is the square root of another measure, the variance. It is called sigma (σ) and is written like this:

$$\sigma = \sqrt{\frac{\Sigma(x_i - \bar{x})^2}{n}}$$

Here are three ways of calculating the standard deviation.

The first is the simplest: you just need a calculator, and you can get it by pressing a button. If you have to calculate it manually, here is a convenient way of going about it:

1. Determine the dispersion of each value from the mean that you have already calculated;
2. Square each difference and add them;
3. Divide the sum by the number of values: that's the variance;
4. Take the square root of this variance, and you'll get the standard deviation.

Check if you've mastered the technique by finding the standard deviation (and, in so doing, the variance) of the following data: 2, 2, 3, 5, 7, 9, 14. You'll find that the variance is 16.57 and the standard deviation is 4.07.

The third way provides only a rough approximation but can be useful because it is quick and easy to do.

1. Take the highest value of your population, then subtract the lowest. In so doing you have found the numerical variation of the results, called the range;
2. Then divide the number you obtain by four. Again, remind yourself that this only produces a rough approximation of the standard deviation.

This measure is extremely useful. Specifically, when the distribution of data resembles the bell curve, a valuable empirical rule applies, which along with the mean and the standard deviation can provide us with important information. Indeed, 68.2 percent of your data will fall within an interval equivalent to the standard deviation, whether above or below the mean. What is more, 95.4 percent of your data will fall within an interval of two standard deviations from the mean. Finally, 99.8 percent of your data will fall within an interval of three standard deviations.

This can be represented as follows:

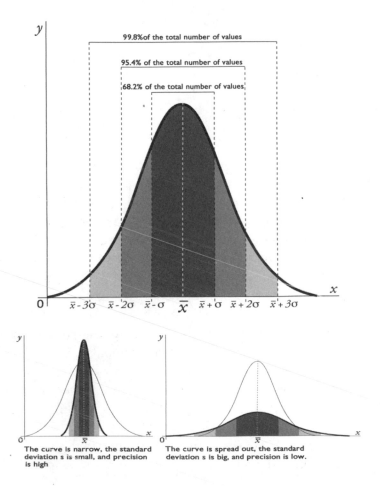

The curve is narrow, the standard deviation s is small, and precision is high

The curve is spread out, the standard deviation s is big, and precision is low.

In other words, if the mean is twelve and the standard deviation is three, about 68.2 percent of the values observed fall within the range of nine and fifteen.

Let's return to your fish. If the standard deviation is 1 mg, would you eat them? What if it was 4 mg?

Statistics allow us not only to describe but also to analyze data. A few tools are indispensable if we wish to assess the values we are given: surveys and sampling, and statistical dependence.

SURVEYS AND SAMPLES

*Using methods known only to himself,
our researcher reported very interesting statistics.*

—MARCEL GOTLIB, French cartoonist

Statistics allow us to infer the properties of a given population from the examination of a small part of it, known as a sample. Forming samples and making judgments based on them are among the most widespread and important applications of statistics. We encounter them frequently, as you may have guessed, in the form of surveys.

These techniques solve a problem for us. We want to know one or more properties of a population, generally a very large one, but for all sorts of reasons—cost, time, and so on—we can't actually examine every constituent of the population, which would basically involve carrying out a census. For example, we would like to know how voters in this country intend to vote—but without having to ask every single one. Or we would like to know how many of the billy clubs manufactured at a given factory are defective, but we don't want to (and can't) examine them one by one. In this case, as in all the other imaginable ones, statistics allow us to make a judgment about a population (all the voters, all the billy clubs produced at the factory) by examining only a few of its representatives. These form the sample. When we judge soup by tasting a spoonful, we are judging on the basis of a sample. When the columnist for the NYPD newsletter evaluates different models of billy clubs, he too is sampling.

Defining samples comprises an important and complex part of statistics. It is easy to understand why. For a judgment about a population to be valid, the sample analyzed has to be representative of that population. This criterion is crucial, and in order to satisfy it, our sample will have to be large enough and unbiased. If you judge an entire pot of soup based on just a drop, you might be accused of using too small a sample; if you take a good-sized spoonful, but you take it from the exact spot where the cook just dumped the pepper, your opinion that the soup is too peppery will not be valid because your sample was biased. Thus, sometimes a sample is quantitatively sound, but the data we can infer from it are unreliable nonetheless, because the sample is qualitatively biased. The famous *Literary Digest* episode illustrates this well. In fact, this story is told in all the statistics text books.

Literary Digest was a well-read magazine, and from the 1920s on, it ran surveys in the lead-up to presidential elections. The predictions it made on the basis of these surveys were quite successful. It used the straw-poll method: before the election, the magazine sent two fake ballots to people who could, if they so desired, fill out a ballot, indicating the candidate for whom they intended to vote, and return it to the magazine. Then these "votes" were counted and predictions were made.

The results obtained by the magazine proved to be right (they announced the winner each time) but also not very precise. In the 1920 election, the difference between the magazine's prediction and the official result was 6 percent; in 1924, it was 5.1 percent; in 1928, it was 44 percent; in 1932, the best year, it was 0.9 percent.

Though ultimately rather mediocre, these results were obtained by sending out a very high number of "straw ballots": 11 million in 1920, 16.5 million in 1924, 18 million in 1928, 20 million in 1932. In this last year, 3 million people sent back their ballots.

In the 1936 election, based on the 2.3 million straw polls that were returned (out of the 10 million sent out) the magazine announced that Franklin Delano Roosevelt's Republican adversary, Alfred Mossman Landon, would win. A young psychologist named George Gallup had interviewed 4,500 people, and he was predicting that FDR would win. And indeed, FDR did take the election with 60.8 percent of the vote—Landon received only 36.6 percent—one of the biggest majorities in any US presidential election.

The reason for *Literary Digest*'s failure was quickly uncovered, and an unforgettable lesson was learned from it. While enormous, *Literary Digest*'s sample was biased; on the other hand, Gallup's—the famous founder of the polling company—while much smaller, was unbiased. Indeed, the magazine chose the people to whom they sent straw ballots from amongst its subscribers and randomly from the phone book. Using these two methods, they over-selected people who were wealthy and more likely to be inclined to vote Republican (since they had chosen to subscribe to the rather conservative magazine or had, in 1936, the means to pay for phone service).

Let us glean from this the lesson that a good, representative sample of a given population will be sufficiently big (its quantitative attribute) and unbiased (its qualitative attribute). Determining the size of the sample is a complex process, in which mathematical considerations must be made but so must economic, social, and technical ones. What is the size of a good sample? There is no simple and singular answer to the question. It depends on a range of factors, including the population studied, the degree of precision we want to achieve, the amount of money we have, the questions on which our inquiry is focused, and many others. Most opinion polls make use of samples of 1,000 to 2,000 people, which is generally sufficient (due to technical reasons we cannot examine here). The precision you gain by using larger samples is usually not worth the expense.

The selection process is crucial if you do not want the sample to be biased; individuals have to be chosen at random to be included. The surest method is random sampling. Imagine a population P and a procedure that allows you to select n elements of P. The procedure that guarantees that all the samples of n are equally possible is a simple random sampling procedure. In this case, each element has the same chance of being chosen as any other, and the fact that a given element is chosen does not impact the choice of the others. If you make a list of all the elements of a population and select a sample with the help of a list of random numbers, you will have performed a simple random sampling. This theory is hard to put into practice, however, which is why different sampling methods have been developed: stratification sampling, cluster sampling, and quota sampling, for example. In each, however, the same basic principle must be respected, which is that the elements of the sample must be randomly selected. If respected, this principle guarantees that the statistical analysis inferred from the sample allows for generalizations to be made about the population. If it isn't respected, such generalizations are invalid. This principle is very useful to critical thinkers, for whom the art of detecting bias in judgments based on samples must become second nature. You must pay attention to everything about the selection process that could keep the sample from being randomly selected and thus make it unrepresentative of the population. A few examples will make this clearer.

Example 1:
A radio station carries out a survey about the legalization of marijuana. A total of 3,636 listeners responds and 78 percent of them say they are in favor of it. So the station announces that it is time to legalize marijuana, and presses the government to act.

In this case, it is quite clear that the sample is not random, since it was made up uniquely of listeners of that radio station and, what is more, of those who chose to phone in and make their opinions known (perhaps because it is an issue they care about). So nothing can be concluded about the general population on the basis of this poll.

Example 2:
A few years ago, a Gallup poll based on a stratified sample concluded that 33 percent of the US population that attend-

ed college did not know the metric system. A survey carried out by a daily newspaper in California established that 98 percent of its readers did know it. The participants in this second poll were invited to clip, fill out, and send in an answer slip. We have every reason to believe that the newspaper poll was biased, and that people who don't know the metric system excluded themselves from the poll simply by not participating.

Example 3:
Two thousand people were surveyed and asked to answer yes or no to a clear and precise opinion question. The poll was done by phone and the numbers called were selected randomly by a computer, from a list of all the numbers in service.

These are commonly considered the best practices of opinion polling. There is, however, still a bias, since the poorest people—who do not all own phones—and the homeless are not properly represented therein.

A good poll will tell you that it is accurate to such and such degree, a certain number of times out of one hundred (or out of twenty). For example, it will say that nineteen times out of twenty (or ninety-five times out of one hundred), the survey has a 5 percent margin of error. These numbers refer to sampling error and to the confidence intervals of the poll. What this means, concretely speaking, is that the results of 95 percent of all the samples of a given population to whom the same question is asked at the same time will be the same, to the closest sampling error. Thus you know that ninety-five times in one hundred, the results of this poll have the same value as those presented, give or take 5 percent.

Suppose that the popularity of the president was established as 53 percent in January by just such a poll. In March, the same poll is redone, and his popularity is at 56 percent. Thus, we can affirm that in January, ninety-five times out of one hundred, the president's popularity was between 48 percent and 58 percent and in March, ninety-five times out of one hundred, it was between 51 percent and 61 percent. It is something to consider when you see headlines reporting the second poll announce that the president's popularity is on the rise.

The margin of error we are dealing with here depends on two factors: how the sample is taken and how the questions are formulated, which is what we will now consider.

A good question is neither ambiguous nor biased. Asked in the same way of each person polled, it should be understood in the same way by each. And everyone should be able to and agree to answer it sincerely. Articulating these conditions is a lot easier than satisfying them, as you will notice as soon as you try to formulate opinion questions. This is why good polls first test their questions on a small sample, and then reformulate them as necessary. Detecting the possible biases of a question is an art that any critical thinker must master. A police union might take some comfort from a poll demonstrating that 86 percent of respondents favor the purchase of the new Smash billy clubs, but the critical thinker will ask to see the question, fearing that it was formulated as follows:

Given the dangerous rise in the number of anarchists and the effectiveness Smash billy clubs have demonstrated in bringing them back in line with

State thinking, do you approve of replacing the police's worn billy clubs with inexpensive and ergonomic Smash billy clubs?

Alas, a question's bias is not usually so easy to discern. It can be attached to a number of different factors, including the ambiguity of a question, the terms used, the nature of the information that is sought, and even the identity of the person conducting the poll. Let me give some examples: "Do you read the *New York Times*?" might sound like a clear and precise question, but it can be interpreted in different ways. Do you read it sometimes? Often? Every day? The whole thing? Only some articles? And so on.

The answer to the question "Do you consume a lot of alcohol?" obviously depends on what the person you ask understands to be "alcohol" and "a lot," and also on what he or she wants to tell you. It is a rotten question that will no doubt produce astonishingly low figures when compared to official alcohol sales figures. Darrell Huff tells the story of a poll that established that more US households received *Harper's* magazine than *True Story*. Yet, the sales statistics of the two magazines contradicted that result.

Let's conclude this section on polls by considering the fact that for several years, a political debate over their legitimacy has unfolded above and beyond the methodological quarrels I have sketched here. The debate has to do with opinion polls—there are other polls that concern behavior, knowledge, and demographic characteristics—and particularly with pre-election polls. At the root of the debate is the privileged place that polls and pollsters occupy in our political life. Sociologist Pierre Bourdieu remarked on this topic

that the presuppositions of these polls are contestable because they assume that everyone is able to have an opinion,
that all opinions are equal, and that there is a "consensus
about the problems, that is to say, agreement on the questions that are worthy of asking." Bourdieu concludes that
the public opinion disclosed in polls is "an artifact, pure
and simple, the function of which is to dissemble that the
state of opinion at any given moment is a system of forces
and tensions and that nothing is more inadequate for repre-
senting the state of opinion than a percentage."[15]

As we've said, once data is gathered, statistics allows us
to analyze and especially to look for connections between
certain characteristics. Sophisticated methods have been
developed to provide rigorous explanations for the extent to
which one characteristic is linked to another—for example,
chest and waist measurements. These techniques are useful but also very complex, and we cannot deal with them
here. That said, everyone should master two ideas: the significant difference between correlation and causality, and
the surprising and amusing statistical phenomenon called
the regression toward the mean.

STATISTICAL DEPENDENCE AND CORRELATION

"Correlation" is the word statisticians use to say that two
variables are linked, that their values are associated or dependent on each other. I suppose that a man's chest measurement is correlated to one's waist measurement, and
after having gathered sufficient data, we could probably
express this correlation in precise mathematical terms. An
important part of statistical work consists of doing this sort

of thing: helping to establish such relations, verifying that they are indeed real, and quantifying them. But—here you will recognize our *post hoc ergo procter hoc* from the preceding chapter—establishing a correlation does not mean that you have discovered a causal relationship. The confusion of the two is one of the major sources of irrational delirium. So let me repeat: when statistics establish that two variables, A and B, are correlated, that does not necessarily mean that there is a causal relationship between the two.

A moment of thought will show that the claim that A and B are correlated can mean different things: that A causes B; that B causes A; that A and B are accidentally linked without there being any causal link between them; or that A and B are both dependent on a third factor, C. Establishing causality is one of the most difficult tasks in scientific research. For the moment, let's simply take note of some examples of cases in which A and B are correlated without having a causal relationship.

Imagine a study of high school and university students that shows that marijuana consumption (A) is correlated to lower than average grades (B). It is possible that pot causes these lower than average grades. But it is also possible that having lower than average grades causes students to live it up and smoke pot. Or it is possible that more sociable people tend both to smoke dope and take their academic work less seriously. The price of coffee in Oregon might be correlated to the amount of rain in a given part of the world, but you would have a hard time establishing a causal relationship between the two. Storks on the rooftop of a house are, in certain countries, strongly correlated to the number of children that live there. But that does not mean that storks cause children. Rather, the rooftops of houses big enough to shelter large families are able to hold more storks.

There may be a correlation between the quantity of hair a man has and his grandmother's age. After all, our hair seems to thin and diminish with age while our grandmothers' ages, by definition, increase. But we would laugh, justifiably, at any group of men who worked themselves up trying to keep their hair in order to keep their grandmothers alive.

Bertrand Russell tells the story of visiting monks in China who were convinced that lunar eclipses were caused by a celestial dog trying to swallow the moon. To prevent it, the monks had to perform a ritual that involved striking a gigantic gong. It had proven to be effective since time immemorial. The strikes to the gong were assumed to cause the dog in the sky to flee and so stop the eclipse. The confusion between correlation and causality can be the source of a great many superstitions. It's also what produces the phenomenon of regression toward the mean, which we will now examine.

SUPERSTITION AND REGRESSION TOWARD THE MEAN

When it comes to statistics applied to critical thinking, this is a classic concept. The idea is as follows: when two variables—of which the respective values depend on a great number of factors—are imperfectly correlated, the extreme values of one will tend to be correlated with less extreme values of the other. The phenomenon is completely ordinary, but if we don't pay attention to it, we can end up fallaciously linking one to the other in a relationship of cause and effect. This explains a great many superstitions.

Now to clarify this concept.

It all started with Francis Galton (1822–1911), one of the illustrious pioneers of statistics. Galton wanted to study the relation between the heights of fathers and their sons. He found one, which didn't surprise anyone: tall fathers tend to have tall sons and short fathers tend to have short sons. But he also found something more surprising: particularly tall fathers tend to have sons who are shorter than them, and very short fathers tend to have offspring that are less short than they are. What does this mean?

This is precisely a case of imperfect correlations between two variables—the heights of fathers and their sons. A great many factors play a role in establishing a person's height: the person's father's height, of course, but also the height of his mother, the many genes that determine the size of each of his limbs, his vertebrae, his skull, and who knows what else. Height also depends on a person's environment, food, exercise, and so on. A great number of these factors must coincide for a person to be especially tall (or short), that is, the extreme value in our case. According to the laws of chance, such a combination of circumstances is exceptional. This explains why, when it occurs, it tends to be correlated with a less exceptional event: the less extreme values in our case, which are the tall sons who are not as tall as their fathers. It is predictable, and known as the regression toward the mean.

An example will make it easy to understand what a critical thinker has to gain from knowing about this phenomenon, particularly as it pertains to guarding against superstition.

Apparently, high-level athletes dread being asked to appear on the cover of *Sports Illustrated*. You see why: they are invited after putting in exceptional performances, which are the result of the fortuitous combination of a large variety of factors. These tend to be followed by less exceptional performances. So it is pure superstition for these athletes to blame the weakening of their performance on their magazine cover appearances. You will notice quickly how broadly this idea can be applied.

Now the time has come to broach the last theme of our overview of citizen mathematics: illustrations and graphics, which as you will see can be used to tell many innocent—and not so innocent—lies.

2.2.3 Graphics and Illustrations: Worth a Thousand Lies

Get your facts first, and then you can distort them as much as you please.

—MARK TWAIN

We often make ready use of graphics and illustrations in order to visualize data, particularly in scientific articles, financial reports, and in the media. We have to attend carefully to the way in which they are constructed, because these illustrations and graphics, while conceived to transmit information quickly, can also be deceptive. And the false impressions they give will be very difficult to undo because we will be convinced that we have seen the phenomenon they describe with our own eyes.

PERILOUS ILLUSTRATIONS

Let's start with the following illustration.[16]

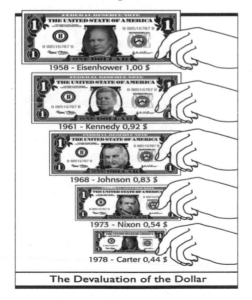

1958 - Eisenhower 1,00 $
1961 - Kennedy 0,92 $
1968 - Johnson 0,83 $
1973 - Nixon 0,54 $
1978 - Carter 0,44 $

The Devaluation of the Dollar

Here we would want to make sure that the pictures get smaller proportionate to the decrease they are meant to illustrate. Yet this is not entirely the case, even if it is hard to see it. The hurried reader may draw erroneous conclusions—especially if he or she is just skimming the text and the illustration.

Let's take a closer look.

The length of the dollar bill is used to represent the declining value of the dollar, from one dollar in 1958 to forty-four cents in 1978, when it required a little bit more than two dollars to buy what you could purchase in 1958 with only one. But the artist also reduced the width of the bills, such that the surface of the 1958 bill is not twice but five times as big. He should have paid attention to the fact that this picture has two dimensions.

Tufte put forward the following principle: "The representation of numbers, as physically measured on the surface of the graphic itself, should be directly proportional to the quantities represented." Each time an illustration veers from this principle, it tells a lie, and the further it veers, the more what Tufte refers to as its "lie factor" goes up. Tufte would express the lie factor of the preceding example as five over two.

You will no doubt have guessed that drawing adequate and accurate illustrations that transmit exactly the information we want to convey and nothing else is a very demanding art form that requires scientific knowledge, artistic talent, and a dose of good judgment all at once.

You will see it—and discover other traps to guard against—in the following work, adapted from the work of Stephen K. Campbell.[17]

Let's imagine that, in 1999, research established that the total amount of government health-care spending in a fictitious country called Tralala was 7.2 billion dollars, while at the same time in another country called Molvania, it was 30.4 billion. Let's leave aside all the legitimate questions I would guess are bubbling to the surface in your critical thinker's brain, and focus only on the numbers that we must represent by means of illustrations. How will we proceed?

Let's say that we choose to represent the situation in Tralala by drawing a hospital to a certain scale, which by convention, represents 7.2 billion. Here it is:

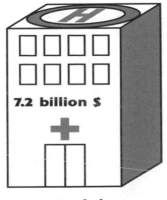

7.2 billion $

Tralala

Starting from this point, how should we represent the situation in Molvania? We are trying to illustrate an amount (30.4 billion) that is 4.2 times bigger than the first (7.2 billion). Thus we could draw as many hospitals as it requires, that is, a little more than four. In this case, the solution would be drawn as follows:

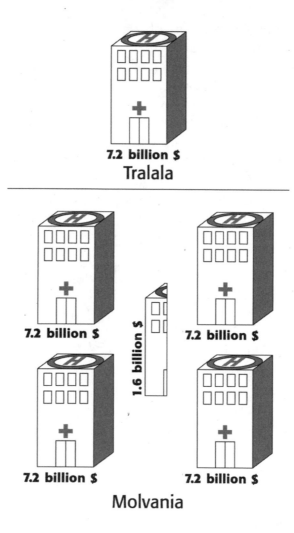

7.2 billion $
Tralala

7.2 billion $ 1.6 billion $ 7.2 billion $

7.2 billion $ 7.2 billion $

Molvania

Is this satisfactory? In deciding, think about the readers. They might draw the (erroneous) conclusion that there is one hospital in Tralala for every four in Molvania. That would be deplorable.

So we might be tempted to draw just one hospital to represent the situation in Molvania, but make it 4.2 times taller than the first. Here is what it would look like:

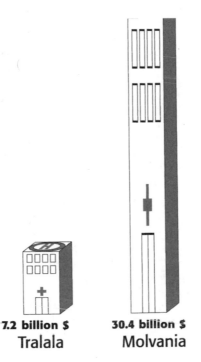

7.2 billion $
Tralala

30.4 billion $
Molvania

In this display, the second hospital just looks weird. The reader would wonder what happened to its width. If the height is multiplied by 4.2, shouldn't the width be too? In that case, we would suggest the following illustration:

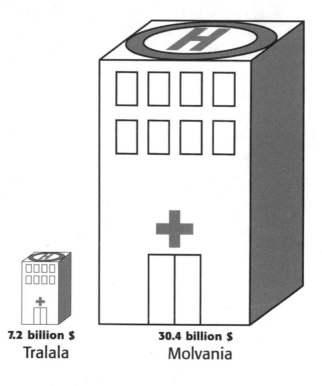

7.2 billion $
Tralala

30.4 billion $
Molvania

But once again, there is a major problem. Since our new hospital is 4.2 times taller, and 4.2 times wider, it is now 17.64 bigger (4.2 x 4.2) than the first. The text might say that the numbers are 7.2 billion and 30.4 billion, and might explain carefully that the growth factor is 4.2, but the illustration says something entirely different: it says 17.64 times bigger. Ideologues who want to pass off their theories have much to gain from this kind of strategy. So to correct our aim, we must increase the second hospital by a factor of 2.049, the square root of 4.2. That will give us the following illustration:

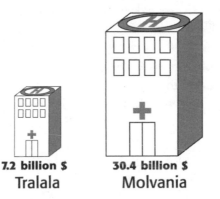

7.2 billion $ **30.4 billion $**
Tralala   Molvania

But, alas, that is not all. Readers don't generally think about hospitals as two-dimensional objects, and will no doubt interpret the illustration above as having three dimensions: height, width, and depth. Consequently, the building as it is drawn still exaggerates the difference between Tralala and Molvania. An accurate illustration has to increase the second by a factor of 1.432, the cubic root of 4.2. In that case, this is what should appear:

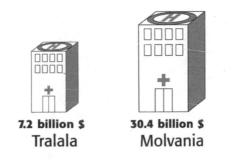

7.2 billion $ **30.4 billion $**
Tralala   Molvania

Good illustrations bring a text to life and can transmit large quantities of information quickly and efficiently. But an illustration is also a formidable weapon, and the critical thinker must always ask him or herself whether the illustration is adequate, whether the scale is accurate and relevant, whether the two or three dimensions represented are misleading or even give an impression that runs contrary to the text and to the facts.

In the example we just looked at, it would doubtless have been simpler to suggest a histogram.

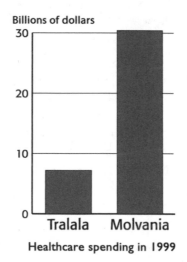

Healthcare spending in 1999

But like graphics, histograms also have to be examined with care, if not with outright suspicion.

GRAPH AND TABLES

Graphs and tables, of which there are many kinds, allow us to display information precisely and synthetically.

Let's start by giving an example of a good table and listing its characteristics.

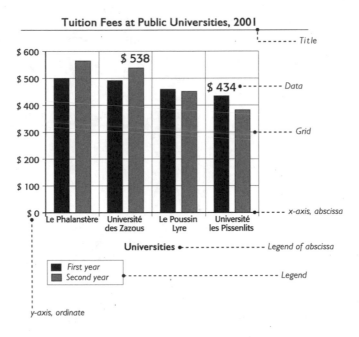

This table has a title that tells us what it is about. It also has a legend that tells us what the vertical bars correspond to. Finally, the Y-axis has a clear scale that starts at 0; the X-axis is equally clear and the units involved are clearly and properly marked.

If a table or a graphic strays from these norms, it will tend to be less clear, and at that point will be easily misinterpreted and risk misrepresentation.

There are also ways of using graphs to willfully trick readers. As critical thinkers, we owe it to ourselves to know the main ones.

THE PERSONALIZED BELL CURVE

When a phenomenon is described by a bell curve, you can stretch or compress the curve at will. By convention, the height of a bell curve is equivalent to three-quarters the lengths of its base. Such a curve gives an accurate representation of a normal distribution, and its standard deviation in particular.

If we follow this convention, we get a curve that looks like this:[18]

Yet we can give the impression—very useful in some cases, but nonetheless dishonest—that the standard deviation is smaller. All we have to do is change the proportions of the drawing and give the curve a height that exceeds three-quarters of its base. Then, the standard deviation looks like this:[19]

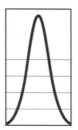

Do you want to give the reverse impression? Nothing could be easier, as you've already guessed. In that case, the curve would look like this:[20]

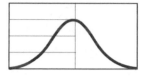

TAMPERING WITH THE Y-AXIS

Here is a completely honest graphic that represents education spending in a given country over a twelve-month period.[21]

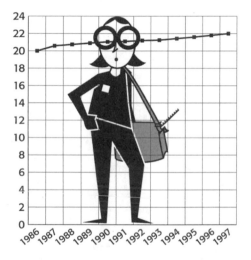

Now we will cheat and give the unwitting reader an entirely different impression of what happened. To do so, we will simply make the entire bottom of the Y-axis disappear. The origin of the Y-axis is no longer zero, and this changes everything. Take a look:[22]

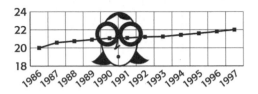

We can do even better—or worse. All we have to do is multiply the intervals on the Y-axis we've shortened to produce an even more significant effect, which you know won't be lost on some ideologues. Here is the result you can achieve:[23]

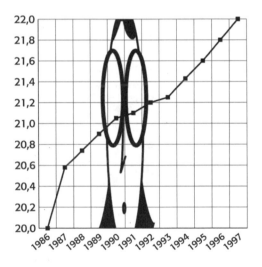

This trick, a favorite in business reports, can obviously be done in different ways, using various graphic representations. Here are some more examples, in which the data are reduced to their simplest expression.

The increase in this company's production seems quite modest, and management might be a little embarrassed to present such results to the shareholders:

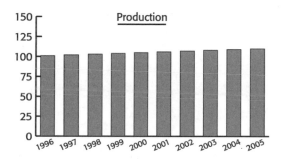

But with a snip of the Y-axis, it can all be fixed. Here's proof:

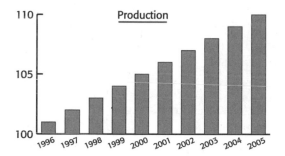

In the following example, the tendency of the variable seems pretty much fixed. Let's say it describes sales results over a given period. These results might not please the Board of Directors.

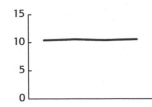

But here are the exact same results, just one snip later. Look at this. Who would deny the salespeople their wage increase?

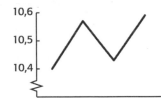

Note the jagged line at the base of the Y-axis in this last illustration. It warns the reader that the point of origin is not actually zero. That is the absolute minimum that an honest graph should indicate. The jagged line is like a signal that warns: be careful; something out of the ordinary is going on here. When this signal is not given and the Y-axis has been tampered with, flashing lights should go off in your head. You should become very suspicious of what you are being told, and above all, you should read the text that accompanies the suspicious graph with the greatest of care.

Let's summarize what we have learned in this chapter with a few rules.

A Few Golden Rules

The Source of the Information

Who produced this data? The person who is presenting it? Someone else?
Did she produce it in her own name? Or in the name of an organization?
What sort of reputation does that organization have?
Does it have interests in the question being discussed or a more or less
    hidden agenda?
Did it provide the data, the interpretation of the data, or both?
If the latter is the case, are they suggesting an interpretation of the data that
    is different from that put forward by the authority that produced it?
What biases, conscious or unconscious, could affect the presentation of
    the data?
How many cases were studied?
How was the data gathered?
Is that sufficient?

The Context

Is the data contextualized or not?
If so, is it relevant?
What do you know about the subject being discussed?
Would it be desirable to know more in order to be able to judge the
    numbers?
Do you know other data related to the same topic that it would be useful
    to keep in mind in order to compare it (for example, data about the
    same topic but from another time period, or another country, or another
    state)?

The Data: Qualitative Aspects

Is it plausible?

Does it seem complete, or is something potentially important missing?

Was some information omitted that might favor one interpretation over another?

What words are used to describe the numbers?

Are the words laden with connotations that favor one interpretation over another?

Could the numbers reasonably be used to say something other than what is stated?

In arriving at the numbers and interpretation that are put forward, was every significant factor taken into account (e.g., inflation)?

If data is compared over a given period of time, is the definition of what is being compared kept constant?

If it is changed, is that change reasonable, relevant, justified, and do the calculations take the change into account?

Is the definition of what is measured reasonable and relevant?

Can we reasonably conclude that the tool used to measure the data is reliable and valid?

Are the conclusions summarized?

Does the summary seem fair?

Do the conclusions seem acceptable in light of the data?

Are they plausible and do they conform to what usually appears in the literature?

If not, is the reasoning strong enough to support the extraordinary nature of the conclusions advanced?

Should this be the case, do the conclusions answer the questions that were asked?

The Data: Quantitative Aspects

Are the relevant absolute numbers provided where percentages are presented?

Is the number on the basis of which increases or decreases in percentage were calculated made clear?

Are the explanations of these changes the only possible explanations?

Has the fact that there are other possible explanations been taken into account?

Is there really something to explain, or is the study trying to explain a phenomenon that is self-explanatory?

If required, how was the sample formed?

What measure of central tendency was used?

Was that the right choice?

What is the standard deviation?

Are the upper and lower limits of the data made clear?

Is a relation of cause and effect established?

How was it established?

Should other factors have been considered?

Is the precision of the end results plausible given the instrument used to measure the data?

Graphs, Diagrams, Illustrations

Are they clear?

Do they match the text?

If required, are the illustrations proportional to the data?

Was the Y-axis tampered with?

Polls

What is the topic of this poll?

Is it really a topic that is of concern to people?

What section of the public was studied?

What methods of sampling, surveying, and analysis were used?

On what date(s) was the survey carried out?

What is the response rate?

How many people were interviewed?

What questions were they asked?

Are those questions clear?

Are they tendentious?

How, under what conditions, and in what order were the questions asked of those surveyed?

How was the issue of "indecision" dealt with?

Who sponsored the survey and who covered the cost of carrying it out?

How many people refused to answer each question?

What limitations are there on the interpretation of the results obtained?

Depending on the answers to this question, you might also want to ask the following questions: Have these or similar questions been part of a poll before? What were the results?

Part Two
ON THE JUSTIFICATION OF BELIEF

CHAPTER 3

PERSONAL EXPERIENCE

The true critical thinker accepts what few people ever accept—that one cannot routinely trust perceptions and memories.

—JAMES E. ALCOCK

Introduction

"I saw it with my own eyes!"

We often call on our own personal experience in this way to justify a belief: a given thing exists (or actually happened) and the proof is that I saw it. More generally, we often argue that a given thing is as we make it out to be because we experienced it with our senses: i.e. we saw, heard, felt, touched, or tasted it.

There is no doubt that personal experience (and its memory) is one of the sources of our empirical and immediate knowledge, and neither is there any doubt that it comes into play in the development of scientific knowledge. Besides, it is reasonable to think that the ability to orient ourselves correctly in the world by means of our senses, distinguishing between the real and the illusory, the true and the false, gives us a developmental advantage. It is not surprising that our organs of perception are such formidable machines, reliable enough to allow us to act effectively in the world.

Thus, oftentimes, appealing to our personal experience to justify our beliefs is far from being completely absurd. "He has gained weight. I know, because I saw him." "The village is fifty miles from the city. I know. I just came from there." "They built a pulp and paper factory. You can tell from the smell!" "The new Bing! billy clubs hurt more than the other kind. I know, I got whacked a couple of times."

Yet appealing to personal experience to justify our beliefs presents some danger. The knowledge that we can draw from it is limited, especially if we compare it with more systematic forms of scientific knowledge. In fact, personal experience frequently does not endow our beliefs with the degree of certainty that we might want to attribute to it. After all, we know very well that our senses can deceive us, our memory can fail to match what actually happened, and our judgment can prove mistaken. So it is important to know and understand the limits of appeals to personal experience in the justification of our beliefs.

There are grounds for believing that the proliferation of so many irrational beliefs flourishes in and is nurtured by the lack of knowledge of these limits. We will examine a number of them here. They are presented under three different headings: perceiving, remembering, and judging. Note, however, that these distinctions are rather arbitrary, in so far as to perceive and to remember is also to judge, as we will see.

3.1 Perceiving

Perception is a construction. That is one of the most valuable lessons critical thinkers have learned from psychology.

In fact, psychologists demonstrated the constructed character of our perceptions long ago, allowing us to better grasp how and to what extent our knowledge, our expectations, and our desires are put into play in our perception.

Consequently, it is best to understand these perceptions as models of the outside world, highly abstract and constructed, instead of as consistently reliable copies of it. To demonstrate this, let us briefly consider visual perception.[1]

The first example, borrowed from Terence Hines, deals with the perception of a red apple.[2] Under normal conditions, the wavelengths that correspond to red are reflected from the apple to the eye and the apple is perceived to be red. But by varying these conditions, for example by changing the lighting, the composition of the light that is sent from the apple to the eye can be modified. What happens then is astonishing: we continue to perceive the apple as red, for the good reason that it (usually) is this color and this knowledge colors, so to speak, what we perceive.

Hines relates another experiment that confirms the role of knowledge in the perception of color. An apple is placed in a box. A hole is pierced in the side of the box, through which subjects can observe the apple, but without knowing that it is an apple, because they just see a sample of color. If the light in the box is changed, the color of the sample is also perceived to have changed. Ignorance of the fact that it is an apple allows us to perceive the new colors correctly. In fact, deprived of this knowledge, our brain cannot insert into our perception what we know about the normal color of the apple.

In the same way, the fact that we perceive the size of objects that are approaching or getting farther away as being constant is the result of an elaborate construction. Our brain judges that the objects remain a constant size, even if the images our retina receives are not. Bruno Dubuc explains:

> Perceptual constancy is our tendency to see familiar objects as having a constant shape, size, and colour, regardless of any changes in perspective, distance, or lighting that they undergo. Our perception of these objects under such changing conditions is much closer to the general image of them that we have memorized than to the actual stimulus reaching our retinas. Thus, perceptual constancy is what lets you recognize a plate of vegetables, for instance, regardless of whether you are looking down on it at your own table, or noticing it on someone else's table in front of you in a dark restaurant, or seeing it in side view on a huge billboard several dozen meters away from you as you drive past it in broad daylight.[3]

This phenomenon explains numerous and sometimes rather spectacular illusions, which the great illusionists have noticed, of course.

Optical illusions have been known for a long time and were systematically studied by painters from the Renaissance on. They provide more amusing and enlightening examples of the constructed character of perception.

Today, thanks especially to Gestalt psychology, we know that we tend to order our perceptions and organize them, for example, as content and form. When the content and the form are unstable, we may perceive two different things in succession in one image—the content having become the form and the form the content—as we go from one to the other.

This well-known picture is a very good example. You will alternate between seeing a young girl and an old woman.

Seeing an Orange Door Out of the Corner of Your Eye

Research has demonstrated very convincingly that knowledge plays a crucial role in the perception of constancy of positions and shapes, as well as colors and sizes. "The brain takes into account what it knows of the object and constructs a perception based at once on sensory input and knowledge," writes Terence Hines, who gives the following example of the constancy of colors.

"As I sit here writing this, there is an orange door off to my left. I can just see the door out of the corner of my eye and I clearly perceive it as colored, in spite of the fact that the light being reflected off the door to my retina is falling on a part of the retina where there are no color receptors. Since I know what color the door is—it is very familiar to me—my brain constructs a perception of color. . . . The phenomenon demonstrates the great importance of knowledge in even the simplest types of perception."

Source: T. Hines, *Pseudoscience and the Paranormal: A Critical Examination of the Evidence* (New York: Prometheus Books, 1988), 170.

The constructed character of perception also explains how a triangle appears in the following picture—our brain constructs it.[4]

A Disc that Produces Subjective Colors

The phenomenon of subjective colors has been known since the nineteenth century; Fechner studied it in 1838. To my knowledge, it has still not been entirely explained, but you can experience it with ease. Photocopy this disc, glue it onto cardboard, and pierce the center with a tack. Then spin it fairly quickly. You will soon perceive a variety of colors, pale and pastel but distinctly present.

3.1.1 Pareidolia: The Face on Mars

At the end of 2004, a Florida couple, Gregg and Diana Duyser, sold a ten-year-old grilled cheese sandwich on eBay. How much did it go for? Twenty-eight thousand dollars.[5] In the eyes of the couple—and no doubt the bidders too—it was no ordinary grilled cheese. Indeed, it bore the image of a face, supposedly that of the Virgin Mary.

The anecdote will make you smile—if it doesn't make you cry. But it is also a reminder of the strength of human capacity to recognize images in random shapes and imprecise stimuli. You don't have to go much further to encounter it: each of us remembers amusing ourselves as children by looking for shapes in the clouds.

Here's another famous example. In 1977, a photo taken the year before by the Viking probe while it was circling Mars drew the attention of an engineer named Vincent DiPietro. In it, he noticed the shape of a face. NASA explained that the phenomenon was due to natural erosion and the effects of light and shadow. But DiPietro wasn't convinced. Others even took NASA's statements as proof that they were trying to hide an important discovery from the public. (Do you recognize the fallacy?)

Soon, people put forward even more audacious hypotheses: they saw in the face on Mars proof that intelligent life forms had developed there. Thus, heaps of rocks near the famous face were taken to be pyramids, avenues, even the vestiges of a city. A whole little industry of publications, conferences, and "research" was thus developed around the face on Mars. The Bible itself is sometimes appealed to as proof.

Let us note seriously that the more aware we are of the constructed character of our perceptions, the less hasty we are to see indications of a Martian civilization in the "face on Mars." In any mass of chaotic data, it is easy to notice phenomena that seem remarkable for one reason or another, without them necessarily being so. That provides us with a very plausible explanation for the mysterious face on Mars, as well as a valuable critical thinking tool.

3.1.2 Doctor Blondlot's N-Rays

> *"I can't believe that!" said Alice.*
> *"Can't you?" the queen said in a pitying tone.*
> *"Try again, draw a long breath, and shut your eyes."*
> —LEWIS CARROLL, *Through the Looking Glass*

Scientists would never fall into such a second-rate trap, you say? Indeed, as we will see, science offers important and necessary guarantees against perceptual illusions. Nonetheless, when scientists misuse subjective perception to validate their theories, they can also become victims. Take, for example, the case of Doctor Blondlot.

The end of the nineteenth and beginning of the twentieth century was a particularly fertile period in the history of physics. Eminent physicians of the era, including Henri Becquerel (1852–1908) or Wilhelm Conrad Röntgen (1845–1923), discovered and studied many sorts of radiation. X-rays and cathode rays, now well known, are some examples.

René Prosper Blondlot, a highly reputed physician and professor at the University of Nancy, announced his own discovery of N-rays in 1903 and named them in honor of his city and his university. If you have never heard of Doctor Blondlot and his rays, however, do not worry. It's because those N-rays simply don't exist. This episode in the history of science is rich in lessons pertaining to the topic we are discussing because it shows the extent to which personal experience can be an untrustworthy basis for justifying our beliefs.

Here are the broad strokes.[6] Blondlot thought he had discovered the N-rays, which were emanated by certain metals: he saw them with his naked eyes. He had refined a fairly simple device by which these rays were projected at objects covered in aluminum paint that made them appear more luminous. But the difficulty that other physicians had trying to reproduce these effects, and thus in observing these rays, soon gave rise to a wave of skepticism. Enter a young American named Robert Wood, who went to Blondlot's laboratory. Blondlot invited him to participate in his experiments. Let's try to imagine the scene.

A device allows for the supposed N-rays to be emitted. They are reflected on paint, the luminosity of which is augmented by the rays. Blondlot sees with his own eyes the augmentation or non-augmentation of that luminosity and, from this observation, concludes whether or not the N-rays are present.

The experiment also involved the use of a sheet of lead that was manually inserted into the device. Blondlot thought its effect was to block the N-rays.

Blondlot entrusted Wood with the task of inserting or removing the sheet of lead. You have no doubt already guessed what happened next. When Wood told him the sheet of lead was present, Blondlot didn't observe the presence of N-rays—even when Wood was not telling the truth.

Wood claimed he was inserting the sheet of lead when he wasn't and vice versa. But Blondlot saw rays when he believed that they were visible—and didn't when he believed that they were not.

The letter Robert Wood published in *Nature*—already one of the most prestigious scientific journals in the world—on September 29, 1904, remains a classic text of critical thinking. In it, he recounted the experiment I just described, as well as other experiments he carried out in Blondlot's laboratory. All pointed to the same conclusion: that Blondlot had been a victim of perceptive distortion.

ON THE UTILITY OF LEARNING A BIT OF MAGIC

Enlighten the dupes and
there will be no more rogues.

—ROBERT-HOUDIN

Of all the mistakes made by scientists who have tested people claiming to have paranormal capacities, the easiest to correct, but perhaps also the most widespread, is that they had excessive confidence in their own sensory perceptions. Put a different way, they didn't take into account the fact that each time they made a judgment, it could be colored by their expectations, their desires, their knowledge, and their beliefs. Add to this the fact that nature, which can be infinitely complex, does not deliberately delude those who study it, while human beings are perfectly capable of cheating, and you have a plausible explanation for the disconcerting ease with which researchers, sometimes very eminent ones, allow themselves to be duped by charlatans. Studying a bit of magic thus becomes an intellectual self-defense move. And if you are a researcher examining people who claim to possess paranormal powers, securing the support of a magician is an absolutely indispensable methodological precaution.

Some examples will show clearly that we would be wrong to rely only on our own observations to draw the conclusions we are asked to draw. Imagine a psychic who distributes a piece of paper to each participant in a session. He asks them to write something on it, which they are to keep to themselves. The slips are collected by a participant who folds them carefully so no one can see what is written on them. Then the psychic sits before the spectators. Without unfolding them or even looking at them, he raises the first slip of paper to his forehead, and pretends to read it by the power of thought alone. He concentrates. After a period of time and a demonstration of effort, he announces, "Among us is a person who, as a child, had a dog named Arfy."

The psychic asks the audience if this is indeed true. A woman raises her hand, stunned: that is indeed what she wrote on the piece of paper. The psychic unfolds the slip of paper, which confirms his prediction, then puts it on the table and takes another one, equally carefully folded. The same scenario unfolds and the psychic goes on to read each slip of paper in the same way.

Well executed, this trick can seem very convincing. But in fact it rests on one of the most effective and precious principles of psychics. It's called having a head start, or one ahead. The psychic actually knows ahead of time what there is on one of the slips of paper. He may have read it in secret, or have an accomplice in the room—the specifics don't matter. Let's say that in this example, he has an accomplice. The accomplice's slip of paper must also be recognizable.

From there on, everything is simple. When he takes the first slip, the psychic takes care not to choose the one that belongs to his accomplice. He raises the piece of paper to his head and states that he is reading what his accomplice wrote on a different piece of paper—in our example, that, "As a child, I had a dog named Arfy." While his accomplice speaks, pretending to be stunned, and all the attention is focused on her, the psychic puts the paper down on the table and reads what is written on it, let's say, "I own shares in a billy club manufacturing company." He then places it face down on the table. He takes a new slip of paper, raises it to his forehead, and pretends to read it: "Someone among us owns shares in . . . some sort of factory . . . it isn't clear yet. Ah . . . there we go . . . a billy-club factory." And so on, until the last slip of paper, which belongs to his accomplice. If someone asks to see the slips of paper after the experiment, they will confirm that the psychic read each one. If you do this trick, it might be wise to make a mistake or two: it adds to your credibility.

For our next example, let's go to France. It is Friday, January 27, 1989, and a story in the French daily *Nice-Matin* reads, "Incredible: a mysterious mind reader predicts the winning lotto numbers. In a letter posted Tuesday and opened at *Nice-Matin*'s offices by a bailiff, the mystery man announced the results of the following day's draw." You can imagine the stir caused by this extraordinary news. Pressed with questions, the paper explained what happened. The day before, a journalist had received an envelope marked, "Clairvoyance Experiment: To be opened only in front of a bailiff." When the bailiff was called in, he noted that the postmark did indeed read, "4:30 p.m., January 24, 1989."

So they opened the envelope; the letter explained this was an experiment meant to prove the clairvoyance of the sender, a gift he in no way wanted to use for base pecuniary ends. The lotto numbers followed: they were indeed those that were drawn the following morning!

In spite of the growing public interest in the matter, however, the mysterious mind reader didn't appear. Not until the day when Henri Broch, a physics professor at the University of Nice, came forward and declared that he was the author, and it had been nothing but a malicious—but didactic—joke intended to show how easily we succumb to the temptations of irrationality.

Here is how you do it.

On an envelope that you do not seal, you stick one of those adhesive labels that can be removed without leaving marks. On the label, you write your name and address, and then you post the envelope to yourself.

It is the twenty-fifth of the month, and here you are in possession of a stamped envelope with an official postmark that asserts it was mailed the day before. You wait to hear the results of that evening's lottery, then you write the letter explaining your clairvoyant gifts, your scruples, the experiment you are trying to carry out, and your "prediction," at this point an easy one to make. Then you take off the adhesive label and write the address of your favorite journalist on the envelope, adding the mention: "Clairvoyance experiment: To be opened only in front of a bailiff." Finally, you place the letter in the envelope, you seal it, and you go take it to your correspondent's mailbox yourself.

What Broch wanted to prove here is what he appropriately called the "doormat effect," which kicks in each time we use a word, out of habit or for any other reason, to designate anything other than that to which it refers. "Wipe your feet on the doormat,"says the sign, but no one literally wipes his or her feet, only the shoes. Our bailiff was the victim of a double doormat effect; he could see the date on which the envelope (but not the letter—the first doormat effect) had been stamped (but not sent—the second doormat effect).

For our last example, let's engage in a bit of telepathy. You announce to an audience that you communicate telepathically with your friend Pete, who lives miles away. To prove it, you suggest communicating the description of a card to him. Someone in the audience gives you a deck, the card is chosen by someone beyond suspicion, and people are invited to supervise the selection of the card as much as they want. Let's say that the three of clubs is chosen. You concentrate and you send your "telepathic emission." Then it is time to telephone your receptor. A member of the audience is assigned to do it. You tell him to ask for Pete Augman, who immediately replies: "Three of clubs." Fantastic? Not at all.

Until that moment, your receptor had only been identified by his first name; you didn't give his surname until after the card had been drawn. That's your code. You and your receptor have in fact learned fifty-two surnames together, each corresponding to one of fifty-two cards. Pete Augman? Three of clubs. Pete Rubello? Three of hearts. And so on.

Here is a variation on the trick, in which the supposed telepath calls his receptor himself. The psychic says, "Pete? Just a second." Then he gives the receiver to someone in the audience to whom the person on the other line tells what card was chosen. Do you have an idea how the psychic did it?

As soon as the "psychic" finishes dialing the number, the phone rings at Pete's, who answers immediately. (Warned that the "experiment" is taking place, he is awaiting the phone call.) As soon as he has picked up, Pete starts saying the names of cards in the usual order, leaving a brief pause between them: one, two, three, and so on, until he gets to the king. When the name of the right card is spoken, the "psychic" says, "Pete?" Pete then begins to recite all the symbols in the deck, again pausing briefly between each one: heart, diamond, spade, club. When the right color is spoken, the "psychic" says, "Just a minute." Many people will be convinced that they saw someone performing telepathy with their very own eyes.

Magicians have played an important role in the examination of the claims of paranormalists, pseudoscientists, and their like. Robert-Houdin was the first to do so, and then Houdini himself. Today, James Randi and Penn & Teller, among others, follow this rich tradition. The first three have published a number of works about their research. You can also watch the amusing and instructive television series *Bullshit!* produced by the latter duo.

The Astonishing Art of Cold Reading

The art of cold reading is an assemblage of techniques that seem to confer astonishing capacities on those who use them effectively. For example, having intimate knowledge of people they have never met before, guessing some of their most secret thoughts, predicting with remarkable precision their projects and intentions, giving sharp descriptions of their personality, communicating with deceased who were close to those for whom the cold reading is being done, and so on.

You can see these remarkable artists in theaters, where they work as magicians or psychics. Without laying bare their tricks, of course, they will easily admit that they are merely putting on a show and that they rely on techniques to create the illusion that they are deploying the stunning powers attributed to them.

You will also find people who produce the same effects and swear that there is no trick. They will say, for example, appealing to a gift that remains a mystery even to them, that they really can speak to the dead, or that they can find out your intimate thoughts. These people will be with the fortune tellers, the astrologists, and the palm readers—all those who trade in human credulity and often misery. But do they really have this mysterious gift? Note that we are being asked to prove a negative existential proposition (there is no X, or X doesn't exist) and that this is very difficult—even, strictly speaking, logically impossible. It is, however, entirely possible to show that the same effects can be produced without calling on any special "powers"—through altogether ordinary means. What is more, it is possible to test these people by imposing conditions according to which they can no longer rely on the usual ways we know they produce their effects. If they still produce them, it will indicate that they don't rely on those means, which would still not prove that they have supernatural powers, but might invite further investigation.

Indeed, every person who purports to produce the effects that magicians manage to produce through cold reading, and who thus purport, for example, to really communicate with the dead, have merely to prove it to become millionaires in an instant. What are you waiting for? In fact, through the James Randi Educational Foundation, Randi the magician has for years running offered a million dollars to anyone who can prove, under adequate observation, to possess any sort of paranormal, occult, or supernatural power—including communication with the dead and other similar effects usually produced by means of cold reading. The tests are carried out with the participation of the candidates and approved by them. On his web site, www.randi.org, Randi explains,

> In most cases, the applicant will be asked to perform a relatively simple preliminary test of the claim, which, if successful, will be followed by the formal test. Preliminary tests are usually conducted by associates of the JREF at the site where the applicant lives. [...]
>
> To date, no one has ever passed the preliminary tests.

Let's get back to cold reading. The basic principle is as follows. The reader first states vague and even contradictory propositions. She is fishing and drawing on a significant reserve of facts (for example, she knows the most popular masculine and feminine names for any given year, lists of objects that are often found in each home, etc.), themes dear to those who consult her (money, love, health, death, etc.), and various hints gleaned from her subject's appearance, manners, language, and so forth. Then, thanks to a clever interpretation of her subject's reactions, she refines her statements. When all is said and done, the client, who only remembers the predictions that turn out to be accurate and forgets the failures, will himself have furnished the answers the charlatan uses to display her gifts. Note that the "reader" sometimes acquires the information she pretends to read ahead of time, either by circulating amongst her subjects before the session or by having an assistant listen to their conversations, or by some other means.

Analyzing a cold reading of communication with the dead suggests the following examples—here I'm paraphrasing the famous magician's explanations. The reader says, "I have an older man." Note that this is a pseudo-question, a suggestion, and a fishing line that aims to elicit a reaction from the subject, who might put forward an opinion, give a name or a last name, or identify the person: "It's my brother" or "It's my father." But he himself will provide that information.

The reader now says, "I am hearing Bob, or Robert. Does that mean something to you?" Once again, this is bait. If there is in fact a Robert, the subject will confirm it. If not, the reader will pursue her fishing expedition, assuring the subject that she will ultimately identify the person.

The reader now asks, "Did your husband die after a long stay at a hospital, or did he die quickly?" The subject, replies, "He died almost instantaneously." To which the reader responds, "Yes. Because he is saying to me, 'I haven't suffered. I was spared any pain.'"

Clever and effective, no? Especially when you're talking to people made vulnerable by the loss of a loved one.

James Randi, "The Art of Cold Reading," http://www.randi.org/Library/ColdReading.

Cold reading makes use of the Forer effect, as well as a form of selective thinking that remembers only what confirms the hypothesis that the subject vehemently wants to believe. This technique seems very simple, it is easy to describe, but it is extremely difficult to use it convincingly. Nevertheless, it is so effective that we can assume that a number of those who practice it are really convinced of having a gift.

Good resources exist for those who wish to know more. For example, Ian Rowland's *The Full Facts Book of Cold Reading* is available at http://www.ianrowland.com/ItemstoBuy/ColdReading/ColdReadingMain1.html. The author, a specialist of these techniques, exposes some of his secrets. But you can also speak directly to someone who produces these remarkable effects. All you have to do is call one of those "psychic" phone services. Of course, the demonstration might cost you in somewhere around $120 an hour, and Rowland's book is much cheaper.

3.2 Remembering

Memory is the almost irreconcilable
enemy of judgment.
—BERNARD FONTENELLE

The hardest thing for politicians is
having the memory required
to remember what not to say.
—COLUCHE

Our results are showing that
changing a belief or memory can have
important consequences for subsequent
thoughts and behavior. When you change
memory, it changes you.
—E. F. LOFTUS

The purpose of memory
is not to let us recall the past,
but to let us anticipate the future.
Memory is a tool of prediction.
—ALAIN BERTHOZ

Memory has been studied a great deal by asking subjects to memorize, for example, lists of words. More recently, however—in the last decades of the twentieth century—because of the influence of cognitive psychology, new methods and new approaches to the topic have been developed. Thanks to them, important discoveries about memory and the way it works have been made. This work has crucial practical consequences, as we shall see. No one who wants to safeguard his or her intellectual independence can afford to ignore them. Here again, what is demonstrated is the reconstructive character of our memories and the influence that our expectations, desires, beliefs, and knowledge can have on them. Elizabeth Loftus is the pioneering figure in this area and her research results are remarkable. Let's take them as a point of departure.[7]

Loftus was initially interested in testimonies—for example, those of witnesses to a crime or an accident. She showed films of traffic accidents to subjects, then questioned them in different ways about what they had seen. The formulation of the questions had a remarkable influence on the answers given by the subjects asked to testify. For example, to the question, "At what speed were the cars going when they smashed?" people gave, on average, an estimated speed faster than when the question was formulated in a more neutral way, such as, "At what speed were the cars going when they hit each other?" What is more, following the first question, more people claimed to have seen broken glass when there wasn't any.

Subsequent research showed that memory could be significantly falsified in predictable ways, by means of diverse techniques that transmit information to subjects without their noticing. The effects of this exposure to false information have since been confirmed by hundreds of other research experiments that demonstrate the effects of what is now called the misinformation effect. Without getting into detail, let's look at an example from an article by Elizabeth Loftus.

The subjects see a car accident. Half of them are then given a false piece of information about the event: the stop sign that they saw was a yield sign, that is to say a sign commanding them to yield to oncoming traffic. The other half are not given this false information. In the end, when the subjects are asked to remember what they saw, the memory of a significant number of the first group will remember that there was a yield sign, while a significant number of the second group will tend to be more accurate. The research shows that these results transfer from the laboratory into real life; they even tend to show that the misinformation effect could be more pronounced outside of the lab.

As soon as we become aware of these findings, it becomes hard to avoid a rather terrifying question: could false memories be planted? Yes, of course. For example, memories of events that have never happened have been implanted in some subjects with the complicity of their family. In some cases, up to 25 percent of participants believed they had a childhood memory of being lost in a shopping mall for a long period of time. Most research, says Loftus, proves that a significant minority of people develops memories that are partially or totally false. What is even more troubling is that what researchers call substantial false memories— that is to say, memories of recent or out of the ordinary and even exceptional events—have also successfully been planted. Thus, using fake ads for Disney World, the vibrant but nonetheless unreal memory of meeting Bugs Bunny (who is not a Disney character) has been planted. Having watched a person possessed by the devil is another example of a planted memory.

The practical implications of results of all these studies are as numerous as they are significant. In the legal sphere, for example, erroneous testimony is the major cause of convictions of innocents (which have later proven to be unjustified by DNA analysis). What is called false memory syndrome follows from this same mechanism: psychotherapists have proven able to lead their patients to recollect memories of sexual trauma that they endured as children. But then in a significant number of cases, these memories proved false and had been planted.

Once again we note the crucial importance of distinguishing between the true and the false, the plausible and the improbable, and of not relying exclusively and blindly on our memory to do so.

A Thought Experiment

"For an example of your memory's reconstructive powers, try this: Remember an instance when you were sitting today. Recall your surrounding, how you were dressed, how you positioned your legs and arms. Chances are, you see the scene from the perspective of someone looking at it, as though you were watching yourself on television. But this memory can't be completely accurate because during the experience you never perceived yourself from this perspective. You now remember certain pieces of the experience, and your brain constructed everything else, television perspective and all."

T. Schick and L. Vaughn, *How to Think About Weird Things: Critical Thinking for a New Age*, 2nd ed. (Mountain View, CA: Mayfield, 1999), 44.

The Pleasures of Mnemonics and How to Keep a Universal Calendar in your Head

The word mnemonics comes from the Greek, "mnêmê" (memory), like the name Mnemosyne, the daughter of Uranus, goddess of memory and mother of the muses. It refers to the collection of techniques and processes that allow for optimal memory use. To remember the first decimal places of the constant

---

pi (π) we can rely on a poem or saying in which the number of letters in each word corresponds, in the proper order, to each of the decimal places.

How (3) I (1) wish (4) I (1) could (5) calculate (9) pi (2).

All mnemonic tricks are basically founded on the same principles: indexing, moving to a simpler memorizing task, deconstructing, and working out. Here are a few of the most common examples.

Acronyms

Each letter of a known word (called an acronym) or the first letters of the words in a phrase are made to correspond with a list of words to memorize.

Examples

HOMES is the acronym by which to remember the names of all the Great Lakes: Huron, Ontario, Michigan, Erie, and Superior.

"My very easy method, just set up nine planets." The first letters of the words in the phrase allow us to memorize the names of the planets in our solar system in the order of their proximity to the sun: Mercury, Venus, Earth, Mars, Jupiter, Saturn, Uranus, Neptune, and Pluto.

Note that since 2006, Pluto is no longer considered a planet, so someone will have to come up with a new acronym.

You'll find other useful primers on mnemonics on this Web site: www.thebrain.mcgill.ca.

The Pieces of the House

The ancient rhetoricians relied on this trick to help them memorize a list of elements. All it requires is to imagine each element in a specific place in one or several well-known rooms that you can travel through in your imagination according to a precise, predetermined plan that always stays the same. This process has been attributed to the poet Simonides of Ceos (c. 554–c. 467 BC).

The legend goes that he recited poems at a banquet held in a house. Then the roof of the house fell in, killing all the residents and rendering their corpses unrecognizable. Simonides was able to say, from memory, who had been there by remembering the place where each person had been seated.

The Universal Calendar

People who are very good at calculation make constant use of mnemonics.

Here is a fun example of what can be done:

Take the following list:

January	1
February	4
March	4
April	0
May	2
June	5
July	0
August	3
September	6
October	1
November	4
December	6

You can imagine a number of different procedures to help remember them. Have fun inventing one and learning the list by heart.

Finished? You now have a universal calendar in your head. If you are given a date, you will immediately be able to say what day it falls on, be it a date in the past or in the future. Take for example my friend Peter, who was born on September 6, 1951. The procedure for determining the day of his birth is the following:

1. Take the two last numbers of the year and divide them by 4, excluding the remainder. In this case, that gives us 51 ÷ 4 = 12, remainder 3, which we forget about.

2. Add the result (12) to the number with which we began: 12 + 51 = 63.

3. To this number, add the one that corresponds to the month of Peter's birthday in the table we've memorized, that is to say 6 (because it is September). This gives us 63 + 6 = 69.

4. Then we add the date of birth, which is 6: 69 + 6 = 75.

5. Finally, the number is divided by 7, which gives us 10, with a remainder of 5.

This final result (5) indicates the day we are looking for, as it corresponds to the following list:

Sunday	1
Monday	2
Tuesday	3
Wednesday	4
Thursday	5
Friday	6
Saturday	0

So September 6, 1951, was a Thursday.

The trick works for all the dates in the twentieth century, as long as you remember to subtract one from the value of the months of January and February in the case of leap years—the years in which the last two numbers are a multiple of four. Remember, however, that 1800 and 1900 are not leap years, while 2000 is. This procedure makes use of the properties of modulo numbers. With a bit of practice, you can figure out the answer very quickly.

Arthur Benjamin and Michael Shermer, Mathemagics: How to Look Like a Genius Without Trying (Los Angeles: Lowell House, 1993), 172–175.

3.3 Judging

Four men visit Australia for the first time. Traveling by train, they see the profile of a black sheep grazing. The first man concludes that Australian sheep are black. The second claims that all one can conclude is that some Australian sheep are black. The third objects, and says that the only possible conclusion is that at least one sheep in Australia is black! The fourth man, a skeptic, concludes: in Australia there exists at least one sheep that is black on at least one side.
—RAYMOND CHEVALIER, quoted in *Québec Sceptique*

The little story told by Chevalier reminds us how hard it can be to make judgments that match the evidence before us—much harder than it seems. In the following pages, I would like to show a few, sometimes unexpected, examples of this difficulty. Each one is a warning against the tendency to rely too quickly or too exclusively on immediate experience in forming our judgments.

We are constantly building "theories" or, if you prefer,

"explanatory schemas" to understand and interpret the world that surrounds us. They are enormously useful: they allow us to order our environment and to evolve more effectively within it. But sometimes the facts demand that we revise these schemas.

Yet diverse phenomena show that we can be quite reluctant—and even stubbornly unwilling—to do so, which sometimes leads us to deny the evidence at hand. This can be explained, in part, by errors in reasoning that we already know about and which we won't go over again here—for example, the trouble we have evaluating probability, or the tendency to draw conclusions based on the observation of too small a sample of cases or unrepresentative cases. This translates into a tendency to easily remember facts that are immediately available, or to consider only the ones that are particularly spectacular or striking for a variety of reasons, to the detriment of data that is more reliable and trustworthy, but also harder to obtain and less extraordinary. If you only read certain newspapers, for example, you will believe that the number of individual crimes is rising at a sky-rocketing rate—though it has been diminishing for decades.

Two Examples of Our Trouble Evaluating Probability

Happy Birthday—To Both of You!

There are undoubtedly twenty-three people in your life to whom you are close enough that it would make sense for them to invite you to their birthday parties. How do you evaluate the probability of having to turn down an invitation from one of those twenty-three because you have to go to the party of another one of twenty-three who was born and is celebrating on the same day? Most people think that the probability is very low. But let's take a closer look.

The first person can be born any day of the year. So there is one chance in 365 that the second person is born the same day, and 364 chances out of 365 that the she is born on another day. If we add the third person to the mix, there are now two chances in 365 that she is born on the same days as one or the other of the first two, and 363 chances in 365 that she is born another day. Let's now include all twenty-three people and do the necessary multiplication: 364/365 x 363/365 . . . 342/365. The result is 0.46 or 46 percent, which is the probability that no birthday coincides with any other. In a group of twenty-three people, there is therefore more than one chance in two (54 percent) that two birthdays fall on the same day. This defies common sense, which has a great deal of trouble intuitively evaluating this sort of probability.

If we are to believe the physician G. Gamow, who used to entertain himself by challenging his mathematician friends with this question, most of those who relied on their intuition were mistaken. Having math skills is not worth very much if we neglect to use them.

False Positives

Here is another truly spectacular example of the difficulty we have evaluating probabilities intuitively. It is known as the paradox of false positives.

Let's suppose that there is a serious lethal disease that affects one person in one thousand in a given population. Luckily, tests exist that can detect the illness. The tests, however, are slightly imperfect: they detect the illness, when it is present, in 99 percent of cases—so they don't recognize a sick person in 1 percent of cases. On the other hand, they don't detect the illness, when it is not present, in 98 percent of cases—so two people in one hundred will be diagnosed ill who actually are not. These are what we call false positives.

The doctor announces to a patient that test results are positive. The question is how worried this person should be. Most people will think that this patient is almost certainly ill. The patient only has, however, a one in twenty-three chance of really being sick, which is not good news, but a lot less terrible than our intuition would suggest. This paradox should be known and considered by those who advocate mandatory screening for certain illnesses.

For those who are interested, here is the demonstration of this stunning conclusion:

Let A be the patient with the illness.

Let B be the patient with positive test results.

We can write the problem as follows:

$P(A) = 0.001$

$P(B|A) = 0.99$

$P(B|\text{not } A) = 0.02$

What we are looking for is: $P(A|B)$

The answer is given in Bayes formula:

$$P(A|B) = \frac{P(A)P(B|A)}{P(A)P(B|A) + P(\text{not } A)P(B|\text{not } A)}$$

This rejection of evidence can take even more stunning forms, with the consequence that we no longer take into account what frustrates our dearest convictions or, on the other hand, that we only consider that which confirms them.

Below, we'll look at several examples.

3.3.1 Cognitive Dissonance

"I have done that," says my memory.
"I cannot have done that," says my pride,
and remains adamant. At last—memory yields.
—FRIEDRICH NIETZSCHE

Leon Festinger advanced the concept of cognitive dissonance in 1957. This theory is no doubt a simplification of a much more complicated one, but it allows us to delineate many otherwise strange aspects of human behavior and make sense of them. Moreover, it is useful for explaining how it is that we can deceive ourselves, which is of particular interest to us here. In simple terms, here is the broad idea.

Imagine a situation in which you entertain two incompatible ideas, beliefs, or opinions. For example, you are very attached to opinion X but, at the same time, you can see that X is wrong in light of observable facts. Or imagine a situation in which your convictions contradict your behavior. This inevitably results in tension and unease. According to the theory of cognitive dissonance, you will try to find a way of making this tension disappear, or at least minimize it, in the simplest and most efficient way possible.

This can be done in a number of ways. For example, if we judge that one of our behaviors is immoral or stupid, we could change our point of view in such a way as to find it just and sensible. When new data is placed before them, two people with opposite beliefs will tend to see in it something that confirms their own position and ignore what invalidates it. Our capacity to invent reasons that justify our otherwise unacceptable behavior plays a leading role in cognitive dissonance. A person who thinks of himself as kind and humane will find all sorts of faults in his victim to justify the violence he uses.

Some otherwise incomprehensible behaviors can be illuminated by these ideas. Let's look at a famous example, drawn from Festinger's work.[8]

In the early 1950s, Miss Keech, a woman of a certain age, claimed to be receiving messages from extraterrestrials from the planet Clarion. One day, one of the messages informed her that on December 21 of that year, the earth was going to be destroyed by a terrifying flood, but that a squad of flying saucers would come to save her and everyone who was close to her at that time.

A group of believers gathered around the lady to wait for the end of the world in her company, while leading an existence that fit their beliefs; they renounced all their possessions, left their jobs, cut themselves off from their friends and acquaintances, and so on. Among these disciples there were also psychologists, who, working incognito, wanted to observe the behavior of the members of the group, especially on December 22. These psychologists noted that members of the group were inoffensive, gentle, refused all publicity and media interviews, did not proselytize, and lived serenely in the shadows, as their convictions dictated.

On December 20, the lady in question received a new message from the residents of Clarion, which she passed on to her followers: the end was near, they should prepare themselves, and they would be rescued at exactly midnight. Additionally, they should not carry any metal on them. So they removed all buttons and zippers from their clothing.

Midnight came and went. In the hours that followed, the despair and disarray of the group were palpable. But at 4:45 a.m., Miss Keech received a message from the Clarionians that their action and their faith had saved the world from calamity. Consequently, the flying saucer rescue mission was no longer necessary. The group exploded in joyful cheers. What happened after that night is only astonishing if we forget the concept of cognitive dissonance.

The group, which until then had been quite discreet, launched numerous passionate campaigns to make their ideas known and defend them. Its proselytizing efforts knew no bounds. Members of the group contacted the media, gave talks, and made speeches in the streets. Their faith in Miss Keech had been strengthened by what had taken place.

3.3.2 The Forer Effect

This very odd effect owes its name to B. R. Forer, a professor of psychology who, in the 1940s, engaged in a fascinating little experiment.

Forer first had his students undergo a personality test. Then he gave each one of them the written description of his or her personality that the test allowed him to infer. The students had to evaluate the test and say whether or not it seemed to have adequately delineated their personality by grading it on a scale of 1 (worst) to 5 (best). On average, they gave it a 4.2 on 5, a result that was by and large confirmed in hundreds of repetitions of the experiment. What a remarkable personality test, you say?

No. In fact, Forer simply copied phrases from newspaper horoscopes, made a paragraph out of them, and gave the same text to everyone. In other words, he *gave everyone the same personality description!*

Here is a passage from it:

> You have a need for other people to like and admire you, and yet you tend to be critical of yourself. While you have some personality weaknesses you are generally able to compensate for them. You have considerable unused capacity that you have not turned to your advantage. Disciplined and self-controlled on the outside, you tend to be worrisome and insecure on the inside. At times you have serious doubts as to whether you have made the right decision or done the right thing. You prefer a certain amount of change and variety and become dissatisfied when hemmed in by restrictions and limitations. You also pride yourself as an independent thinker; and do not accept others' statements without satisfactory proof. But you have found it unwise to be too frank in revealing yourself to others. At times you are extroverted, affable, and sociable, while at other times you are introverted, wary, and reserved. Some of your aspirations tend to be rather unrealistic.[9]

So the Forer effect is our tendency to accept vague and general descriptions and analyses that would apply to anyone as specific and meaningful to ourselves.

Here is another example:

> Some of your aspirations tend to be pretty unrealistic. At times you are extroverted, affable, sociable, while at other times you are introverted, wary and reserved. You have found it unwise to be too frank in revealing yourself to others. You pride yourself on being an independent thinker and do not accept others' opinions without satisfactory proof. You prefer a certain amount of change and variety, and become dissatisfied when hemmed in by restrictions and limitations. At times you have serious doubts as to whether you have made the right decision or done the right thing. Disciplined and controlled on the outside, you tend to be worrisome and insecure on the inside.
>
> Your sexual adjustment has presented some problems for you. While you have some personality weaknesses, you are generally able to compensate for them. You have a great deal of unused capacity which you have not turned to your advantage. You have a tendency to be critical of yourself. You have a strong need for other people to like you and for them to admire you.[10]

I don't think I need to stress any further the enormous benefits, including material ones, that could be reaped by people using such statements to appear to be able to read all sorts of things in palms, tea cups, the stars, cards, the tarot, billy clubs, and so on—if such people existed, of course.

3.3.3 The Wason Selection Task

Our tendency to look for examples that confirm and neglect those that invalidate a hypothesis is particularly well demonstrated by this test.

You are shown four cards, placed face up on a table. They read:

D – F – 3 – 7

Each card has a letter on one side of it and a number on the other. You are then asked which cards you wish to turn over to verify that the following rule was respected: if a card has a D on one side, it has to have a three on the other.

The experiment, which has been carried out repeatedly and on a large number of subjects, shows that unless you have done somewhat advanced math, logic, or programming, most people reply D and three, the first and the third cards. But that is wrong: you have to turn over the first and last cards.

The first, because there could be something other than a three on the other side, which would invalidate the hypothesis. For the same reason, it seems to make sense to turn over the third card (the three): we would look for a D on the other side. But think about it: that wouldn't change anything. The hypothesis says that if there is a D, there has to be a three on the other side; it doesn't say that if there's a three there has to be a D on the other side!

The fourth card, on the other hand, is crucial. If there were a D on the other side, our hypothesis would be refuted. The problem is that we are trying less to refute than to confirm, and so we ignore this card.

This entertaining little test has been taken up by researchers in evolutionary psychology to show that if an example that involves detecting cheaters is the object of our reasoning, the reasoning becomes much easier. Let's take a look at what that's all about, before we leave this topic.

Someone explains to you that you have been put in charge of security in a bar. The bar is open to youth under the age of eighteen and to adults. The youth, however, must absolutely not consume alcohol. If a young person of fewer than eighteen years is found drinking alcohol in the bar, the bar will lose its license immediately. Your job, as the person responsible for security, is to make sure that no young person drinks alcohol. Luckily, every client moves about displaying a card: on one side of the card is a number that indicates the person's age; on the other side is an indication of what the person is drinking.

You're in the bar and you notice the following four cards:

Cola Beer 28 16

What cards would you turn over to ensure that the person is not consuming alcohol illegally?

Note that while this is easy and everyone can answer it, formally speaking this problem is identical to the preceding one. What that means exactly remains contested.[11]

3.3.4 The Pygmalion Effect

In Greek mythology, the story goes that King Pygmalion, unable to find a woman who could live up to his hopes and expectations, had an ivory representation of his vision of the ideal woman sculpted. (In another version of the story, he sculpted the statue himself.) But he fell hopelessly in love with it, and his unhappiness increased. Seeing this, Aphrodite, the goddess of love, came to his rescue; she gave life to the statue and made her fall in love with Pygmalion.

You can read this story not only as a metaphor about the relationship between the creator and his creatures, but also as a reminder of the role our expectations can play in defining others.

Bernard Shaw made this the theme of one his best-known plays, appropriately titled *Pygmalion*. At one point, the main character, who is a young flower girl, declares:

> You see, really and truly, apart from the things anyone can pick up (the dressing and the proper way of speaking, and so on), the difference between a lady and a flower girl is not how she behaves, but how she's treated. I shall always be a flower girl to Professor Higgins, because he always treats me as a flower girl, and always will; but I know I can be a lady to you, because you always treat me as a lady, and always will.[12]

Are the myth and the playwright right? Is it true that our expectations have this power, and if so, to what degree? Arguments put forward in the social sciences push us to answer yes to the first question and to think that this power can be immense. Here are two examples, one drawn from sociology, the other from psychology; the latter is particularly relevant to the world of education.

In 1948, the sociologist Robert K. Merton (1910–2003) published a resoundingly successful article in which he dubbed predictions that come to be true simply because they are made and believed to be true "self-fulfilling prophecies." The stock market could no doubt be held up as the archetype of institutions in which such self-fulfilling prophecies come true. Take X, who with many others buys shares because she thinks the stock will rise. They do indeed rise, because so many people are buying them. And the reverse can also be true.

The psychologist Robert Rosenthal, while working with lab rats that he was teaching to orient themselves in a maze, asked whether the researchers' beliefs about and expectations of their subjects influenced their subjects' performances. To find out, he randomly distributed sixty animals to twelve researchers, telling half of them that the animals were gifted and half that they were stupid. The results obtained confirmed in a major way the "Pygmalion effect" hypothesis: the rats that were believed to be gifted progressed twice as quickly as the rats believed to be stupid.

Could a similar effect be at play in the education of human subjects? That is the question Rosenthal asked next. To answer it, he conceived one of the most famous psychology of education studies, which dealt specifically with teachers' expectations and the intellectual development of students. The results appeared in 1968 under the title *Pygmalion in the Classroom*.[13]

Led by Robert Rosenthal and Leonore Jacobson, the study was carried out at Oak School, a primary school. All the school children—except for those who were graduating—and all the kindergarten children who were meant to go to Oak School the following year, were given a banal and little-known intelligence test (the TOGA). They were told that it was a new test developed at Harvard University that allowed for the identification of children about to undergo "an unusual forward spurt of academic progress." Then one child in five was randomly labeled as having been identified by the test as "bloomers." The hypothesis, obviously, was that these children would make greater progress because the teachers would expect more of them. This prediction seemed to be confirmed when the children were retested at the end of the school year, and was particularly true amongst younger children. In fact, in first grade, according to the scale of measurement that was used, the "bloomers" progressed 27.4 points, while the others progressed only 12.0 points. In third grade, these numbers were 16.5 and 7.0, respectively. No significant difference, however, was observed in children in the last year of their primary school education.

To summarize, wrote Rosenthal and Jacobson, "we may say that by what she said, by how and when she said it, by her facial expressions, postures, and perhaps by her touch, the teacher may have communicated to the children of the experimental group that she expected improved intellectual performance."[14]

3.3.5 The Milgram Experiments; or, The Wrongdoing Enabled by Blind Submission to Authority

It's the mid-1960s at Yale University. You have answered a classified ad that you found in a newspaper and you go to a psychology laboratory to participate in an experiment about the effects of punishment and learning. Another volunteer is there too, and a researcher in a white coat welcomes you. He explains that one of you is going to teach the other sequences of word pairs and will have to punish the other person, by administering electric shocks of increasing intensity, if he makes a mistake. A draw of sorts designates you as the teacher. You are directed into the room where the student will be and you are shown the chair where he will sit. You are given a weak electric shock to show you what it feels like. You are present while the student is seated in the chair and an electrode is placed on him.

Then you return to the adjacent room with the researcher who greeted you. He sets you up in front of the control center that you will operate. The shocks you will give run a scale from 15 to 450 volts, progressing in increments of 15 volts. The levels are labeled "Light shock" up to "Very strong shock: Danger." At 435 volts the label reads: "XXX." The experiment begins. Each time the student makes a mistake, you administer a shock 15 volts stronger than the last one. At 120 volts, the student complains of pain; at 150 volts he asks to stop the experiment; at 270 volts he screams in pain; at 330 volts he is incapable of speech. Do you hesitate to continue? Throughout the experiment, the expert uses only four phrases to incite you to continue: "please continue"; "the experiment requires that you continue"; "it is absolutely essential that you continue"; "you have no other choice, you must go on."

As you may have guessed, the draw was rigged, and the student is an accomplice, an actor who simulates pain. In short, you were the subject of the experiment. Before carrying it out, Milgram asked middle-class adults, psychiatrists, and students how far they thought they would go. He also asked how far they thought others would go. No one thought they or others would go as far as 300 volts. But during the experiment on forty men aged twenty- to fifty-five-years-old, 63 percent continued to the end, administering 450-volt electric shocks.

ANOTHER CASE OF SUBMISSION

The details of the experiment, which I won't get into here, are spine-tingling. Milgram's experiment has been commented on, repeated, and discussed abundantly. But this study of submission to authority remains a contribution to our knowledge of the nature of authority and of its power to make us act in irrational ways that cannot be overlooked. Someone suggested that the lesson a critical thinker must draw from it is the following; never, ever agree to take part in a psychology experiment at Yale.

But no, it isn't that.

All right, this is it: you have to think before you obey, always asking yourself if what is being asked of you is justified, even if the order is given by an authority figure.

3.3.6 The Asch Experiment; or, The Wrongdoing Enabled by Conformism

Once again, you're volunteering for an experiment. You are ushered into a room where there are nine chairs arranged in a semicircle. You are told to sit on the next-to-last chair, and gradually, other participants fill the rest. Then you are shown two cards at once. One has only one eight-inch line on it; the second has three lines of six, eight, and ten inches each. You are asked to point to the line on the second card that matches the line on the first. Easy! The participants on the other side of the semicircle answer before you. To your stupefaction, they give the wrong answer. All choose the wrong line. Of course, once again, they are accomplices. The question is: what will you do when it is your turn to speak?

Here again, the results of the experiment have proven troubling time and time again. More than a third of the subjects were brought around to share the group's opinion; 75 percent were won over at least once.

The moral of the story? Conformism is dangerous and you always have to think for yourself. It is difficult, and sometimes uncomfortable, but indispensable.

As soon as a human being gets a Ph.D., a strange phenomenon takes place in his or her brain that makes the person incapable of saying the following two sentences: "I don't know," and, "I made a mistake."

—James Randi

Hoaxes

Hoaxes are actions, documents, or artifacts designed to deceive the public. They can be inconsequential and committed in jest, but they can also be ill-intentioned and designed to get something from the victim, generally money. A hoax is a form of swindle.

Hoax artists always claim to want what is best for you, and they have invented many ingenious ways to take it away from you. They have displayed enormous ingenuity to do so. Indeed, being thought clever is the premier characteristic of a successful hoax artist. Most often hoaxers rely, with good reason, on the dishonesty of the sheep they are about to fleece. This is the second characteristic of a good hoax artist. Here is a typical hoax scenario that allows us to see both traits in action.

Two hoax artists go to a neighborhood where they steal a dog. One of them goes to a bar with the animal on a leash. He orders a drink and starts a conversation with the bartender. He lets slip that this dog was just left to him by an old and very wealthy aunt. He adds that the animal is a burden he would be happy to be rid of. And he explains that he came to this neighborhood, where he never goes, for a business meeting at which he is going to close a lucrative deal. But he can't bring the dog. Would the bartender be willing to take care of it for just half an hour? Then the hoax artist leaves, leaving the dog to the bartender.

His accomplice then enters. Very quickly, he pretends to notice the dog, takes an interest in it, and then approaches the bartender: what a wonderful animal, he says, a rare breed of which he himself is, by chance, a breeder. Would the bartender be willing to sell it? He would pay a lot for the animal. But the bartender says she cannot sell the dog: the animal belongs to a client, who will, however, be back soon. "I don't have time to wait," says thesecond client, "but for such an animal, I can be patient for half an hour."

Time goes by and the owner of the dog does not come back. Half an hour passes, and then an hour. Much to his regret, the dog breeder must leave. He leaves his card with the bartender and asks her to give it to the animal's owner. If the deal interests him, he will merely have to call the phone number written on the card.

Then the breeder exits. Not long after, the owner of the dog returns. He is sad and dejected. His lucrative deal fell through. He admits that he has serious financial problems, and that he doesn't even have enough money to pay for his drink.

The hoax artists are betting that events will unfold as follows:

The bartender offers to pay for her client's drink and even to help him by buying his dog. She realized while she was watching it that she really likes the animal. So she proposes a certain sum. The other refuses at first, and feigns outrage: the dog is, after all, family heritage. So they negotiate. The affair ends when the client leaves with money from the sale. As soon as he steps out the door, the bartender calls the phone number on the card left behind by the breeder. Of course, the number is out of service.

The Internet provides hoax artists with new possibilities and opens the door to altogether new territory for their ingenuity. Who has not received an urgent e-mail message from a Third World dignitary soliciting your assistance in accessing a fabulously endowed bank account and promising you a portion of the loot in return for your help? But for it to work, you first must advance a small amount of money, in order to pay fake fees. In a case such as this, critical thinking can save you huge amounts of money and worry, if not your life.

Here are a few questions that will help you to identify e-mail hoaxes:

—Does the text appear to have been written by the author? Is it signed? If not, be careful.

—Does it contain declarations of authenticity like: "This is not a joke, an urban legend, or a hoax"? If so, be careful.

—Is liberal use made of capital letters and exclamation marks? Be careful.

—Does it make use of emotional language? Be careful.

—Is the information contained in the e-mail extraordinary? Is it presented as secret and unknown to most people? Does it seem too good to be true? Does it promise that you will get rich quick and without any risk, or that you will be miraculously healed? Be careful.

—Does it provide sources for its claims? Are they credible? If not, be careful.

—Does it give a real reply-to address? If not, be careful.

—Does it provide an Internet address? Does the URL make sense in the context of the rest of the message? If, for example, the message comes from an institution and asks that you provide information—say, a password, which you should never give out—to a site whose address is not that of the institution in question, be careful.

—Check the Internet to make sure the message hasn't already been identified and denounced as a hoax.

—Pay careful attention to the general appearance of the message. Hoax artists try to make their missives look like authentic documents, but they don't always succeed. For example, the letter from the bank might contain strange and unusual spelling or aesthetic errors, the logo used might appear to be the simple copy that it is, and so on.

See http:/http://hoaxbusters.ciac.org/hoaxbusters.ciac.org.

After all this analysis and reflection, after all this information and the results of all the research we have examined, what must we think about relying on personal experience to justify our beliefs? I think that from now on we will be more suspicious of its limitations and I would submit for your approval the following conclusion, offered by Schick and Vaughn:

> Because of all the limitations of our personal experience—perceptual construction, memory construction, the effects of stress, the impact of expectancy and belief, selective attention, misjudgments of probabilities, subjective validation, altered states of consciousness, and much more—we must [put forward this principle]:
>
> It's reasonable to accept personal experience as reliable evidence only if there's no reason to doubt its reliability.
>
> Reasons for doubting include any of the limitations just mentioned. Other reasons include poor observational conditions (like limited visibility, bad lighting, faint stimuli, unusual circumstances, and so on), and conflicts with other propositions we have good reason to believe.[15]

This last sentence inevitably raises the following question: what are the propositions that we have good reason to believe, and from there, what knowledge is sufficiently certain to allow us to hope to overcome the limitations of personal experience? Empirical and experimental science will provide an answer to these questions. And it is on this that we will now focus.

But first, I would like to close this section by offering you a critical thinking tool that is useful when a "fantastic" proposition is presented for approval on the basis of testimony. It is Hume's famous maxim.

3.3.7 A Valuable Tool: Hume's Maxim

In a text titled "Of Miracles," the philosopher David Hume weighed in on the theological debates that were shaking his era. He offered a remarkable argument to help evaluate so-called miracles. This argument can be applied to all extraordinary affirmations, so it is one of the most effective tools at the disposal of critical thinkers. ·

All the different religions, Hume remarked, put forward miracles as proof that they are true. However, the miracles have to be believed on the basis of mere testimony, because most people haven't witnessed them, or been the beneficiaries of them. So, what is a miracle?

By definition, Hume explained, it is a violation of the laws of nature that is attributed to divine will. Our confidence in those laws of nature is founded on experience; therefore, it is fallible. But the testimony of the miracle is also founded on experience. What we have to compare are the respective probabilities of the two events: first, the probability that there was indeed a violation of the laws of nature; and then the probability that the witness (or one of the people communicating the information) made a mistake or is trying to deceive us. As soon as the problem is posed in this way, which is the correct way, we conclude that the second hypothesis is the most plausible. We can call upon many things we've learned through experience to support it, like the fragility of our senses' perception, witness contradiction, the incoherence of different religions' claims to miracles (which cannot all be simultaneously true), the desire to marvel and to believe, the pleasure of thinking that one has been chosen to witness a miracle, the desire to deceive, and so on.

Let's allow Hume to speak for himself:

> A miracle is a violation of the laws of nature; and as a firm and unalterable experience has established these laws, the proof against a miracle, from the very nature of the fact, is as entire as any argument from experience can possibly be imagined. Why is it more than probable, that all men must die; that lead cannot, of itself, remain suspended in the air; that fire consumes wood, and is extinguished by water; unless it be, that these events are found agreeable to the laws of nature, and there is required a violation of these laws, or in other words, a miracle to prevent them? Nothing is esteemed a miracle, if it ever happen in the common course of nature. It is no miracle that a man, seemingly in good health, should die on a sudden: because such a kind of death, though more unusual than any other, has yet been frequently observed to happen. But it is a miracle, that a dead man should come to life; because that has never been observed in any age or country. There must, therefore, be a uniform experience against every miraculous event, otherwise the event would not merit that appellation. And as a uniform experience amounts to a proof, there is here a direct

and full proof, from the nature of the fact, against the existence of any miracle; nor can such a proof be destroyed, or the miracle rendered credible, but by an opposite proof, which is superior.

The plain consequence is (and it is a general maxim worthy of our attention), 'that no testimony is sufficient to establish a miracle, unless the testimony be of such a kind, that its falsehood would be more miraculous, than the fact, which it endeavors to establish; and even in that case there is a mutual destruction of arguments, and the superior only gives us an assurance suitable to that degree of force, which remains, after deducting the inferior.' When anyone tells me that he saw a dead man restored to life, I immediately consider with myself, whether it be more probable, that this person should either deceive or be deceived, or that the fact, which he relates, should really have happened. I weigh the one miracle against the other; and according to the superiority, which I discover, I pronounce my decision, and always reject the greater miracle. If the falsehood of his testimony would be more miraculous, than the event which he relates; then, and not till then, can he pretend to command my belief or opinion.[16]

This argument can and must be generalized because it has a range of applicability that is much broader than merely that of miracles confronting the laws of nature. Jean Bricmont reformulates in the following way what we might call the "Expanded Hume's Maxim":

You have . . . to ask the following question of scientists as much as to the charlatans, astrologers, and homeopaths: what reasons can you give me to believe that the truth of what you're suggesting is more probable than the fact that you are mistaken or are deceiving me? Scientists can answer by referring to specific experiments as well as the technological applications to which their theories give rise. (The latter is sometimes more obvious to the layperson.) But the others can give no such answers.

Moreover, a question also raised by Hume is how to face the problem presented by the multiplicity of doctrines founded on an arguments of the miraculous kind. If I am to believe in homeopathy, why not believe in the healings by faith that have the same efficaciousness on the other side of the Atlantic as homeopathy has here? Why believe our own astrology more than that of Tibet or of India? All these beliefs are founded on testimony that are equally valid, and consequently equally invalid too. Or, in other words, those who appear to be very credulous in our own societies are often very skeptical when they are told about beliefs from abroad. Their position is inconsistent, because they do not apply the reasoning that justifies their skepticism toward exotic beliefs to those that were ingrained in them as children or which permeate their immediate environment.[17]

Carl Sagan contributes by adding the following corollary,

and it is once again another golden maxim: "Extraordinary claims demand extraordinary evidence."[18]

CHAPTER 4

EMPIRICAL AND EXPERIMENTAL SCIENCE

It is not so much what the scientist believes that distinguishes him, but how and why he believes it.
—BERTRAND RUSSELL

One thing I have learned in a long life: that all our science, measured against reality, is primitive and childlike—and yet it is the most precious thing we have.

—ALBERT EINSTEIN

The displacement of the idea that facts and evidence matter by the idea that everything boils down to subjective interests and perspectives is—second only to American political campaigns—the most prominent and pernicious manifestation of anti-intellectualism in our time.

—LARRY LAUDAN

Introduction

Science occupies a significant but singular place in our culture. On the one hand, science, or more specifically the technologies it has produced, has an influence on almost every aspect of our lives. On the other hand, its results, concepts, and methods seem somehow not to have penetrated our consciousnesses and remain all too foreign to the public at large.

This might go some way to explaining why there still exists an overabundance of pseudoscientific and even anti-scientific beliefs; that they persist and propagate as they do remains mysterious in many respects. Paradoxically, it is not rare to see the partisans of pseudoscience decrying science and rationality in one breath and claiming to be scientific and rational in the next. Science is reductive and oppressive, the astrologist will say—but astrology, at least the kind he practices, is a science.

Finally, rationality itself, that which science tries to put into action, is the object of fundamental attacks in some academic and intellectual circles today. In these instances, science and reason are generally presented as sordid ideological masks that provide cover for various kinds of domination: Western, male, capitalist, and so on. Such analyses sometimes affirm a relativism hospitable to paranormal and esoteric doctrines, according to which science is just one discourse among others, a simple social and political "construct" without any privileged access to the truth. Such a conclusion is readily justified by the enormous difficulty (often portrayed as an impossibility) of articulating precisely and in a philosophically satisfying way just what science is, how it works, and how its results are achieved and verified—all tasks that disciplines called epistemology and philosophy of science set out to accomplish, although it has not yet been entirely successful. (The word epistemology is derived from the Greek *epistêmê*, knowledge, and *logos*, discourse or study; epistemology is the critical study of knowledge, while philosophy of science is the critical study of science and its principles, methods, and conclusions.)

The Enormous Difficulties of Epistemology

At the beginning of the twentieth century, believing correctly that science is a rational endeavor, some thinkers also believed, incorrectly this time, that if they joined the (new) formal logic to an empiricist theory of origins and knowledge justification, they would be able to describe and fully explain rationality. They ultimately had to admit that this was not the case. To show you the sort of terrible and unexpected trouble epistemologists encountered, consider the following example, called the Hempel paradox.

How do many scientists end up holding a proposition to be (probably) true?

Ask scientists who are not really versed in philosophy this question and they will generally answer that data-gathering bestows an increasing probability on a proposition: "To begin with, a proposition is put forward as a hypothesis (it doesn't matter how here). Then data is gathered (again, it doesn't matter how). If it confirms the hypothesis, its probability increases. Otherwise, it decreases." Common sense is quite comfortable with this description, which a famous example involving crows allows us to grasp better.

Our hypothesis will be that all crows are black. Let's suppose that we observe a crow, and we notice that it is black; this observation confirms the hypothesis. Shall we conclude that the hypothesis is true? Certainly not, obviously, because one crow could not allow for a generalization about all crows.

You no doubt sense the trouble ahead: it's that a finite number of observations, however immense, can never logically allow absolutely for a generalization about all crows. But let us leave that aside for the moment. The important thing is that this observation of a black crow seems to us to bestow a certain plausibility to the hypothesis that all crows are black, plausibility that will increase as more crows are observed that also display the property of being black. However, an astonishing paradox emerges; it was studied by the logician and philosopher Carl Hempel. This paradox throws into question the intuitive notion of confirmation that I just described.

Hempel used a law of logic for calculating propositions called contraposition. The law is quite easy to understand: it says simply that the proposition, "If this, then that," is logically identical to the proposition, "If not this, then not that." Not very clear? Let's take a closer look. Let's start from the conditional proposition, as the logicians say, "If P, then Q." To make it more concrete, let's say, "If it rains, then the sidewalk is wet." Its contraposition is "If not Q, then not P," so, "If the sidewalk isn't wet, then it isn't raining."

Let's return to our crows. Our hypothesis says, "If something is a crow, then it is black." Its contraposition is, "If something is not black, then it is not a crow." So, because this contraposition is logically identical to the proposition we started with, every observation that confirms one must necessarily confirm the other. To get a good understanding of the notion, let's imagine, as suggested by Martin Gardner, a box of socks. This box is stored on top of your dresser, and you can't see inside it; in order to see your socks, you have to be satisfied with pulling out your socks one by one. You are trying to verify the hypothesis that every black sock is a size nine. You pull a sock out of the box; it is black and size nine. The hypothesis has been confirmed. You pull out another sock; it is blue and size seven. What do you conclude?

Hempel's paradox arises here. You see, since the proposition, "All crows are black," is equivalent to "All non-black objects are non-crows," it seems that we have to conclude that the observation that a frog is green confirms that all crows are black. In fact, we have to conclude that the observation of any object whatsoever, so long as it is not black, confirms that all crows are black.

But isn't it strange that you can draw ornithological conclusions from your kitchen simply by observing multicolored utensils and using seemingly unassailable logic? And if it is true that we have now considerably simplified the work of ornithologists, who no longer need to travel to practice their science, what price do we have to pay for this simplification? Our troubles don't end here. As my shrewd readers will have noticed, the observation of a green frog confirms not only that all crows are black, but also, with the same implacable logic, that all crows are white.

The tragedy of a certain contemporary and frankly irrationalist epistemology is that, noticing that these attempts at reconstructing the rationality of science had failed, some "theorists," often ill-equipped to be thinking about science, wrongly concluded that science is not a rational endeavor.

I have articulated my position on these irrationalist epistemologies in "Contre le charlatanisme universitaire (Against University Charlatanism)," *Possibles* 26, no. 2 (Summer 2002): 49–72.

You'll have guessed that questions of science (and pseudoscience) raise numerous complicated questions, and it will be impossible to address them all here or even to get to the bottom of a few of them. More modestly, I hope to give those of you who want to adopt a critical perspective toward science and pseudoscience some markers to help you situate yourselves in relation to all this, as well as some tools for intellectual self-defense. Thus, you will have the means to exercise critical judgment when faced with scientific research, with the extravagant epistemological theories you will not be able to avoid encountering if you venture into this territory, and lastly, with the weird and extraordinary "theories" that will be presented to you.

I will proceed in four stages.

To begin, I want to give you some idea, simple but concrete, of what scientists do to test a hypothesis. Indeed, among other things, science is a way of formulating questions and interrogating reality to arrive at answers. To this end, I will present three concepts that you will have to master: experimentation with controlled variables, experimentation with a control group, and double-blind experimentation.

Several conceptual clarifications related to the idea of science will follow. I will put forward a definition of empirical or experimental science, as well as definitions of certain other concepts necessary to the apprentice epistemologist and philosopher of science. By suggesting a series of questions to ask, I will then give you markers that will help you evaluate the validity of the research results that are presented to you. Finally, the last part of the chapter introduces a model that will help you to evaluate the bizarre theories that the followers of the paranormal or of esotericism ask us to accept with a frequency that shows no sign of decline.

4.1 Science and Experimentation

Imagine that you are the head of an organization like James Randi's, described above. Your Billy Club Foundation promises a prize of $50,000 to whomever demonstrates paranormal or occult powers. Let's go further and establish another convention; you yourself will pay any eventual winner with your own funds.

One morning, you receive a letter from a candidate. The man practices water divination. He is a dowser. The letter mentions that with a regular wooden rod (traditionally, they were made of hazel), he is able to detect water underground. Indeed, he explains, when he walks about holding his rod extended in front of him, it suddenly begins to move in a completely visible way. It's the sign that there is water underfoot; if you dig in that spot, you're sure to find it.

Your correspondent is stunned that you would give such a prize—and he hopes it isn't a joke—but he is thrilled to be able to claim it. He understands that you'll need some proof before writing the check, but in the case of divination, a very old art form, proof is easy to obtain. All societies have practiced it and recognized it since the dawn of time—so it must work.

He personally, in the course of his long career, has been able to install almost fifteen wells. He appends to his letter a list of the owners of all the lots that have a well because of him and his rods, and all would be willing to testify to his abilities. Your correspondent reminds you that it is well-known among the residents of the area who know he is a dowser that his art always hits the mark, and that they call him each time they need to dig a well. His address follows, and he asks you to send the check as soon as possible.

Would you pay him? Surely you would ask him for proof beforehand, and you would be right to do so. Let's proceed sequentially.

Your correspondent puts forward arguments to support a conclusion. To think clearly, you first have to determine what exactly that conclusion says, given that it is the thesis he is upholding and in support of which he is advancing arguments. Then you have to find those arguments and determine whether or not they are valid.

Your candidate seems to be saying that the power to detect water with a rod exists, and that he himself possesses that power. To support this conclusion, he puts forward the notion that this art has been practiced for a long time, and that he himself practices it successfully. Should you be satisfied with this and pay him? Certainly not. First of all, the thesis he maintains is not very clear: Where? When? How? Under what conditions? As soon as you read the letter, piles of questions come to mind. Moreover, you know perfectly well that things known and believed for a long time, and held as true by individuals, groups, and entire societies, have proven to be false. You also know how easily people can deceive themselves, can see poorly, remember poorly, judge poorly, and so on. You also know that false testimonies are always possible.

Taking all that into account, you decide to inquire. You find ten witnesses from among those named by the candidate. They seem trustworthy and all assure you that your candidate did indeed discern the locations of their wells. Now do you pay him?

You shouldn't. If you are prudent, you will say to yourself that even if the candidate correctly indicated where water was to be found in each of those cases, other factors could have been at play. You cannot exclude the possibility, for example, that he simply found the water by chance. Or because there was water everywhere on the lot where he was searching, at various depths. Or because he is very good, consciously or unconsciously, at locating the clues that make it reasonable to think that there is water at a given spot.

As you cannot exclude these explanations, and they account for what has been observed just as well as the explanation put forward by the dowser, you want to make sure that these factors or others are not the reasons for his apparent success before you pay your candidate. According to Ockham's razor, you want to look for the most economical explanation, that which demands that you postulate the fewest possible entities: Why make a foreign and heretofore unknown power intervene where simple and well-known factors suffice to explain what is observed?

A Powerful Razor

Pluralitas numquam est ponenda sine neccesitat: it means, "Plurality should not be postulated unless it is necessary," or, "We should not multiply beings unnecessarily." This maxim was attributed to William of Ockham (circa 1285-1349), a Franciscan monk who was the most important philosopher of his time. Excommunicated by Pope John XXII, Ockham responded with a treaty that demonstrated that the Pope was a heretic.

Often called "Ockham's razor," this principle became one of medieval philosophy's major contributions to critical thinking. It is doubtful, however, that the monk would have subscribed to the uses that modern science makes of his famous razor. In its beginnings, the principle of parsimony was used in the context of the "Battle of Universals"; Ockham and many others used it to defend the nominalist thesis, according to which there are no general entities corresponding to general names, which are only words always corresponding to singular things (the opposite point of view is called realism). But in modern thought, Ockham's razor became a principle of parsimony and economy. This principle, both methodological and ontological, recommends that one look for the simplest explanation and preserve the hypothesis in which the fewest entities are postulated. Very useful in science, this principle is equally useful for examining the pretensions of certain parascientists. You can't prove that extraterrestrials never visited and built the pyramids in Egypt or erected the statues on Easter Island; but if those phenomena can be accounted for without having Martians intervene, that simpler explanation must be privileged over the rest.

Thinking about all this, you probably feel the need to be more precise about what affirmation it is exactly that you need to test, as well as the specific conditions of the test and the results that would validate the original claim. Are you with me? Are you starting to see the problems that arise as you try to work out a method? In that case, you're starting to formulate the problem as it is done in science. It is fair to say that this scientific way of thinking about and searching for a way of testing an idea is essentially the way all human beings think when faced with common problems. The only difference is that in the case of science, it is pursued with obstinacy and a rare vigor.

You see that in principle, this idea of experimentation is quite simple. To sum it up, you have to try to verify what is alleged to be real, present, vouched for, etc. But in fact, the procedure can be very complex, basically because observing is difficult and because you have to make sure that what you presume to be present is indeed what is at play in what you observe. And sometimes that is stunningly complicated to do.

Let's examine three methods of experimental verification, which will introduce us to some of those difficulties while also showing us ways of trying to overcome them: experimentation with controlled variables, experimentation with a control group, and double-blind experimentation. That will give us an idea of what exactly scientists do, following which we will try to define the concept of science itself a little more precisely.

4.1.1 Experimentation with Controlled Variables

Let us return to our dowser.

We want to limit as much as possible the other potential explanations of the result and observe whether it always takes place in these conditions. To do so, we will have to mount an experiment with the systematic control of these variables.

Like many before and after him, Randi actually tested dowsers. The chosen protocol, accepted by the dowsers who were tested, was as follows. On a ten-by-ten-meter rural plot on which there was apparently no indication of water, three plastic tubes were hidden about fifty centimeters underground. Following different trajectories, each tube started from point A and went to point B. The water ran through one tube at a time. This had been communicated to the dowsers. With their wands, they had to determine the trajectory of the water and mark it out with stakes. The protocol laid out what would count as a success and what would count as failure, for example how close to a tube a marker had to be in order to be considered valid. Thirty stakes were given to each candidate and each dowser had three tries. We will skip the rest of the details of the protocol, but let's note that that method of doing things allowed for statistical analysis to be carried out. Anyone would have placed a certain number of markers accurately, simply by chance. Thus, the dowsers had to do better than chance would allow for anyone to think that something else was operative in their performances. Before the test, the dowsers declared their agreement to these conditions in writing, as well as their confidence in their ability to pass the test with total success. They even claimed to be convinced that they could place (almost) all the stakes correctly.

When Randi tested dowsers in Italy between March 22 and March 31, 1979, however, no statistical analysis was necessary.[1] The first candidate placed one out of thirty stakes correctly, then two out of thirty. Then he gave up, choosing instead to pick up his first path again as a third try, which allowed him to place six stakes out of thirty. Thus, it was a failure. The second placed two stakes correctly out of the fifty-eight he put into the ground. The third forfeited before he even began. The last ended the test of his own accord. Randi did not have to write any checks that day.

Similar tests of dowsers produce the same results. What does this mean? First, that you have to beware of mere testimonials; also, that the power that was alleged did not manifest itself—which does not mean that we have demonstrated that it does not exist; finally, that it would be interesting to try to explain what happens when dowsers practice their art. Maybe they find water because it is there anyway, but how do you explain the movement of their rods?

To tell you the truth, the most plausible explanation of this phenomenon is that it is caused by ideomotor effect. Briefly, this is when a subject makes minute, involuntary, and unconscious movement through self-suggestion. Even the sort of tool that dowsers use (a Y-shaped branch that they hold on both arms of the Y, with the lower stem—that part which "reacts"—pointed out in front of them) suggests that this is the case. Held as it is, the rod is very unstable and responds strongly to the slightest wrist movements, because it amplifies them.

But you have another candidate. Let's see what it is all about this time.

4.1.2 Experimentation with a Control Group

The person claiming the prize has invented an electro-magnetic pyramid for slobs. He has attached a photo. In it you can see a few pieces of metal that do in fact form a pyramidal shape. The candidate explains that this pyramid gathers the cosmic energy of the great Egyptian masters and is capable of doing great things. At this point, he has discovered that it prolongs the life of his razors, because the energy in question preserves and miraculously restores the blades. He assures you that a blade that used to last ten days can now be used for twenty.

Do you pay up?

You would be right to ask for proof. After all, given the evidence, this inventor might be right to believe in his product, but you yourself have no reason to think that this supposed energy exists. Thus, you can reasonably believe that it is quite possible that the man shaves longer with a blade that is as dull as it was before, but which he imagines to be in better shape. Besides, you have a skeptical friend who acquired the same pyramid for a laugh. He didn't notice a difference in the longevity of his razors. Here again, though, his convictions might have biased him against detecting the alleged effect of the pyramid.

What you need is a way of comparing the state of two identical blades after being used identically in every respect, with one exception: the first blade would be kept in the pyramid, the other would not. In this way, it is fair to think that if you observe a substantial difference between the two, the pyramid could indeed have something to do with it. Note that this sort of test will have to be done on more than two blades. Indeed, you wouldn't want to use one razor that was, by chance, better or worse than the others. Therefore, to eliminate the possible effects of random chance, you'll have to test a great many blades.

Many difficult technical and methodological problems will arise quickly. For example, we'll have to be sure that the two groups (the blades kept in the pyramid and the blades that are not) are identical, that they are a random sample, and that they are of a sufficient number. With blades, it is easy enough, but suppose that this was a study of human beings? Putting such samples together is often a major endeavor. You also have to make sure that the treatment of both groups of blades is identical in every way—except in terms of exposure to the pyramid, of course. Finally, you have to find an objective measure of the blades' wear.

Let's say that you manage to satisfy all these conditions. You will then have what is called an experiment with a control group. It represents one of the high standards of science, and one of its glories. I think you already understand the principle a bit, and it is simple: you form two groups, one called experimental, and the other a control group. They are identical, except for the treatment that one gets (the experimental group) that the other does not (the control group). Then you compare results and analyze the differences with the help of statistical techniques that allow us to determine if and to what extent the difference observed is real and significant.

In this sort of study, you must pay a great deal of attention to the way groups are put together. If they are not identical, you leave yourself open to the suspicion that something other than the treatment was involved in the differences observed. For example, consider the following research in education that appeared in a reputable journal, which is often cited in the literature, and which has been a basis for the educational reforms that have been carried out in California and across the United States. Activate your baloney detector and in this description find reasons to believe that the study may not be valid:

> Ten second-grade classes participated in a year-long project in which instruction was generally compatible with a socioconstructivist theory of knowledge and recent recommendations of the National Council of Teachers of Mathematics. At the end of the school year, the ten project classes were compared with eight nonproject classes on a standardized achievement test and on instruments designed to assess students' computational proficiency and conceptual development in arithmetic, their personal goals in mathematics, and their beliefs about reasons for success in mathematics.
>
> The students in the study attended three schools

that contained both project and nonproject classes. The ratios of project to nonproject classes in these schools were 5:2, 3:2, and 2:4. Students within each school were heterogeneously assigned to second-grade classes by the principals on the basis of reading achievement scores. The schools each served an almost exclusively Caucasian student population with a wide range of socioeconomic backgrounds. Ten second-grade teachers volunteered to participate in the project and use the instructional activities. The eight nonproject teachers used the Addison-Wesley (1987) second-grade textbook as the basis for their mathematics instruction. Both project and nonproject teachers taught mathematics for approximately forty-five minutes each day.[2]

Have you found them? Well done! Indeed, by giving the experimental classes to volunteers, you guarantee that the groups won't be comparable. The reason is obvious: you haven't controlled for possible bias, and people who volunteer for such research are by definition particularly interested and motivated. Thus, in all likelihood, they will achieve better results than less motivated colleagues no matter what teaching method they use. Since you cannot exclude the possibility that this factor was at play, this research has no scientific value.

Experimentation with a control group is used everywhere it can be, including in the evaluation of medical treatments. In these cases, in order to control for bias, subjects all receive a treatment (for example, identical pills) but without knowing whether or not they are part of the control group or the experimental group. Those who are in the second group receive the medication; the others do not—in its place they are give a sugar pill or placebo (Latin for *I shall please*).

Now another correspondent has gotten in touch with you. This time it involves a horse named Hans, in Europe. Listen to this: this horse knows how to count, give dates, and a whole pile of other really amazing things. Things aren't looking good for your bank account. Your correspondent tells you that serious researchers have tested Hans and have not been able to account for what is happening with the usual explanations: no tricks, no cheating, nothing. Hans answers twelve by tapping his hoof twelve times when his master asks him to add six and six! Therefore, you have to believe that Hans is a genius of a horse. But before writing a check to the horse's owner, you decide to go see for yourself.

This story of a horse named Clever Hans is true, fascinating, and rich in methodological lessons.[3]

4.1.3 Double-Blind Experimentation

As you arrive, you think about a test you did the year before. It dealt with a group of police officers convinced they could converse with the dead through a Ouija board. As you recall, it is a smooth game table inscribed with letters and numbers. A participant places her hands on a little three-legged board, or planchette, that slides easily over the game's surface. She asks a question of a dead person and the board slides of its own accord, according to the player. Thus it moves from letter to letter, in the correct order, of each of the words that make up the deceased's answer.

"Corporal MacPhearson, what is your greatest regret?" asks the police officer.

"The billy clubs. Even more than the hobnailed boots, Lieutenant!"

At the time, you thought the ideomotor effect could explain what you saw, and you had a very good idea that allowed you to verify it. You thought, if the "dead interlocuter" is moving the board as the player claims, then he will still answer correctly if the player doesn't know the answer to the question or cannot see the game. For example, suppose you blindfold the player. According to her claim, it shouldn't change the outcome and the "deceased" should continue to compose the right answer with the help of the board. Again, suppose that the police officer who is asking the questions doesn't speak ancient Greek and purports to be addressing Plato; you could request that someone ask the questions of Plato in ancient Greek, a language he spoke very well, and ask that he answer in that language. (You also noted that you would have to ask all those who communicate with extraterrestrials or with all sorts of other gifted and powerful spirits to report back to us with the precise, verifiable, and stunning declarations, not just with those vague and pompous generalizations that they always seem to proffer.) To their great surprise, when they were tested in this way, the police officers failed miserably: they responded with meaningless and randomly produced series of letters.

The following month you were invited to testify at a trial that involved the parents of an autistic child. They were accusing a therapist of fraudulent medical practice, and of having scammed money from them by fostering false hopes. The therapist purported to be able to communicate with their autistic child: she held the child's hand, and the child would then type the answers to questions using a computer keyboard. The child said that she loved her parents a lot, that she hated being trapped in her body, and so on. Were it true, such a thing would have been wonderful. But her parents started having doubts. Called upon to testify, you remembered your experiment with the Ouija board and decided to test it more rigorously. In this case, when the child was asked questions to which she alone was supposed to know the answer, the extraordinary effect did not take place.

So you think that a method of this kind is what it will take to test Hans. After all, the horse might discern his master's movements and hesitations, and the pinching of his lips, and interpret them correctly to mean that he must stop tapping his hoof. You conceive of a test based on this idea. You've hit the bull's eye. Hans is a remarkable horse, but not for the reasons we thought. Indeed, you don't have to suppose that he knows algebra in order to explain his behavior.

What you've conceived is what is called double-blind experimentation. Suppose that you're testing medication; not only do the subjects not know if they're part of the experiment group or the control group (that is a case of single-blind experimentation), but the person who administers the test (who will give the subjects either the medication or the placebos) or who will evaluate the results won't know either, in order not to provide any clues, even involuntary ones, to the participants that might influence the results.

These comments barely skim the surface of an immensely vast topic. I hope that they have still been able to give you some idea of what it means to adopt a scientific method and attitude. Indeed, this effort to publicly and systematically seek to know the world, which I have tried to help you understand, is one of the notable things about science.

But by "science" we mean much more than a simple methodological orientation. Let's try to dig into some of that.

4.2 Science and Epistemology

Science allows us to answer certain questions with rigor and objectivity. But these are not the only questions that deserve to be asked, or the only important questions that humanity does ask itself, and even less the only ones that we deeply need to answer.
—MANON BONER-GAILLARD

I am quite conscious that I am about to deal with difficult technical problems here, a good number of which are always heatedly debated by experts. But it seems necessary in a book to offer a few markers to help you navigate these questions. Those who wish to extend their study will find material to orient them in the abundant epistemological literature suggested in the bibliography at the end of this work.

First, it would be good to remember that the word "science" is polysemic, having multiple meanings, and that much confusion and many polemics would be avoided if we were more careful about using it. Thus, we sometimes talk of science when in fact we're referring to its practical and technical applications. In those cases, we should speak instead of techniques, technologies, or applied sciences.

What, then, is science?

4.2.1 Science and Sciences

Science is first a mode of knowledge that aims at objectivity, which it tries to achieve by a diversity of means. Among them are those logical and empirical methods that I tried to give you a glimpse of above, as well as the systematization of their observations, the mathematization and univocity of their concepts, and the public and repeatable quality of their experiments. Science, however, is a human enterprise, and fallible. Even if certain scientific propositions seem practically and for excellent reasons to be certainties, all scientific propositions are by definition revisable. In other words, scientific truth is fallible, because unlike in religion or pseudoscience, there are no absolute certainties: there are only propositions that might ultimately have to be revised.

Science studies phenomena, that is to say objects it has constructed and displayed. Often, it requires a considerable intellectual effort to acquire the knowledge necessary simply to observe these phenomena. It also assumes a complex casting off of and, psychologically speaking, a rupture with our ordinary knowledge and ways of thinking insofar as they bear on the objects of our ordinary experience. Here are some simple examples: classical mechanics maintains that all bodies fall according to the same law; the law of inertia maintains that bodies in uniform rectilinear movement continue their uniform rectilinear movement if no other force acts on them; and so on. All of that is elementary, but already profoundly counterintuitive to our ordinary wisdom, which is conceived on the basis of our immediate experience.

Science seeks knowledge of phenomena. To do so, it

establishes constant relationships between them that are expressed as laws. These phenomena and these laws are in turn explained and understood in vast networks of inter-related concepts called theories. If you can reasonably say that the scientific method is a particularly obstinate and resolved extension of common sense, you also have to understand that the knowledge gained through it is in no way common. What is more, scientific facts, laws, and theories are often counterintuitive, sometimes even off-putting and hard for us to accept using common sense. Finally, through these laws and theories, science is sometimes able to predict or even control the phenomena it studies, by manipulating their cause and effects.

All the same, this initial characterization of science does not tell us anything about the diversity of sciences. We have to touch on it here.[4]

We can make a convenient distinction between formal sciences and applied sciences. The first category, which includes mathematics and logic, does not deal with the empirical world, and one might say that the disciplines with it are concerned only with the form of propositions. Knowing that the logical proposition P or not-P, which can be translated as "it is raining" or "it is not raining," is valid does not tell us anything about the actual weather.

Applied sciences, on the other hand, focus on the facts of the world: zoology, anthropology, biology, mycology, and chemistry are applied sciences. It is customary to distinguish among them between social sciences and natural sciences. Some disciplines, such as physical anthropology or psychobiology, are difficult to classify in one category or the other.

We also categorize sciences according to their methods. Thus, formal sciences use a particular method that involves setting out systems of axioms as hypotheses and deducing theorems from them while ensuring that the systems obtained conform to certain formal criteria (coherence, completeness, etc.). Formal sciences use a method we will refer to as hypothetical-deduction. Some sciences must be content with observing: classical astronomy, for example, was a science of observation. But they aspire to experimentation and to being able to control their experiments, which many manage to do.

We can also distinguish sciences according to their status, or if you prefer, their degree of development. This latter grows over time toward ever greater abstraction. Some sciences are simply taxonomic, which is to say that they are content with classifying observations. Mycology (the study of mushrooms) is a taxonomic science. At the next level, sciences are inductive and able to establish laws and generalizations. With the emergence of theories that allow us to subsume phenomena and laws, and to explain them, some sciences become deductive. Finally, when the concepts, laws, and theories of an applied science become so certain and developed that they can be presented by means of hypothetical-deduction, then the science has become axiomatized.

4.2.2 Three Important Foundations of Empirical and Experimental Science

Empirical and experimental science rests on at least three propositions that are reasonable, but cannot be demonstrated in any strict sense. We can formulate these three ideas as follows:[5]

1. There exists a real world, independent of us, our beliefs, representations, feelings, opinions, conceptual frameworks, and so on.
2. Some of our propositions describe (states of) this real world; in principle, they are true or false, according to whether what is affirmed does or does not conform to what is actually observed in the real world.
3. We can communicate to others what we think we have discovered about the world, and others can in turn undertake to verify it.

The first idea is that of external realism. It is the metaphysical attitude that most people and almost all philosophers and scientists adopt. This idea is not a thesis about the world or about the best way of knowing it, but about the prerequisite condition of all knowledge. It is also the simplest and best-confirmed hypothesis that allows us to explain the regularity of the outside world.

Renowned mathematics and science writer Martin Gardner put it this way:

If you wonder why all scientists, philosophers, and ordinary people, with rare exceptions, have been and are unabashed realists, let me tell you why. No scientific conjecture has been more overwhelmingly confirmed. No hypothesis offers a simpler explanation of why the Andromeda galaxy spirals in every photograph, why all the electrons are identical, why the laws of physics are the same in Tokyo as in London or on Mars, why they were there before life evolved and will be there if all life perishes, why all persons can close their eyes and feel eight corners, six faces, and twelve edges on a cube, and why your bedroom looks the same when you wake up in the morning.[6]

The second thesis is that supported by the correspondence theory of truth, which affirms that our propositions that relate to the world are true or false according to whether or not they correspond to what is actually observed in the world. This idea is also shared by common sense, and the vast majority of philosophers and scientists. For Aristotle, for example, telling the truth is "saying of what is that it is and of what is not that it is not."[7] For the scholastics, the truth is *"adaequatio rerum et intellectus,"* that is, the conformity or suitability of our thoughts to things. You have to make a distinction, however, between the meaning of the concept of truth, on the one hand, and the criteria and procedures for determining the truth on the other. Let me explain what that means.

Defending a correspondence theory of truth is to defend the idea that the truth is a predicate that is given meaning by the correspondence between a proposition and a fact or a state of affairs. Tarski, the logician, came up with the canonical technical formulation of these ideas; for example, the proposition, "The snow is white," is true if the snow is white—the truth is defined here by the removal of the quote marks. But it is not enough to know what it means to be true to determine the criteria and procedures that will allow us to decide whether there is in fact correspondence, and so truth. In some cases, it is very simple; in others, harder; and in still others, impossible. To illustrate all this, I will take up an example of Martin Gardner's, whose talent for explaining difficult ideas simply I must once again commend.

Let's say that I show you a deck of fifty-two cards. I spread the cards face down on the table and I draw one card at random. Without looking at it, I put it face down on the corner of the table. Then, I write a description of the card on a piece of paper: "This card is the queen of hearts." What does "being true" mean in the case of this proposition? Be careful. I am not asking *how* we will know it is true. If you do this experiment with scientists, philosophers, and ordinary people, you will notice that everyone agrees that that proposition is true if and only if the card is the queen of hearts. How will we decide if that is the case? To this question, each person will answer that simply by turning over the card, we will find out if it is indeed the queen of hearts.

This example makes clear the distinction between the meaning of the truth as correspondence, and the criteria and procedures that allow us to decide the truth. It is a crucial one. Indeed, it can be difficult to determine the criteria and procedures and to formulate a judgment. The meaning of the concept of truth, however, remains the same.

Let's suppose now that I take the card I've set aside—which no one has seen—and that I put it back into the deck of cards, and that I shuffle it. On my piece of paper, I change the word "is" for "was" so it reads, "This card was the queen of hearts." The meaning of the proposition, in terms of the concept of truth, has not changed. But note how it is now difficult to determine if the proposition is true. We could perhaps find a large number of wood particles on the card, left when the card was rubbed on the table; we can imagine that this card is the only one to have the thumbprint and index fingerprint of the person who drew it on either side. If we find these distinctive signs on the queen of hearts, and only on it, we will be tempted to say that the proposition, "This card was the queen of hearts," is true. But to what degree? What would allow you to reach a verdict? And with what sort of certainty? These questions are the lot of scientific researchers; for epistemologists, clarifying them is a difficult knot of problems that remain unresolved.

To finish, imagine that I replace the card in the deck, and that I throw the deck into the fire where it is entirely burned. In that case, the meaning of the truth of the proposition, "This card was the queen of hearts," remains unchanged, but there remains no way of knowing, I think, whether or not it is true.

The third postulate simply lays out the possibility of using language to communicate propositions that describe the world and the possibility of verifying alleged results, generally by repeating the experiments that produced them.

Note that these scientific postulates are also the same ones that we adopt spontaneously and necessarily as soon as we speak or act. If I am planning a trip to Mexico, and I consult a book to find out about the country's climate, I assume that the book's authors have adopted external realism, the correspondence theory of truth, and the idea of communication and public verification. Thus, I suppose that there exists, apart from me, apart from others, and apart from our representations, a physical place where I want to go, endowed with properties that are also independent of me and of others, and that the book I am consulting tells the truth about the weather in that place if it describes the actual weather there. In fact, I could go verify it myself.

Let's deal with several final conceptual distinctions that will be useful to us. They have to do first with science, understood this time as a practice and as a social and political reality; and then with the flipside of science, or pseudoscience.

4.2.3 Science as Practice

It is a truism to say that science is a social practice, constructed by humans in a given social, political, and economic context. But it's an important fact, and one that can weigh very heavily on the decision to invest in a given research sector, on the direction of that research, and even on its results. The critical thinker must be very conscious of it and ask each time if these factors could have had an effect.

Note that this is neither a matter of denying the rationality of science or of searching with such assiduousness as to invent economic interests that *a priori* falsify all research. We simply have to remain lucid and critical before the possibility that interests, generally economic ones, might have influenced the research that was conducted or the results that were announced.

We all know, with regard to this matter, the scandalous

story about the funding of reports that minimized or denied the dangers of cigarettes, research that was funded by the tobacco companies. So I will take up a different example, one which has caused a lot of discussion and concern over the last few years: pharmaceutical companies. Their research has been at the heart of many controversies. It is a perfect demonstration of that to which critical thinkers must attend with great care.

Four years ago, the *New England Journal of Medicine* propelled this debate—until then limited to circles of the well-informed—into the public arena when it published several editorials that drew attention to the troubling phenomenon of the links between the pharmaceutical industry and university research, the resulting conflicts of interest, and their impact on the research itself. The prestigious journal even claimed to have trouble finding peers without any links to industry to review and evaluate the articles submitted for publication. No one doubts the reality or the significance of the phenomenon anymore. The process is very simple; pharmaceutical companies pay for university students, who are in significant need of funding in order to carry out research. Armed with this dependency, the pharmaceutical companies are in a position to try (and sometimes succeed) to dictate their research topics, and even influence the results and their dissemination. You can guess how dramatic the consequences can be, as illustrated by the well-known case of Doctor Olivieri—a case that attracted attention from the international university community.

Nancy Olivieri, a hematologist working in a Toronto hospital and a researcher-professor at the University of Toronto, was conducting research on a new medication

called Deferiprone. She discovered that it had dangerous side effects and wanted to publish and make these
important results known. The problem? Her work was
financed by Apotex, the company that produced the medication. Apotex then undertook a major legal campaign
and launched a smear campaign in order to ban the publication of the article and the dissemination of these results to the affected patients. Unfortunately, neither the
hospital nor the university defended Nancy Olivieri; both
were more concerned with the financial contributions of
the pharmaceutical companies than with the truth or the
independence of the researchers. After two years of inquiry, a commission presented its report. It clearly said that
the whole episode took place "because public institutions
must now depend on funding from private enterprise."

The Olivieri affair is likely only the tip of the iceberg. At
the same university, an eminent psychiatrist named David
Healy had his contract terminated because of statements
he made about anti-depressants in general and Prozac in
particular. In the US, it has gone even further: a drug company called Immune Response Corporation, the maker of
Remune, an anti-AIDS therapy, went so far in 2001 as to
sue the scientists whose findings suggested the drug was
of little benefit to patients. They sought $10 million for
damages.[8]

When Scientists Cheat

The number of cases of scientific fraud has risen over the past twenty years, and they flourish most in biological and medical sciences, say Yves Gingras, a sociologist of science at the University of Quebec in Montreal (UQAM) and Serge Larivée, a teacher at the University of Montreal's School of Psychoeducation.

Medical sciences win top prize, with 52% of the cases of fraud involving data fabrication, which has been universally denounced around the world since the earliest days of science, specifies Serge Larivée. Hard sciences account for only 26% of these deceptions, "which involve the invention of every part of the results of experiments that were never carried out," and human and social sciences account for 22%.

Health sciences again rank highest in terms of data manipulation, a lesser but no more pardonable mistake, with 81% of known fraud. On the other hand, only 19% of data falsification was observed in hard sciences and 10% in human sciences. "An indicator of the amplification of the phenomenon of fraud in science is the rise of the number of retractions in scientific journals," emphasizes Yves Gingras. "The augmentation of errata because of the pressure to publish is another clue that points, if not to fraud, at least to questionable data. Biologists claim that half of scientific articles could contain questionable data."

Why are life sciences the most affected? Competition is most intense in that field, and the number of researchers who devote their lives to it is gigantic. Therefore, the battle for funding, which has not really expanded over the years, is ferocious. "The resources allotted to university research were enormous until the oil crisis in 1973," explains Yves Gingras. "Today, we have less money and many more researchers."

P. Gravel, "De Ptolémée à Newton et Poisson: Des scientifiques moins rigoureux que leur discipline," *Le Devoir*, November 16, 2002, sec. B.

4.2.4 Science, Proto-science, and Pseudoscience

Tell me what pseudoscience you buy,
and I will tell you what your philosophy
of science is worth.
—MARIO BUNGE,
Argentinian philosopher and physicist

Here is the last set of conceptual distinctions I want to establish.

It is important for the critical thinker to understand what science is. One of its crucial ramifications is that it allows for a distinction between science and pseudoscience to be made. Indeed, knowing what real money is, we will be better positioned to recognize fake money. Finding a dividing line, however, has proven to be more difficult than many might have thought, as the works of Karl Popper, one of the most eminent and influential epistemologists of the twentieth century, show.

Popper lived in Vienna and was passionate about all the revolutionary ideas that were stirring the city—and all of Europe—at the time. First, there was Marxism, which advanced a dialectical materialist interpretation of history based on the development of productive forces and class struggle. Marxists derived laws by which they analyzed the past and present conditions of humanity, and which predicted what they claimed must come to pass, such as the advent of communism. Then there was psychoanalysis, which advanced the concept of the unconscious, as well as a model of the human psyche influenced by drives; repressions; and id, ego, and superego, and which uses these categories to explain dreams, Freudian slips, and many behaviors—even certain illnesses which psychoanalysts claimed to be able to treat. Finally, there was physics, and in particular the theory of general relativity that Einstein had just put forward. In this case too—and this is what makes the three systems similar at first glance—abstract and general categories were appealed to within a theoretical framework and were used to explain and predict certain phenomena.

Popper asserted that what distinguished these three theories, and what makes the latter scientific while the first two are not, is the risk that the latter takes to be *incompatible* with some of the possible results of observation. In other words, Popper proposed that falsifiability is the distinctive criterion of science—that is, its capacity to make predictions that can be tested experimentally and that can be contradicted. In sum, a scientific theory is falsifiable because it is possible to discover that it is false. As for the Marxists and the Freudians, they merely discover confirmations of their ideas in every experience; nothing ever contradicts their theories. That is precisely the mark of pseudoscience, believed Popper. The idea is interesting, but alas, it has its limits.

To understand what I mean, consider the following historical example. The orbit of Uranus that astronomers observed was systematically different from what was predicted by calculations made on the basis of Newtonian mechanics, which at the time was the exemplary model of a scientific theory. So we were faced with a theory falsified by experience. But in spite of this, the physicians and astronomers did not renounce Newtonian mechanics. On the contrary, they searched for something that would save the theory. One possibility was that there was another planet, still unknown to them, which the calculations did not take into account. So Adams and Leverrier advanced the hypothesis that the gravitational force of this still-undiscovered planet explained the difference between what was observed of Uranus's orbit and the theory's predictions. This difference would be eliminated if the calculations were to take into account the attraction of this new planet. The unknown planet was finally discovered: Neptune.

Following Mario Bunge's example, I want to suggest that the distinction between science and pseudoscience has to be drawn on a continuum that runs the gamut from really and irremediably phony pseudosciences to the most solid, genuine, and credible sciences, and including proto-sciences (sciences in the process of becoming scientific) and less certain sciences. The criteria that would allow us to make these distinctions are necessarily many. Below are the characteristics of pseudoscience, according to Bunge:[9]

—A field of pseudoscientific research is made up of a pseudo-community of researchers, which is a group of believers rather than an association of critical and creative researchers.

—The society in which it exists supports it for commercial reasons, or tolerates it while simultaneously marginalizing it.

—Its research domain includes unreal or at least not demonstrably real entities, properties, or events.

—Its general outlook includes an ontology that accepts immaterial entities or processes (like disincarnate spirits); an epistemology that accepts paranormal cognitive possibilities, appeals to authority, and arbitrary data production; and an ethos that obstructs the free search for truth in order to protect dogma.

—Its formal background is very weak, fraudulent (making use of pseudo-quantities), or purely ornamental.

—Its disciplinary background is miniscule or non-existent. Pseudoscientists learn little or nothing from science and don't contribute anything to science, either.

—The problems it deals with are essentially imaginary or practical: it does not involve basic research problems of any significance.

—Its alleged knowledge find contains a good number of false or unverifiable conjectures, which are opposed to well-confirmed scientific hypotheses, but it does not propose any well-confirmed universal hypotheses.

—The discovery of laws and their use to explain or predict facts is not among its goals.

—Its methods include procedures that cannot be verified or that cannot be defended by established scientific theories. Criticism and empirical tests are especially unwelcome. There is no continuous field of research, except insofar is one pseudoscience flows into another.

—Finally, a pseudoscience is generally stagnant and changes only through internal quarrels or because of external pressures, rather than in response to research results. In other words, it is isolated and closed in on itself.

It might be an amusing and highly instructive exercise to take a few notorious pseudosciences and examine them in light of these criteria. (Take for example: iridology, reflexology, astrology, Dianetics, graphology, and so on.) The critical examination of pseudoscientific hypotheses and theories will also benefit from the use of the SEARCH model presented later in this chapter.

The critical thinker will scale her belief in different allegedly scientific claims to the degree of development of the science under consideration, and to the seriousness of the arguments, facts, and most notably the research to which it appeals. Knowing full well that any scientific assertion can, by definition, be called into question, she will put forward skeptical arguments worthy of the contested theses' credibility. When almost all the experts in a truly scientific field of research agree among themselves, she will consider it unreasonable to think that the truth is to be found elsewhere; when the same experts disagree, she will find it reasonable to suspend her judgment.

To evaluate hypotheses, assertions, or theories, the critical thinker will remind herself that theses cannot purport to be scientific unless they are clear, precise, and inter-subjectively testable, and if the tests carried out demonstrate that they are true, or, at the very least, reasonably allow them to be held as partially true.

Vaughn and Schick proposed five criteria that allow such an evaluation to be systematized:[10]

> **Testability:** In other words, is the hypothesis, assertion, or theory testable? At least in principle, is there a way to determine if it is true of false? If not, it is probably trivial and valueless.
>
> **Fruitfulness:** All things being equal, the best hypothesis, assertion, or theory allows us to make observable, precise, and surprising or novel predictions.
>
> **Scope:** Briefly, all things being equal, the more phenomena a hypothesis, assertion or theory explains, and the broader the range of phenomena to which it applies, the better it is.
>
> **Simplicity:** As a general rule, a hypothesis, assertion, or theory that assumes the fewest uncertainties and postulates the fewest entities is to be preferred.
>
> **Conservatism:** A hypothesis, assertion, or theory that is coherent with our most well established beliefs is generally preferable to one that is not.

A Real Dummy Trap

"LIFE TECHNOLOGY® introduces its brand new concept talisman:

The Psionic Kabbalah Manifesting Capsule.™

The Psionic Kabbalah Manifesting Capsule™ contains four unique elements designed to make it the most potent talisman or manifesting enhancement device we have designed to date. These unique elements are listed as follows:

Element 1. The Psionic Kabbalah Manifesting Capsule™ contains in printed form a mini scroll of the most sacred magickal formula of Kabbalah, the written formula of the 72 Names of God.

Element 2. The Psionic Kabbalah Manifesting Capsule™ contains pure quartz crystal microspheres. Quartz is a material of powerful healing, spiritual enhancement, and manifesting properties, which acts to enhance the transmission and delivery of our intent to the creative centre of the universe.

Element 3. To bring immediate protection to its owner, The Psionic Kabbalah Manifesting Capsule™ contains a fragment of red string from Rachel's Tomb in Jerusalem.

Element 4. The Psionic Kabbalah Manifesting Capsule™ also incorporates a special Ethero-Magnetic™ caduceus orgone generating coil, which utilises the magickal and sacred 'lost cubit' measurement, a meaurement [sic] so profound that its precise value can not be found in ancient or modern literature. Only select few individuals and scientists are aware of its actual value."

Wow. All that for only $89.95, plus postage and packing!

http://www.lifetechnology.org/kabbalahcapsule.htm/.

4.3 A Few Questions for the Critical Reading of Research Results

When there are research results that you want to examine more carefully, you should try to find the answers to most, if not all, of these questions.

GENERAL AND PREREQUISITE QUESTIONS

Who did this research? Were they serious researchers, trained to carry out this sort of research? Who funded it? Could the funding of the research have influenced the results or the way the results were presented? How developed are the research areas and science in question? What established and generally agreed-upon bodies of knowledge are used in this domain? Where has this research been published? Is it a trustworthy publication? Are its articles peer-reviewed? What subject or problem does it deal with? What conclusion does it defend?

THE OBJECT OF THE RESEARCH QUESTION

How is the research question formulated? Is it clear? Is it at least possible to answer it? Is the vocabulary used in the formulation biased? What definitions are attributed to the concepts used? Are they common? Plausible? Should this be the case, what values seem to be assumed, or perhaps just agreed to, at least implicitly, in the formulation of the problem or the subject? Can that have an impact on the research? Is important information omitted? Does the literature review seem complete? Do the researchers explain how their problem is similar to or distinct from that which is described in the literature review?

THE METHODOLOGY

Are the samples big enough? Representative? How were they put together? If an experiment with a control group was undertaken, what measures were taken to guard against bias? If an experiment with a control group was necessary but was not conducted, how is that accounted for? If an experiment with a control group was conducted, was a double-blind experiment conducted? Was it done properly?

THE DATA ANALYSIS

What measuring instruments were used? What definitions of the things being measured were given? Are specifications related to the reliability and the validity of these instruments made?

THE CONCLUSIONS

Is an honest summary presented? Does the research answer the question asked? Could the interpretation of the data have been different? In that case, are the other interpretations mentioned and is it explained why they were discarded? Also use the five criteria of evaluation: testability, fruitfulness, scope, simplicity, and conservatism.

4.4 The SEARCH Model

By way of concluding this section on science, I want to suggest a model that will help you to think in a more rigorous and coherent way about those "theories," claims, or hypotheses that we could call bizarre or extraordinary and which are often presented to us for approval. This model was conceived and developed by Theodore Schick, Jr., and Lewis Vaughn in order to help us to think about weird things. I find it very relevant and useful. I hope that you will too.

The model is called SEARCH. I will introduce it and then apply it to homeopathy. My presentation of the model, like the example that follows, paraphrases its authors.[II]

The SEARCH model involves four steps:

1. State the claim.
2. Examine the Evidence for the claim.
3. Consider Alternative hypotheses.
4. Rate, according to the Criteria of adequacy, each Hypothesis.

The first step is to state the claim as clearly as possible. The idea is quite simple: in order to critically evaluate a proposition, we need to understand it. Yet often the propositions we are asked to accept are neither clear nor precise. So the first step is to formulate the proposition clearly. In short, what exactly and precisely is being claimed?

The second step is to examine the arguments and evidence advanced in support of the claim. Are they valid? Is the evidence trustworthy and credible? To judge, it is necessary to be well-informed.

The third step is to weigh alternative hypotheses. Ask yourself if hypotheses other than the one proposed could also support the claim. It is always wise not to jump to conclusions too quickly, to consider other possible explanations, and to tell yourself that there might well be one even if you can't find it right away.

The fourth step is to rate each hypothesis according to the criteria of adequacy. You already know them: testability, fruitfulness, scope, simplicity, and conservatism.

It goes without saying that all these steps must be applied neither mechanically nor dogmatically, but with reason and openness. Let's apply the SEARCH model now; following the authors' lead, let's dwell a little on homeopathy.

Established by S. Hahnemann (1755–1843), today homeopathy[12] is a widespread medical practice. Those who use it will tell you it works. But since you are a critical thinker, it will take more than anecdotes to convince you.

Homeopathic products are made by taking an active ingredient (a plant for example) and diluting it in ten parts of water. Then, one unit of the resultant potion is diluted in ten more parts of water. Now the ratio is 1/100. The process continues this way; each time the mixture is shaken. A homeopathic remedy generally contains a dose referred to as 30X, which means this process was repeated thirty times. In total, then, the ratio is one part of active substance to 1,000,000,000,000,000,000,000,000,000,000 parts water. Other remedies have a preparation called 30C; in that case, the dilution is carried out each time with one hundred parts of water. In that procedure, you end up with one part of the active substance to one-followed-by-ninety-zeros parts of water. At that point, your potion does not have one single molecule of the active substance in it.

To explain how "it works," homeopaths appeal to effects

that are unknown and even considered impossible in biology and chemistry—"water memory," for example—or to mysterious processes and entities like vital force, harmony, and so on. A strange way of taking care of yourself? Definitely. If you search a little bit, you will discover that homeopathy is based on two principles.

The first is that like heals like. Homeopaths say: *similia similibus curantur.* The second is the belief that the smaller the dose, the more effective the medication. All in all, the homeopath thinks that infinitesimally small doses of substances that cause the symptoms of an illness in a healthy person are able to heal a person who is suffering from the illness.

What to think of all this? Now is the time for you to apply the SEARCH model. Here are a few hints to guide you.

First you have to state clearly the claims made by practitioners of homeotherapy. Then you have to examine the evidence they put forward to support their beliefs. You will find a lot of anecdotes, but also studies appealed to by those who defend homeopathy—though the studies have almost all been systematically refuted on methodological grounds by their opponents and more neutral observers alike.

Can you imagine alternative hypotheses that would explain the benefits claimed by people who use homeopathy? You can certainly formulate some. You should know that most illnesses we contract in the course of our lifetimes— including those that homeopathy purports to heal—disappear on their own in time. You should also know that any evaluation of a medication must take into consideration the possibility that the placebo effect is operative. Finally, you must rate each hypothesis against the criteria of adequacy, and draw your conclusion.

CHAPTER 5

THE MEDIA

A popular government without popular information, or the means of acquiring it, is but a Prologue to a Farce or a Tragedy; or, perhaps, both. Knowledge will forever govern ignorance; and a people who mean to be their own Governors must arm themselves with the power which knowledge gives.

—JAMES MADISON

The critical habit of thought, if usual in society, will pervade all its mores because it is a way of taking up the problems of life. Men educated in it cannot be stampeded by stump orators. . . . They are slow to believe. They can hold things as possible or probable in all degrees, without certainty and without pain. They can wait for evidence and weigh evidence, uninfluenced by the emphasis or confidence with which assertions are made on one side or the other. They can resist appeals to their dearest prejudices and all kinds of cajolery. Education in the critical faculty is the only education of which it can be truly said that it makes good citizens.

—WILLIAM GRAHAM SUMNER

You can't say the truth on television: too many people are watching.

—COLUCHE

Of course the people don't want war. But after all, it's the leaders of the country who determine the policy, and it's always a simple matter to drag the people along whether it's a democracy, a fascist dictatorship, or a parliament, or a communist dictatorship. Voice or no voice, the people can always be brought to the bidding of the leaders. That is easy. All you have to do is tell them they are being attacked, and denounce the pacifists for lack of patriotism and exposing the country to greater danger. It works the same way in any country.

—HERMANN GOERING

Introduction

Other than school, the world of the media is one of the best places for citizens to learn to think critically. A good number of people think that the media describe and reflect the important things—if not everything—that happen in the world. They believe that what the media transmit to us is the product of independent research undertaken by journalists, such that media-makers themselves independently establish the content that they broadcast; and that the description of the world the media offer is essentially neutral and complete, and that facts and opinions are always distinguished from each other in a recognizable way.

But grievances against the Western mass media are piling up. Among other things, they are reproached for chasing ratings and allowing themselves to be dragged further and further down the slippery slope of demagoguery and sensationalism. Over the past few years, worry about growing media concentration has added to these others. But there is another reason, maybe even more basic, to worry about the media's performance and contribution to democratic life. It has to do with the very specific notion of democracy that certain highly influential contemporary institutions tend to rely on. They maintain that it is better to marginalize the public than to inform it, so as to make spectators rather than political actors of people. All this makes it imperative to exercise critical thinking when dealing with the media, as the following example demonstrates.

On August 2, 1990, Iraq invaded Kuwait. Immediately, and with uncommon speed and vigor, the brutal aggression was condemned by the United Nations, which imposed sanctions on Iraq on August 6.[1] By the fall of 1990, lively debates about the possibility of military intervention were raging. Though Saddam Hussein had been a longtime dear friend, a precious ally and trade partner, the United States was advocating intervention.

At this exact moment, an unforgettable event unfolded, one that you will probably remember, even if you only follow the news at a glance. Let's go over the facts. A young girl called Nayirah made a presentation to the Human Rights Caucus of the House of Representatives in Washington. Members of Congress and the American public alike were totally upset by the testimony of this fifteen-year-old Kuwaiti who told stories of unspeakable horror through her tears. She described how Iraqi soldiers stormed a hospital in Kuwait where she was working as a volunteer, how they stole incubators and killed or left 312 babies for dead, suffering on the maternity ward floor.

The media broadcast the news around the world. After August 2, Saddam Hussein, yesterday's dear friend, became the "Butcher of Baghdad"; in the wake of Nayirah's testimony, he was a tyrant "worse than Hitler." Those who favored a war against Iraq made good use of this precious testimony, particularly against those who wanted to stick to sanctions and find a negotiated political solution to the conflict—which Iraq had, for that matter, proposed to the United Nations in mid-August.

During the weeks that followed Nayirah's testimony, President George H. W. Bush referred to the events described by the young girl at least five times, recalling each time that such "great atrocities" were like "Hitler revisited."[2] During the debates over military intervention that took place shortly thereafter, no less than seven US senators also referred to Nayirah's testimony.

The motion in favor of entering a war finally passed by five votes. The bombing campaigns that could not reasonably be called a war began with the massive approval of the American public. As for international opinion, which had already undergone a profound shift since the fall of the Berlin Wall, it had changed considerably and President Bush the First was quite conscious of the fact. On February 2, 1991, appearing on *NBC Nightly News*, he could state confidently, "The US has a new credibility. What we say goes."

At that point, however, quiet rumors and doubts about Nayirah's testimony and her terrible story started to emerge. Today, we can reconstruct what happened with as much certainty as can reasonably be had about such subjects.[3] Nayirah was in fact Nayirah al Sabah, the daughter of Kuwait's ambassador to Washington. She never had anything to do with that hospital, and nothing she described took place there. Her testimony was bogus; it had been carefully prepared and staged down to the last detail by hacks from Washington's Hill and Knowlton company. They had carefully trained the young girl—and a few other people who were to corroborate her story—for the sound and simple reason that the firm had just signed a lucrative ten-million-dollar contract with the Kuwaitis to argue for the US's entry into war with Iraq. Hill and Knowlton were only doing their job. After all, they are a big public relations firm.

Note that, contrary to accusations often leveled at media critics, the tale I just told has nothing to with conspiracy theory. Once exposed to the light of day, there is nothing secret going on here, although the PR firm's maneuvering does quite largely fit the standard definition of conspiracy. Everything I discussed is recorded in the public domain and can be discovered, updated, and verified by anyone and everyone. Doing that, however, requires time and perseverance: you have to know how to get news and information from sources other than the big media chains; you have to learn to remain critical of all information; finally, you have to know the institutions involved and know the structural dynamics of the processes in which they are actors. You can see that this is far from any conspiracy. Everything I will say about the media in the following pages can essentially be explained in terms of the free functioning of the institutions involved, and in terms of their roles, their motives, and those of their actors. Upholding a theory of media conspiracy would, in fact, be as idiotic and indefensible as arguing that all journalists are sell-outs or that the owners of the news outlets dictate what each one of them writes.

It is true that structural and institutional conditions for the broadcast of information and the functioning of the media do exist, and that they exert what is sometimes immense influence on what is said and how it is said. That is why it is useful to review those conditions and their impact, all the while recognizing that we will be able to find stunning information in the corporate media about topics that are frequently covered up. This information can be true and valuable; that said, it is also true that you will have to look carefully and know what you're looking for in order to find it. Thus, for example, to my knowledge, the real story of Nayirah was reported once in Quebec.[4] Jooneed Khan, the journalist who did the story, wrote, "Young 'Nayirah' whose testimony shook a Congressional committee on the eve of the vote, was none other than the daughter of the Ambassador of Kuwait in Washington, used for the purposes of propaganda by the public relations firm Hill and Knowlton, whose services had been bought by the Kuwaiti lobby." In the US, author John R. MacArthur was among the first to expose the dupe, writing an op-ed in the *New York Times* where he suggested, "Congress and the news media deserve censure for their lack of skepticism."[5]

If I chose to begin this chapter with this story, it is because it rather conveniently connects all the themes I will deal with in the following pages. Let me present an overview of those themes in the order in which I will cover them.

It's a truism that information is a major political issue in any society that claims to be democratic. Yet few people know what these public relations firms are, where they come from, and what role they play. We'll note that they are born of conceptions of democratic life and the role of information that are deeply opposed to our common usage of those terms. From that point on, we will be in a position to measure the gap between true democracy and what we could call theoretical democracy. The first section of this chapter will be devoted to such considerations.

The modern media share this same historical background. Today the media are made up of vast corporations that we must examine carefully if we wish to know and understand how they function. When we devote ourselves to meticulously carrying out this work, we see that a reasonable person has to conclude that a propaganda model of the media sheds some crucial light on the actual functioning of these institutions and their role in shaping opinions within real, experienced democracies—as opposed to systems that simply claim to be democracies. Chomsky and Herman's propaganda model of the media systematizes all these ideas. We will take a more detailed look at it in the second section of this chapter.

Knowing all this, a critical observer of the media will pay careful attention to the cover-ups and biases that won't fail to appear in the corporate media's representation of reality. Having understood their nature and their way of functioning, you will be able to deploy a variety of means to develop and maintain, in a systematic and rigorous way, a critical attitude toward these institutions particularly, and toward all sources of information more generally. At the end of this chapter, I suggest some tools that might help critical thinkers in this task. It is a difficult one, but indispensable if we wish to contribute to bridging the gap between real and theoretical democracy.

5.1 Another Kind of Democracy

When they hear about it for the first time, most people have trouble conceiving of and accepting that numerous institutions and conceptions of mass communications within democracies were founded and developed on a propagandic manure heap.

In the United States, the foundational experience took place during the First World War, when the Commission on Public Information, or Creel Commission, named after the man who presided over it, was created to lead the predominantly pacifist US public to war. The Commission was totally successful. And from it emerged many of the instruments and techniques of propaganda used in contemporary democracies: the mass dissemination of press releases, emotional appeals in targeted advertising campaigns, the reliance on cinema, the targeted recruitment of local opinion-makers, the setting-up of sham groups (for example, grassroots citizens' groups), and so forth.[6]

Walter Lippmann, one of the most influential members of the Creel Commission, and often described as the most respected journalist in the world after 1930, described the Commission's work as "a revolution in the art of democracy" in which an "intelligent minority" in charge of the political sphere is responsible for "manufacturing the consent" of the people, when a minority of "responsible men" didn't automatically have it.

This "shaping of healthy public opinion" would protect them from "the trampling and rage of the bewildered herd" (in other words, the people), those "ignorant and meddlesome outsiders" whose role it is to be spectators and not "participants." The overarching idea of the birth of the public relations industry was explicit: public opinion had to be "scientifically" manufactured and controlled from on high in order to ensure the control of a dangerous populace.[7]

Edward Bernays,[8] Sigmund Freud's nephew, also played a primary role in the development of the public relations industry and the political *ethos* that characterizes it.[9] There's no doubt that he learned the lessons taught by the Creel Commission well. In many important works (*Crystallizing Public Opinion, The Engineering of Consent, Propaganda,* and a dozen or so others), Bernays explained that, given what had been conceived and developed in this laboratory of the new democracy, it had become possible to "regiment the public mind every bit as much as an army regiments the bodies of its soldiers."[10]

The highlights of Bernays's public relations career are legendary. On Easter Sunday, 1929, in New York, he organized a memorable women's march on Fifth Avenue, putting feminism at the service of women's right to smoke cigarettes. At the same time, working for Lucky Strike and American Tobacco, he helped cigarette companies to conceal the evidence already accumulating that proved that tobacco is a deadly substance.

In the 1950s, he began working for United Fruit, persuading the public at large of the dangers of communism in Latin America. He made people believe that the country confiscated the company's land by "injecting" bogus news into the US media and setting up sham grassroots groups that hid their true intentions behind noble or benign fronts. He was successful beyond what anyone could have hoped; in June 1954, a military coup d'état, "helped" by the CIA, overthrew Guatemala's democratically elected government.[11]

It is important to notice how very particular conceptions of democracy and information are operative in these practices. The great majority of people in this democracy are spectators, not participants. The information to which they have the right is that which is prepared for them by the true actors of the democratic sphere. This information is meant to distract them; it is simplified in order to be accessible to the feeble understanding of the world they are believed to have—a feebleness that it is advantageous to the true actors to preserve. From this point of view, a healthy democracy is understood to be something extremely different from that which most people ordinarily and maybe naively have in mind.

In one of the first editions of the *Encyclopedia of Social Sciences*, which appeared in the 1930s, Harold Laswell, one of the most eminent media specialists, explained that above everything else, it was important not to succumb to "democratic dogmatism," that is, the idea that ordinary people might have the capacity to determine their own needs and interests themselves, and that they might thus be capable of choosing what suits them on their own. This notion is entirely wrong, Laswell assured his readers. The truth is rather that they need an elite to decide for them. This can certainly seem problematic, at least if you have a naive conception of democracy. But Laswell proposed a convenient solution: for want of force to control the populace, opinion can be used to control it perfectly well.

Today, public relations firms are powerful political and economic actors. They serve business, governments, and anyone else who has the means to pay them. Alex Cary wrote, in a pithy turn of phrase as accurate as it is biting, "The twentieth century has been characterized by three developments of great political importance: the growth of democracy, the growth of corporate power, and the growth of corporate propaganda as a means of protecting corporate power against democracy."[12] I couldn't say it any better.

Without going on about the history of public relations firms and their role,[13] I think we can conclude the following: confronted with information, in general and the media in particular, anyone wishing to exercise intellectual self-defense should demonstrate great vigilance.

5.2 The Propaganda Model of Media

The right to information assumes that information
worthy of the name is available and its corollary is the
critical lucidity of every citizen.
—MANON BONER-GAILLARD

The phenomenon of media concentration is undeniable at this point, and present to varying degrees in all liberal democracies in which information has been handed over to nearly unfettered market mechanisms. It has gradually come to be acknowledged by all observers. All the same, we are still far from being able to gauge its political repercussions, to which I would now like to draw your attention.

By media concentration, I will from now on refer to two distinct movements that are nonetheless close to each other. The first is the concentration of media (newspapers, radio, television, magazines, publishing houses) among an increasingly limited number of owners. The second is the convergence of the same media that, under one company umbrella, circulate content among themselves that they can reuse and to which they can add.

The following table was published in *Mother Jones* in March 2007. It shows that in the US, as of the time of publication, merely eight corporations control the vast portion of what is printed in newspapers, books, and magazines, and broadcast on TV or on the Internet. The exact configuration of this monopoly shifts as conglomerates acquire new assets or are subsumed by others, but its effect on journalism remains corrosive.

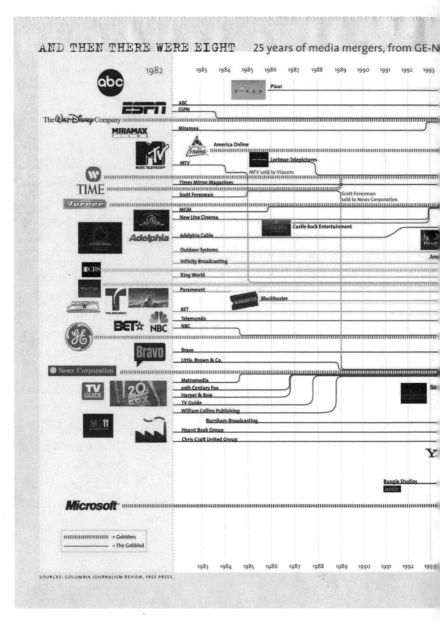

AND THEN THERE WERE EIGHT   25 years of media mergers, from GE-N

SOURCES: COLUMBIA JOURNALISM REVIEW, FREE PRESS

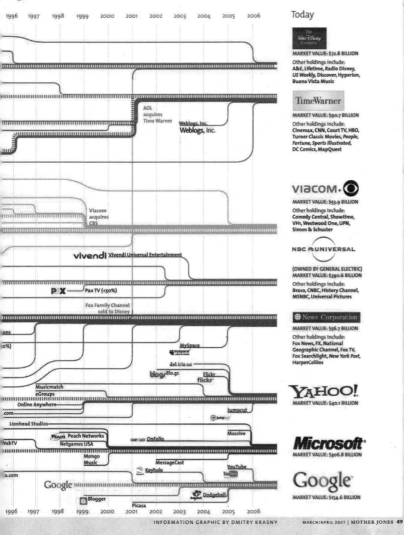

Often, critical observers start by decrying the demagogic and sensationalist aspects of corporate media content. Such accusations seem to me to be largely well-founded; it is no doubt useless to dwell at length here on the effects of the massive weapons of diversion that are reality TV, trash TV, and all those new formulas television has inflicted upon us over the last few years.

Having agreed on that, we have still not dealt with what is most significant. What is most serious is not that the mainstream corporate media are increasingly—and pre-dictably—becoming actors in the great staging of the society of the spectacle, thereby taking up the role of en-tertainers that we know all too well. What is most serious is this: although they should be fundamental political tools in the development of a public space for discussion and debate, they have renounced this task in order to function as propaganda and a means of covering up reality. In other words, even if there is hardly cause to celebrate the fact that television is pouring more and more resources into reality TV shows and other spectacularly stupid productions, the real tragedy actually plays out each night on the newscast, as it retreats from and forgets the media's political and civic mission, which is to inform the public.

To my knowledge, Edward Herman and Noam Chomsky have carried out the most conclusive and significant work on these themes. Let me summarize their main points, which systemize the intuitive hypothesis I just mentioned. According to these authors, there is a sense in which the media are over-determined by a number of structural and institutional elements that condition—certainly not entirely, but at least very broadly—the sort of representation of reality that they offer, as well as the values, norms, and perceptions that they promote. More concretely, these researchers have suggested a model in which the media to a large extent fulfill a propaganda function in our societies. The media, write the authors, "serve to mobilize support for the special interests that dominate the state and private support for the special interests that dominate the state and private activity; and . . . their choices, emphases, and omissions can often be understood best, and sometimes with striking clarity and insight, by analyzing them in such terms."[14]

The Top 25 Censored Stories of 2007

Each year, Project Censored offers a carefully compiled and fact-checked list of subjects and stories that were blacked out by the mainstream media. Generally, they were mentioned only a few times in a few obscure places, and that was it; or the alternative press covered them, or they were covered in reports published by institutions or on news wires. Reading these annual lists makes some people feel deeply shocked and uneasy. Indeed, they are subjects that seem (and are) very important but about which very little information is available, unless you go get it from sources other than the mainstream media. Here are the top Censored stories from 2007:

#1 Future of Internet Debate Ignored by Media

#2 Halliburton Charged with Selling Nuclear Technologies to Iran

#3 Oceans of the World in Extreme Danger

#4 Hunger and Homelessness Increasing in the US

#5 High-Tech Genocide in Congo

#6 Federal Whistleblower Protection in Jeopardy

#7 US Operatives Torture Detainees to Death in Afghanistan and Iraq

#8 Pentagon Exempt from Freedom of Information Act

#9 The World Bank Funds Israel-Palestine Wall

#10 Expanded Air War in Iraq Kills More Civilians

#11 Dangers of Genetically Modified Food Confirmed

#12 Pentagon Plans to Build New Landmines

#13 New Evidence Establishes Dangers of Roundup

#14 Homeland Security Contracts KBR to Build Detention Centers in the US

#15 Chemical Industry is EPA's Primary Research Partner

#16 Ecuador and Mexico Defy US on International Criminal Court

#17 Iraq Invasion Promotes OPEC Agenda

#18 Physicist Challenges Official 9-11 Story

#19 Destruction of Rainforests Worst Ever

#20 Bottled Water: A Global Environmental Problem

#21 Gold Mining Company Threatens Ancient Andean Glaciers

#22 Billions in Homeland Security Spending Undisclosed

#23 US Oil Targets Kyoto in Europe

#24 Cheney's Halliburton Stock Rose Over 3,000 Percent Last Year

#25 US Military in Paraguay Threatens Region

A description of each of these entries is available in Peter Phillips and Project Censored, *Censored 2007: The Top 25 Censored Stories* (New York: Seven Stories Press, 2006).

To summarize, this propaganda model posits a number of filters as the elements that largely predetermine media production. It suggests a systematic and highly political dichotomization in media coverage toward the interests of major state powers. According to the authors, all of this plays out in the topics the media covers, as well as in the depth and quality of their coverage. From that point, the model allows us to make predictions; we must then determine whether they match what we observe.

There are five filters.

The first is constituted by the size, concentrated ownership, and profit orientation of the media. The media belong to corporations and to the very wealthy people who control them. We must assume that this biases them. In *Media Monopoly*,[15] a work published in 1983, Ben Bagdikian worried about the monopolistic control over US media. At the time, he emphasized that fifty businesses controlled the majority of American media. Indeed, he had reason to be worried. As the years went by and the book was republished in one revised edition after another, Badgikian continued to express the same concern, based on the same reasons, with one variation: the number of owners diminished in successive editions. There were twenty-eight, then twenty-three, then fourteen, then ten. The last edition of *Media Monopoly* shows that only five corporations control the major US media—where the term media here covers television, newspapers, magazines, Hollywood films, and books.

The second filter is the media's dependence on advertising. The media don't so much sell information to an audience as they sell an audience to advertisers. Advertising revenue is estimated to be about 70 percent for a newspaper and more than 90 percent for a television station. Those who pay want the shows or the pages where their ads appear to be conducive to selling. Advertisers don't need to intervene directly in order to influence the media. The dynamic set-up ensures that they will get what they want. That said, advertisers sometimes specifically demand that shows where they intend to advertise have certain characteristics. For example, Badgikian quotes texts in which Proctor and Gamble states that it will not advertise on any show that insults soldiers or that suggests that the business world is not a good and religious community. It goes without saying what sort of effect this filter has on alternative or critical media.

The third filter is the media's dependence on certain sources of information: governments, businesses themselves—notably mediated by PR firms, lobby groups, and press agencies. In the end, one can say that this symbiotically creates a sort of affinity between the media and those who nourish them—an affinity born of coinciding interests that is as much bureaucratic as it is economic and ideological.

Help Coca-Cola Sell its Product by Making Brains Available to Advertisers

"There are many ways to talk about TV, but from a business perspective, let's be realistic: basically, TFI's job is helping Coca-Cola, for example, to sell its product.

For an advertisement to be seen, the viewer's brain must be available. The purpose of our shows is to make it available: that is to say to entertain and relax it in order to prepare it in between ads. What we sell to Coca-Cola is available human brain time.

Nothing is more difficult than obtaining this availability. This is where permanent change is located. We must constantly look out for popular programs, follow trends, surf on tendencies, in a context in which information is speeding up, multiplying and becoming obsolete.

Television is an activity without memory. If you compare this industry to the automobile industry, say, for someone who builds cars the creation process is much slower; and if the vehicle is a success, he will have even less leisure to enjoy. We won't have any time!

Each day, everything hangs on the audience ratings. We are the only product in the world that 'knows' our clients by the second, within 24 hours."

Patrick Le Lay, CEO of TFI, France's top private domestic TV network, interviewed with other CEOs in *Les Dirigeants Face au Changement* (Leaders Facing Change) (Paris: Éditions du huitième jour, 2004).

The fourth filter is flak, that is, the criticism that the powerful aim at the media in order to discipline them. When all is said and done, there is a tendency to recognize certain sources as reliable, and journalists avoid extra work and the hassle of being criticized by citing them almost exclusively and crediting their expertise. What these sources and experts say are facts; everything else is opinion and subjective commentary, and by definition, of less value. It need not be said that these comments are largely limited by everything that has already been discussed above.

Stirring the Manure

"There are two basic kinds of ads. Promise ads promise to satisfy desires or reduce fears and usually give us 'reasons why' the product will do that. Identification ads sell the product by getting us to identify with it (or with a company). Of course, most ads contain a combination of both promise and identification devices. . . . But we have to be a bit wary [because]:

a) Ads don't tell us what's wrong with the product, thus tempting us to commit the fallacy of suppressed evidence.
   Example: Ads for over-the-counter nonprescription drugs which rarely tell us about possible side effects.
b) Ads use psychological tricks more than direct appeals to reason.
   Example: The Lite Beer TV commercials that use identification, humor, and repetition, while giving us the quickly stale 'reasons why' over and over again.
c) Ads are often deceptive or misleading, in particular by making false implications while literally stating the truth.

Example: The London Fog commercials that imply their raincoats are made in England.

Note that all sorts of other devices, such as weasel words and fine-print takebacks are also used.

d) Ads commonly use puffery. (Note that puffery is legal).

Example: The *Chicago Tribune*'s motto: 'World's greatest newspaper.'

e) Ads often use meaningless jargon or deceptive humor.

Example: Tide getting clothes 'whiter than white.'

f) Ads tempt us to reason fallaciously.

Example: Testimonials inviting the fallacy of appeal to authority.

g) Ads tend to twist our values toward those values that an easily advertised product might satisfy.

Example: Making us more concerned with buying just the right pain reliever or cold symptom suppressor than with the real necessities of life.

It is important to realize that political candidates and policies are sold via advertising in much the same way as other 'products.' Identification, in fact image making in general, is the most frequently used device."

Howard Kahane, *Logic and Contemporary Rhetoric: The Use of Reason in Everyday Life*, 4th ed. (Belmont, CA:Wadsworth, 1984), 228–229.

Herman and Chomsky call the fifth and final filter anticommunism. In fact, it refers more broadly to the media's hostility to any perspective that is left, socialist, progressive, etc.

One of the substantial benefits of such a model is that it can be tested against the facts. Each time, and with re-markable consistency, what is observed conforms to a great extent with what the model predicts. From the perspective of participatory democracy, this means, on the one hand, that facts everyone should be aware of remain little known or unknown and, on the other hand, that interpretations of events that should be known and discussed, rarely or never are.

Here's an example. James Baker III is the co-chair of the US government's bipartisan Iraq Study Group, the mandate of which is to "conduct a forward-looking, independent assessment of the current and prospective situation on the ground in Iraq, its impact on the surrounding region, and consequences for US interests." Baker is also a senior counselor and partner in Carlyle Group, a privately-owned equity firm with major ties to the Bush Administration. The Carlyle Group owns United Defense Industries, a major military contractor that sells weapons systems to the Pentagon. Carlyle's profits have skyrocketed since the US invaded Iraq. This important set of facts and connections are relevant to us all; they should be well-known and up for public debate. But apart from a few articles, Baker's conflict of interest has barely been reported in the US media.

If I had to summarize the conclusion to draw from the propaganda model of media, I would do so as follows.

The mainstream media has a tendency to present, defend, and propagate the point of view of the political elite and the elite who own the media—which are often, not surprisingly, one and the same. This is so consistently true that it is as predictable as it is remarkable. And it is true whether the topic is business, free trade, international agreements, economic globalization, decisions about whether or not to go to war, national and international politics, questions related to the common good, health, ecology, or education, as well as a thousand other equally crucial topics. This cannot but seriously limit the breadth of political debate, and even deeply distort it. It replaces a democracy of participants, at once governing and governed, with a democracy of spectators ordered to look away or to acquiesce.

Practically speaking, what can we draw from this analysis?

If it is right, the media, which cover only certain topics among many possible topics, which cover them from particular perspectives, and with certain values and worldviews, will tend to hide certain facts, data, and analyses, or systematically falsify their presentation of them. The critical thinker must learn to spot these omissions and these biases. But how?

The following section will offer a few partial answers to this question.

5.3 Thirty-one Strategies for Fostering a Critical Approach to the Media

Dozens of people are gunned down each day in Springfield, but until now none of them was important. I'm Kent Brockman. At three p.m. Friday, local autocrat C. Montgomery Burns was shot following a tense confrontation at town hall. Burns was rushed to a nearby hospital where he was pronounced dead. He was then transferred to a better hospital where doctors upgraded his condition to "alive."
—THE SIMPSONS[16]

I. Become the devil's advocate.

Faced with an assertion or a thesis, look for what could be held up against it while asking yourself if there is another point of view and the reasons one might choose it.

2. Try word substitution.

Have fun replacing certain words with words with other connotations, and even different meanings, and ask yourself whether or not you could defend the new meanings you produce. Is free trade being discussed? Replace it with "managed trade." Quite often the new term better corresponds to reality. Is education up for discussion? Put in "indoctrination" instead. Are ecology and environmental protection up for debate? Replace them with—it's your turn!

3. Write or call the media.

Did you read or watch something unacceptable? Complain. Journalists and their bosses are sensitive to criticism from the public.

4. Be rigorous.

Your brain is territory that an enemy wants to occupy by

persuading you of certain things. Do not take resistance lightly. Practice active reading and listening. Take notes, record, clip. Develop the healthy habit of carefully noting all the information related to an event you want to discuss: Who? What? When? In what context?

5. Become a dancer.

It is vital to practice the art of dancing with ideas of which Nietzsche spoke. Take any given event as it is described in the corporate media. Have fun examining it in different conceptual frameworks and from different points of view. How would it be described in the Third World? In the poorest areas of Chicago? In the wealthiest areas of the same city?

6. Spot favors and complicity.

Media people are part of an elite. It is important to be aware of the relationships the media has with others who comprise that elite. X invites Y to be on their show, who then reciprocates by writing about X's book in her column, Z invites her to a conference in France, and so on.

7. Beware of symmetry's deceit.

In 1996, the Society of Professional Journalists withdrew the concept of objectivity from its Code of Ethics and replaced it with a number of other concepts like "equity," "balance," "accuracy," "completeness," and "fairness." They justified the decision with the explanation that a good number of journalists at that point felt that the word objectivity expressed neither what journalists are able to achieve nor what should be expected of them. The transformation reflected in this change is significant; it is a shift from a search for objectivity, now held to be illusory, to a desire for balance in the presentation of diverging points of view. It is undoubtedly altogether praiseworthy to demonstrate sensitivity to a great diversity of positions. But abandoning the concept of objectivity makes one fear the worst relativist drift for a philosophical reason perfectly articulated by Plato. The example of global warming is interesting in a number of ways.

The Poverty of Epistemological Relativism

Let us briefly examine this notion of epistemological relativism, as widely held today as ever before, according to which the truth is relative. A critical thinker has to have thought about this issue and resisted its temptations.

Let's begin by asking ourselves what this idea that the truth is relative could mean. First of all, relative to what? Protagoras, one of the first to maintain an epistemological relativism, and the object of one of Plato's exemplary critiques, held that the truth is relative to "man, the measure of all things." But he never said clearly if by man he meant individuals (such and such human), the species (humanity), or even a particular group of humans within society (the Athenians, the Spartans). But whatever version of relativism you adopt, it leads to untenable consequences and must therefore be rejected.

In the first case, in which the truth is relative to individuals, this subjectivism leads to strange conclusions. If the fact of believing a proposition to be true made it so, we would be infallible from the moment we asserted something to be true; disagreements between individuals would be impossible and pointless; everyone would be right.

Similarly, in the second case, in which the truth is relative to society, social relativism also leads to many strange conclusions. Here again, society is infallible; propositions like "the earth is flat" would have to be accepted as true as soon as a social group believed them.

But the main argument against relativism is no doubt what we could call the "relativist firecracker." The defense of relativism is either impossible or contradictory, because either we defend it by means of non-relativist arguments, and in that case we admit what we are trying to deny in our defense; or we defend it using relativist arguments, and then we aren't really defending it at all because our interlocutor can always assert the contrary. As Harvey Siegel writes: "Relativism is self-referentially incoherent or selfrefuting, in that defending the doctrine requires one to give it up."

The lesson to draw from this analysis, which goes all the way back to Plato, is a very important one. We are fallible, our knowledge is limited, and it is produced by human beings who live in society: all that is true. But the idea of truth itself, understood as something that exists independently of us, is an absolutely necessary regulating concept of all cognitive activity.

Harvey Siegel, *Relativism Refuted* (Boston: D. Reidel, 1987), 9.

Indeed, there is a great deal of informed agreement on the matter. Counterposing expert opinions with those of lobby groups, as if they were comparable and could balance each other, results in a profoundly deceptive illusion of symmetry. This is demonstrated extremely well by a recent study published by Fairness and Accuracy in Reporting (FAIR).[17]

8. Compare stories.

Using the Internet, compare different presentations of the same events available in two different countries.

9. Recognize ideology.

Learn the top ten tenets of ideology so that you can recognize ideologues in action.

Ideology in Action—The Top 10 Procedures

Ideology

1. turns the particular into the universal;
2. hides the labor involved, making commodities and cultural texts appear natural;
3. sets up false analogies;
4. creates a sense of neutrality to mask a particular bias;
5. frames the acceptable limits of a topic or issue (sets the agenda);
6. sets up the fallacy that the simplest explanation must be the true one;
7. makes the special appeal—leaders as just plain folks;
8. confuses the surface appearance of things with the entire phenomenon;
9. creates the sense that history leads to this moment and the present situation;
10. excels in the practice of TINA—"There is No Alternative."

Peter Steven, *The No-Nonsense Guide to Global Media* (Toronto: New Internationalist, 2004), 113.

---

10. Spot the usual suspects.

Learn how to recognize what the Observatoire des médias (Media Observatory) in France calls "compulsory figures."

The critical media observer will pay special attention to the conventions, genres, and practices that have the following effects.

Domination: the writing and staging of workers and employees, and particularly women; elitist and masculine paternalism that seeps into reports on professional and private life, classism, and intellectual elitism that lead journalists to describe working-class people they don't know with condescension or disdain. Editorial directors often come from the dominant classes; more and more frequently, they come from journalism schools or sometimes from Ivy League schools where they internalize bourgeois social mores; their salaries put them in the same ranks as senior executives or liberal professionals. All of that breeds in them particular interests as well as a particular way of seeing the world.

Depoliticization: the news item meant to entertain, and the transformation of every issue (social or international) into a news item; excessive personalization (and the multiplicity of personal profiles, sometimes with the consent of leaders of collective movements who purport to combat individualism); the 'political' presentation of all political issues and the technical presentation of economic issues.

Promotion: the mutual favors and complicities that allow for the formation of an ostensible "elite" to which the "people" owe an explanation for their "irrationality" and their "populism."

Dispossession: the art of keeping those who are given air time from speaking. Analyze, for concrete examples, public or commercial radio, streeters, testimonies, debates in front of panels, e-mail and texted questions, surveys, etc.

PLPL and Acrimed, *Informer sur l'information: Petit manuel de l'observateur critique des médias,* 14–15.

11. Analyze the news.

Collate the first pages of your favorite daily paper for a month and analyze it. First decide on the criteria you will use. Define them as well as possible, construct your checklist, and use it. Show your results to a friend, ideally one who does not share your social and political opinions, and discuss it together. If possible, compare your results with your friend's, if he or she agreed to carry out the same procedure.

12. Grill the commentator.

Gather together the last fifty editorials or the last fifty columns written by one journalist and analyze them from different angles. What topics to they address? What sources do they cite? What vocabulary do they use? And so on.

13. What's in a name?

Consider the title of an article or a news item. Does it match what you read? What other title would have been possible? Or desirable? Are there reasons why this title was used rather than another? Remember that though columnists and editorial writers title their own pieces, generally this is not true of news writers and writers of other sorts of texts.

14. Go to the source.

Identify the sources that feed the media that you don't know and try to learn more about them. If you read and listen actively, you will soon come across frequently quoted sources: the IMF, USAID, the Cato Institute, the Competitive Enterprise Institute, for example. What are they? The Internet will be useful to you. Read the Web sites of these institutions. Follow their tracks in the media. When, by whom, how frequently, how, and to what end are their studies used?

Hello, friends of the forest!

The BC Forest Alliance wants to promote a balanced approach to forest management in British Columbia. It is hard not to agree, don't you think? Can you feel your inner eco-fiend stirring? But beware!

The BC Forest Alliance is actually an organization set up by Burson-Marstellar, the giant PR firm, to counter the populace's "lack of confidence" and concern about clear-cutting and the pollution produced by sawmills. This virtuous façade hides business interests and their private profit motives.

See Carl Deal's *The Greenpeace Guide to Anti-Environmental Organizations* (Berkeley, CA: Odonian Press, 1998), to learn more about a whole range of organizations like Burson-Marstellar.

---

15. Resist myths.

Learn to recognize urban myths and don't get sucked in by them.

Urban Myths: Stories Too Good to Be True

You know the story of the young girl who was asked to babysit while the baby's parents went out to dinner, and to put the chicken in the oven while they were gone? When they returned home a few hours later, the parents were horrified to realize that the young woman, who was completely drugged up, had put the baby in the oven.

Or the story of the student who arrived late to his university math

---

exam? Three problems were written on the board. The student, who was gifted, solved the first two easily, but was stumped by the third. He worked at it relentlessly, and finally, just before handing in his papers, he found what he thought might be the solution. The next day he got a call from his professor. He was convinced that it is because he had completely blown the last problem. But his professor told him that only the first two problems were on the exam; the third, which he had put on the board simply by way of example, was not. It was a problem that had remained unsolved for a century; Einstein himself had been unable to solve it. Now the student had solved it and had made mathematical history.

Finally, did you know that a fast food chain that will remain nameless here uses earth worms instead of beef in its burgers? A friend of a friend discovered it in the strangest way.

These stories, called urban myths or urban legends, travel through popular culture and are repeated, often with only a few variations. Frequently, the hook is that the storyteller will say that it happened to a friend of a friend: this characteristic is so ubiquitous that people who collect and study urban myths have created an acronym for it: FOAF (friend of a friend).

Urban legends are not all necessarily untrue. Besides, we obviously can't prove that what they claim did not take place—since we can't, in any strict sense, prove a negative factual proposition. But generally, there is no proof that it did actually happen. Anyone who follows the trail of these stories usually hits a dead end: the friend of the friend doesn't exist, or was himself telling a friend's story who was telling what a friend told him, and so forth.

Let's attempt to formulate a definition that will include all the common characteristics of urban legends.

Urban legends are apocryphal stories—that is to say, questionable and suspect but at least slightly plausible—that are most frequently passed on orally from one individual to another (although they are also to be found on the Internet and in anthologies) and that are told as if they were true. The person telling the story often claims to have a close and reliable source, to whom the story actually happened. All the same, the storyteller generally does not give a verifiable name or facts.

Urban myths are also good stories; they are able to elicit an audience's interest and allow the storyteller to use his or her talents. They generally take a bizarre, surprising, or unexpected turn. They describe ordinary people in horrible, ironic, or embarrassing situations. Finally, urban myths often contain a moral or a warning regarding certain pervasive fears or phobias.

To find out more about urban myths, begin by consulting the work of Jan Harold Brunvand, the researcher who christened them in the 1980s when he wrote *The Vanishing Hitchhiker.* He has continued to archive and study them since in books like *Too Good to Be True: The Colossal Book of Urban Legends,* which is referenced in the bibliography.

16. Record ...

some episodes of your favorite newscast. Then watch them with a stopwatch in hand. Write down what topics are covered, the order in which they are covered, and the amount of time devoted to each. Then take a look at other media sources to know what could have been covered differently that day. Draw conclusions.

17. Regularly check ...

sites like those of Amnesty International and Human Rights Watch, and do so particularly during crises. You will find valuable information that is barely reported by the corporate media, if it is reported at all.

18. Follow ...

themes and topics over a long period of time, as they are covered by one media outlet.

19. Compare ...

the coverage offered by one media outlet of two given subjects that are reasonably comparable in every way but one. For example, compare the way in which criminal acts committed by enemies are dealt with compared to the way similar acts committed by friends are dealt with. Compare events that are not comparable. Is a union activist charged with breaking down a door? Compare the coverage of this event with that of an employer who committed a far greater crime, one involving deaths for example.

A Valuable Research Tool

You can use databases to do research (by keywords, authors, and so on) in many newspapers and periodicals at the same time, going back far in time. It's a very useful tool that is accessible to you at home via the Internet. Lexis Nexis is a good example: http://www.nexis.com/research/search/. You usually have to pay for a subscription

---

20. Transcribe ...

everything that is said during a newscast, if you have the patience for it. Then do a quantitative analysis of the text: how many words were said about a given subject? Who said them? To how many words in your favorite daily paper does that correspond? Compare your results with different written texts. Don't blame me if you decide, with good reason, never to watch the news on TV again.

21. Ask questions.

Faced with any information, ask yourself: Who is speaking? What interests does she have in the topic at stake? What are her values and presuppositions? Is the subject dealt with superficially or in depth? What historical and social counter-examples (as the case warrants) does she suggest to help her listeners understand the causes and the complexity of the phenomenon?

22. Are sources cited?

Are there several of them? Are they trustworthy? There is reason to be wary of terms like "official sources" or "observers."

23. Spectacle and experience.

Is the report done with an obviously and almost exclusive concern with eliciting interest, particularly by relying on sensationalism, entertainment value, spectacle, and "human interest"? If so, beware. Better yet, turn off the television or put down the newspaper. You won't be missing anything.

24. Check references.

Learn to recognize not just who is speaking and the place the person is talking about, but also which points of view are not presented, who is not invited, and who is not given the right to speak. So pay close attention to the institutional affiliation of experts, particularly those who appear repeatedly in the media in times of crisis or to comment on a given subject.

25. Study political philosophy.

Each of us sees the world through a prism of fundamental beliefs that we have more or less consciously adopted. These beliefs can conveniently be divided into two categories: values and conceptions of the world. A good number of debates are essentially conflicts between two different and firmly held conceptions of the world or sets of values. To get to know the values and conceptions of the world that underlie different worldviews, resolve to study the big systems by which they are organized. You cannot take a critical stance toward the media without knowing what is meant by libertarianism, liberalism, social democracy, Keynesianism, utilitarianism, monetarism, socialism, anarchism, feminism, communitarianism, and so forth.

26. Vocabulary.

Remind yourself of what you learned in the first chapter of this book: it is the perfect time to use it.

27. Numbers.

Remind yourself of what you learned in the second chapter of this book: it is the perfect time to use it.

28. Read Chomsky.

Read his books, of course, but also his articles. He writes regularly on ZNet, where he also has a blog where you can ask him questions.

Chomsky, in extenso

A useful rule of thumb is this: if you want to learn something about the propaganda system, have a close look at the critics and their tacit assumptions. These typically constitute the doctrines of the state religion.[18]

The propaganda model does not assert that the media parrot the line of the current state managers in the manner of a totalitarian regime; rather, that the media reflect the consensus of powerful elites of the state-corporate nexus generally, including those who object to some aspect of government policy, typically on tactical grounds. The model argues, from its foundations, that the media will protect the interests of the powerful, not that it will protect state managers from their criticisms; the persistent failure to see this point may reflect more general illusions about our democratic systems.[19]

Perhaps this is an obvious point, but the democratic postulate is that media are independent and committed to discovering and reporting the truth, and that they do not merely reflect the world as powerful groups wish it to be perceived. Leaders of the media claim that their news choices rest on unbiased professional and objective criteria, and they have support for this contention within the intellectual community. If, however, the powerful are able to fix the premises of discourse, to decide what the general populace is allowed to see, hear, and think about, and to "manage" public opinion by regular propaganda campaigns, the standard view of how the system works is at serious odds with reality.[20]

Most biased choices in the media arise from the preselection of right thinking people, internalized preconceptions, and the adaptation of personnel to the constraints of ownership, organization, market, and political power. Censorship is largely self-censorship.[21]

Now, underlying these doctrines, which were very widely held, is a certain conception of democracy. It's a game for elites, it's not for ignorant masses, who have to be marginalized, diverted, and controlled—of course for their own good.[22]

29. Read other news sources regularly.

The guide below may help you choose. Read not only alternative and independent press and media but also specialized press and media.

30. Beware ...

of the influence your own values and presuppositions have on your perceptions. Remind yourself that you are not immune to selective perception, cognitive dissonance, and so on.

31. Remind ...

yourself that everyone has values and presuppositions. So you should be wary of me, too. In any case, I don't hide that my fundamental beliefs are anti-authoritarian. You should take this into account when you evaluate what I have presented here.

I am noticing, with some dismay, that this chapter has almost ended and I still have not used the term "billy club" once. There —I did it! Let me end this chapter by suggesting some rules of conduct inspired by what we've learned.

Some Golden Rules

General Considerations Regarding the Media
Who does this media belong to?

What possible biases could the ownership have?

What space is given to advertisers?

What sources are used? (press agencies, polls, experts, government officials, PR firms, etc.)

General Considerations Regarding Documents
Whose byline is attached to the article I am reading, or report I'm reading or watching?

Is that person credible? Biased?

What makes me believe him or her?

What public is being addressed?

What presuppositions or values are at play?

From what point of view is it written?

What sort of a text is it:

— news?

— an opinion piece?

— a report?

— a column?

— an editorial?

— an ad?

— something else?

Ways of Analyzing a Document
Where is the document run?

—— on the first page, or the last?

—— at the top or the bottom of the report?

Is it relevant?

What topic or problem does it deal with?

Does the media source have particular interests in the news, history, subject matter, or problem covered or addressed?

How much sensationalism is at play?

Is there an excessive emphasis on the new, the unusual, the sensational, or the dramatic?

What space is devoted to pictures or illustrations?

What sources are used?

Are they relevant, credible, biased?

What facts are put forward?

Are they relevant and credible? Are they presented in a biased manner?

What arguments are raised?

Are they valid?

Are there contradictions?

Is the vocabulary used neutral?

Could different conclusions be drawn on the basis of the same facts? Or on the basis of other presumptions or values?

How would we judge these facts from other perspectives——elsewhere in the world, for example, or from another social class or age or gender?

What can we gain by multiplying points of view in this way?

CONCLUSION

Now we have covered everything I wanted you to discover in this book. Our journey ends here. There are, however, still two things left for us to do: one for me, and one for you. On my end, I want to give you the ability to pursue this topic further, and to do that, I invite you to consult the selected readings and appendix that follow. They list resources that I think will be able to accompany you as you deepen your critical thinking. On your end, remember to go back and read Sagan's Baloney Detection Kit. I hope that everything in it now seems perfectly familiar. Indeed, it is to Sagan that I want to give the last word, he who subtly evoked that "delicate balance" of critical thinking that we must all seek:

> It seems to me what is called for is an exquisite balance between two conflicting needs: the most skeptical scrutiny of all hypotheses that are served up to us and at the same time a great openness to new ideas. If you are only skeptical, then no new ideas make it through to you. You never learn anything new. You become a crotchety old person convinced that nonsense is ruling the world. (There is, of course, much data to support you.) On the other hand, if you are open to the point of gullibility and have not an ounce of skeptical sense in you, then you cannot distinguish the useful ideas from the

worthless ones. If all ideas have equal validity then you are lost, because then, it seems to me, no ideas have any validity at all.

INDEPENDENT MEDIA GUIDE

I don't necessarily share all the values of every organization and publication listed below. It is, of course, up to you to choose your own sound reading material.

Print Media

American Journalism Review

http://www.ajr.org

American Journalism Review is a national magazine that covers all aspects of print, television, radio, and online media. The magazine, which is published six times a year, examines how the media cover specific stories and broader coverage trends. *AJR* analyzes ethical dilemmas in the field and monitors the impact of technology on how journalism is practiced and on the final product.

Columbia Journalism Review

http://www.cjr.org

"America's Premier Media Monitor"

Dissent

http://www.dissentmagazine.org

Founded in 1954 by a group of New York intellectuals, notably Irving Howe, *Dissent* announced in its first issue that, "The purpose of this new magazine is suggested by its name: to dissent from the bleak atmosphere of conformism that pervades the political and intellectual life in the United States. . . . With that goal in mind, we continue more than fifty years later to publish thoughtful, incisive articles on politics and culture that challenge the *status quo*."

Free Inquiry

http://www.secularhumanism.org

"The aim of *Free Inquiry* is to promote and nurture the good life—life guided by reason and science, freed from the dogmas of god and state, inspired by compassion for fellow humans, and driven by the ideals of human freedom, happiness, and understanding."

In These Times

http://www.inthesetimes.com

"*In These Times* is dedicated to informing and analyzing popular movements for social, environmental, and economic justice; to providing a forum for discussing the politics that shape our lives; and to producing a magazine that is read by the broadest and most diverse audience possible."

Left Turn

http://www.leftturn.org

"Left Turn is a national network of activists engaged in exposing and fighting the consequences of global capitalism and imperialism. Rooted in a variety of social movements, we are anti-capitalists, radical feminists, anti-racists, and anti-imperialists working to build resistance and alternatives to corporate power and empire. Through our publication, *Left Turn* magazine, our website, and other forums, we seek to create spaces for our various movements to reflect and strategize."

Mother Jones
http://www.motherjones.com

"Mother Jones is an independent nonprofit whose roots lie in a commitment to social justice implemented through first-rate investigative reporting." *Mother Jones* magazine is published every two months.

The Nation
http://www.thenation.com

"*The Nation* will not be the organ of any party, sect, or body. It will, on the contrary, make an earnest effort to bring to the discussion of political and social questions a really critical spirit, and to wage war upon the vices of violence, exaggeration, and misrepresentation by which so much of the political writing of the day is marred." (From *The Nation*'s founding prospectus, 1865.)

New Internationalist
http://www.newint.org

"The New Internationalist workers' co-operative (NI) exists to report on the issues of world poverty and inequality; to focus attention on the unjust relationship between the powerful and powerless worldwide; to debate and campaign for the radical changes necessary to meet the basic needs of all; and to bring to life the people, the ideas, and the action in the fight for global justice. *New Internationalist* is a monthly magazine."

New Scientist
http://www.newscientist.com

"Since 1956 we have been keeping our readers up to date with the latest science and technology news from around the world. With a network of correspondents and seven editorial offices worldwide, we have a global reach that no other science magazine can match."

Skeptical Inquirer
http://www.csicop.org/si

"This dynamic magazine, published by the Committee for the Scientific Investigation of Claims of the Paranormal, tells you what the scientific community knows about claims of the paranormal, as opposed to the sensationalism often presented by the press, television, and movies."

Skeptic Magazine
http://www.skeptic.com

"The Skeptics Society is a scientific and educational organization of scholars, scientists, historians, magicians, professors, and teachers, and anyone curious about controversial ideas, extraordinary claims, revolutionary ideas, and the promotion of science. The Society engages in scientific investigation and journalistic research to investigate claims made by scientists, historians, and controversial figures on a wide range of subjects."

The Skeptic
http://www.skeptic.org.uk

"*The Skeptic* is the UK's only regular magazine to take a skeptical look at pseudoscience and claims of the paranormal. An invaluable resource for journalists, teachers, psychologists, and inquisitive people of all ages who yearn to discover the truth behind the many extraordinary claims of paranormal and unusual phenomena."

This Magazine

http://www.thismagazine.ca

"One of Canada's longest-publishing alternative journals. Founded by a gang of school activists in 1966, and originally called *This Magazine is About Schools*, the modern-day *This Magazine* focuses on Canadian politics, pop culture and the arts, but in keeping with its radical roots never pulls punches."

Utne Reader

http://www.utne.com

"*Utne Reader* reprints the best articles from over 2,000 alternative media sources bringing you the latest ideas and trends emerging in our culture . . . Provocative writing from diverse perspectives . . . Insightful analysis of art and media . . . Down-to-earth news and resources you can use . . . In-depth coverage of compelling people and issues that affect your life . . . The best of the alternative media."

Electronic Media

A-Infos

http://www.ainfos.ca

"A-Infos is a specialized press agency, in the service (as we see it best) of the movement of revolutionary anti-capitalist activists who are involved in the various social struggles against the capitalist class and its social system."

Adbusters

http://www.adbusters.org/home

"We are a global network of artists, activists, writers,

pranksters, students, educators, and entrepreneurs who want to advance the new social activist movement of the information age. Our aim is to topple existing power structures and forge a major shift in the way we will live in the 21st century. This site was designed to help you turn the drab number cruncher you're staring at right now into the most versatile activist tool ever reckoned with. From cyberpetitions to Critical Mass tips, from disseminating corporate propaganda, to downshifting your lifestyle and treading lightly on the planet, we hope this site will inspire you to move—upon your return to the real world—from spectator to participant." *Adbusters* magazine is published bimonthly.

The Alternative Information Center
http://www.alternativenews.org

The Alternative Information Center (AIC) is a joint Palestinian-Israeli organization which prioritizes political advocacy, critical analysis, and information-sharing on the Palestinian and Israeli societies as well as on the Israeli-Palestinian conflict. In doing so, the AIC promotes responsible cooperation between Palestinians and Israelis based on the values of social and political justice, equality, solidarity, community involvement, and respect for the full inalienable national rights of all Palestinian people.

CorpWatch
http://www.corpwatch.org

"CorpWatch investigates and exposes corporate violations of human rights, environmental crimes, fraud, and corruption around the world. We work to foster global justice, independent media activism, and democratic control over corporations."

CounterPunch

http://www.counterpunch.org

"*CounterPunch* is the bi-weekly muckraking newsletter edited by Alexander Cockburn and Jeffrey St. Clair. Twice a month we bring our readers the stories that the corporate press never prints. We aren't sideline journalists here at *CounterPunch*. Ours is muckraking with a radical attitude and nothing makes us happier than when *CounterPunch* readers write in to say how useful they've found our newsletter in their battles against the war machine, big business, and the rapers of nature."

FAIR

http://www.fair.org

"FAIR, the national media watch group, has been offering well-documented criticism of media bias and censorship since 1986. We work to invigorate the First Amendment by advocating for greater diversity in the press and by scrutinizing media practices that marginalize public interest, minority, and dissenting viewpoints. As an anti-censorship organization, we expose neglected news stories and defend working journalists when they are muzzled. As a progressive group, FAIR believes that structural reform is ultimately needed to break up the dominant media conglomerates, establish independent public broadcasting, and promote strong non-profit sources of information."

Guerrilla News Network

http://www.gnn.tv

"Guerrilla News Network is an independent news organization with headquarters in New York City and production facilities in Berkeley, California. Our mission is to expose people to important global issues through cross-platform guerrilla programming."

Indymedia
http://www.indymedia.org

"The Independent Media Center is a network of collectively run media outlets for the creation of radical, accurate, and passionate tellings of the truth. We work out of a love and inspiration for people who continue to work for a better world, despite corporate media's distortions and unwillingness to cover the efforts to free humanity."

Infoshop.org
http://www.infoshop.org

"The Alternative Media Project is the umbrella nonprofit for Infoshop.org, *Practical Anarchy* magazine, and several other publishing, journalism, and information dissemination projects."

InterActivist Network
http://www.interactivist.net

"The InterActivist Network is a collaborative effort, an activist communication resource, an independent media project, and a technology skill-sharing project. It is a model for community action using new media and technology to invigorate public dialogue and to inform current debates within our own communities—both local and global."

OneWorld.net
http://www.oneworld.net

"The OneWorld network spans five continents and produces content in eleven different languages, published across its international site, regional editions, and thematic channels. Many of these are produced from the South to widen the participation of the world's poorest and most marginalised peoples in the global debate."

PR Watch

http://www.prwatch.org

"*PR Watch*, a quarterly publication of the Center for Media & Democracy, is dedicated to investigative reporting on the public relations industry. It serves citizens, journalists, and researchers seeking to recognize and combat manipulative and misleading PR practices."

Rebeliòn

http://www.rebelion.org

"Rebeliòn pretende ser un medio de información alternativa que publique las noticias que no son consideras importantes por los medios de comunicación tradicionales. También, dar a las noticias un tratamiento diferente, más objetivo, en la linea de mostrar los intereses que los poderes económicos y politicos del mundo capitalista ocultan para mantener sus privilegios y el status actual."

ZNet

http://www.zmag.org

"ZNet is a huge website updated many times daily and designed to convey information and provide community. Over a quarter of a million people a week use ZNet. Founded in 1995, ZNet offers information through diverse watch areas and sub-sites, translations, archives, links to other progressive sites, a daily commentary program, and much more."

Radio

Free Speech Radio News

http://www.fsrn.org

"Free Speech Radio News is the only daily, syndicated, progressive newscast in the United States. This news program is not owned or controlled by anyone except the progressive reporters who produce it—some of the best in community broadcasting. And FSRN regularly features breaking stories and investigations often absent from, or buried in, the corporate press."

Pacifica Radio

http://www.pacifica.org

"Bringing listeners alternative, community, free speech, listener sponsored radio for over 50 years."

Radio4All.net

http://www.radio4all.net

"The A-Infos Radio Project was formed in 1996 by grassroots broadcasters, free radio journalists, and cyber-activists to provide ourselves with the means to share our radio programs via the Internet. Our goal is to support and expand the movement for democratic communications worldwide. We exist to be an alternative to the corporate and government media which do not serve struggles for liberty, justice, and peace, nor enable the free expression of creativity. The archived material is available to anyone who wants it free of charge."

Video

Big Noise Films
http://www.bignoisefilms.com

"Big Noise is a not-for-profit, all-volunteer collective of media-makers around the world, dedicated to circulating beautiful, passionate, revolutionary images."

SubCine
http://www.subcine.com

"SubCine is the only source for Independent Latino Film and Video. We are an artist-run and artist-owned collective of Latino film and video makers. Through SubCine, you'll find some of the most challenging, experimental, and progressive film and video work being done today."

Whispered Media
http://www.whisperedmedia.org

"Whispered Media uses video and other media tools to support campaigns for social, economic, and environmental justice."

SUGGESTED READINGS

Books and Articles

General

Allen, Steve. "Dumbth": *The Lost Art of Thinking With 101 Ways to Reason Better and Improve Your Mind*. Amherst, NY: Prometheus Books, 1998.

Baron, Jonathan. *Thinking and Deciding*. New York: Cambridge University Press, 1988.

Cannavo, S. *Think to Win: The Power of Logic in Everyday Life*. Amherst, NY: Prometheus Books, 1998.

Capaldi, Nicholas. *The Art of Deception: An Introduction to Critical Thinking*. Buffalo, NY: Prometheus Books, 1987.

Carroll, Robert Todd. *The Skeptic's Dictionary: A Collection of Strange Beliefs, Amusing Deceptions, and Dangerous Delusions*. Hoboken, NJ: John Wiley & Sons, 2003.

Cederblom, Jerry, and David W. Paulsen. *Critical Reasoning: Understanding and Criticizing Arguments and Theories*. 2nd ed. Belmont, CA: Wadsworth, 1986.

Cogan, Robert. *Critical Thinking: Step by Step*. Lanham, MD: University Press of America, 1998.

Dawes, Robyn M. *Everyday Irrationality: How Pseudo-Scientists, Lunatics, and the Rest of Us Systematically Fail to Think Rationally*. Boulder, CO: Westview Press, 2001.

Diestler, Sherry. *Becoming a Critical Thinker: A User Friendly Manual*. 2nd ed. Upper Saddle River, NJ: Prentice-Hall, 1998.

Ennis, Robert H. *Critical Thinking*. Upper Saddle River, NJ: Prentice-Hall, 1996.

Flesch, Rudolf. *The Art of Clear Thinking*. New York: Harper & Row, 1951.

Gilovich, Thomas. *How We Know What Isn't So: The Fallibility of Human Reason in Everyday Life*. New York: Free Press, 1991.

Hughes, William. *Critical Thinking: An Introduction to the Basic Skills*. Peterborough, ON: Broadview Press, 1992.

Hume, David. *An Enquiry Concerning Human Understanding*. Boston: Adamant Media, 2005.

Levy, David A. *Tools of Critical Thinking: Meta-thoughts for Psychology*. Boston: Allyn and Bacon, 1997.

Levy, Joel. *The Con Artist Handbook*. London: Prospero Books, 2004.

Hecht, Jennifer Michael. *Doubt: A History, The Great Doubters and their Legacy of Innovation from Socrates and Jesus to Thomas Jefferson and Emily Dickinson.* New York: HarperCollins, 2004.

Monmonier, Mark. *How to Lie with Maps.* Chicago: University of Chicago Press, 1991.

Moore, Edgar W., Hugh McCann, and Janet McCann. *Creative and Critical Thinking.* 2nd ed. Boston: Houghton Mifflin, 1985.

Paul, Richard, and Linda Elder. *A Miniature Guide for Students and Faculty to Scientific Thinking.* Dillon Beach, CA: Foundation for Scientific Thinking, 2003.

Ruggiero, Vincent Ryan. *Beyond Feelings: A Guide to Critical Thinking.* New York: Alfred Publishing, 1975.

Sagan, Carl. *The Demon-Haunted World: Science as a Candle in the Dark.* New York: Ballantine Books, 1996.

Schick, Theodore Jr., and Lewis Vaughn. *How to Think About Weird Things: Critical Thinking for a New Age.* 2nd ed. Mountain View, CA: Mayfield, Mountain View, 1999.

Sutherland, Stuart. *Irrationality: Why We Don't Think Straight!* New Brunswick, NJ: Rutgers University Press, 1992.

Swanson, Diane. *Nibbling on Einstein's Brain: The Good, the Bad, and the Bogus in Science.* Toronto: Annick Press, 2001.

Vos Savant, Marilyn. *The Power of Logical Thinking: Easy Lessons in the Art of Reasoning and Hard Facts About its Absence in Our Lives.* New York: St. Martin's Griffin, 1997.

Warburton, Nigel. *Thinking from A to Z.* 2nd ed. New York: Routledge, 1998.

Language

Armstrong, J. Scott. "Unintelligible Management Research and Academic Prestige," *Interfaces* 10, no. 2 (1980): 80–86.

Engel, S. Morris. *Fallacies and Pitfalls of Language: The Language Trap.* New York: Dover Publications, 1994.

Kahane, Howard. *Logic and Contemporary Rhetoric: The Use of Reason in Everyday Life.* 4th ed. Belmont, CA: Wadsworth, 1984.

McDonald, Daniel, and Larry W. Burton. *The Language of Argument.* 8th ed. New York: HarperCollins College Publishers, 1996.

Pratkanis, Anthony R., and Elliot Aronson. *Age of Propaganda: The Everyday Use and Abuse of Persuasion.* New York: W. H. Freeman, 1992.

Ravitch, Diane. *The Language Police: How Pressure Groups Restrict What Students Learn.* New York: Vintage, 2004.

Weston, Anthony. *A Rulebook for Arguments.* 3rd ed. Indianapolis: Hackett Publishing, 2000.

Wright, Larry. *Better Reasoning: Techniques for Handling Argument, Evidence and Abstraction.* New York: Holt, Rinehart and Winston, 1982.

Suggested Readings

Mathematics

Benjamin, Arthur, and Michael Shermer. *Mathemagics: How to Look Like a Genius Without Really Trying*. Los Angeles: Lowell House, 1993.

Best, Joel. *Damned Lies and Statistics: Untangling Numbers from the Media, Politicians, and Activists*. Berkeley, CA: University of California Press, 2001.

––––––. *More Damned Lies and Statistics: How Numbers Confuse Public Issues*. Berkeley, CA: University of California Press, 2004.

Campbell, Stephen K. *Flaws and Fallacies in Statistical Thinking*. Mineola, NY: Dover Publications, 2002.

Cobb, P., et al. "Assessment of a problem-centered second-grade mathematics project," *Journal for Research in Mathematics Education* 22 (1991): 2–29.

Dewdney, A. K. *200% of Nothing: An Eye-Opening Tour through the Twists and Turns of Math Abuse and Innumeracy*. New York: John Wiley and Sons, 1993.

Everitt, Brian S. *Chance Rules: An Informal Guide to Probability, Risk, and Statistics*. New York: Copernicus, 1999.

Gardner, Martin. *Aha! Gotcha: Paradoxes to Puzzle and Delight*. San Francisco: W. H. Freeman, 1982.

Gonick, Larry, and Woollcott Smith. *The Cartoon Guide to Statistics*. New York: Harper Perennial, 1993.

Hacking, Ian. *An Introduction to Probability and Inductive Logic*. Cambridge, UK: Cambridge University Press, 2001.

Huff, Darrell. *How to Figure the Odds on Everything*. New York: Dreyfus Publications, 1972.

Huff, Darrell, and Irving Geis. *How to Lie with Statistics*. New York: W. W. Norton, 1993.

Jones, Gerald E. *How to Lie with Charts*. New York: Excel Press, 2000.

McGervey, John D. *Probabilities in Everyday Life*. New York: Ivy Books, 1986.

Paulos, John Allen. *Innumeracy, Mathematical Illiteracy and Its Consequences*. New York: Hill and Wang, 1988.

––––––. *Beyond Numeracy: Ruminations of a Numbers Man*. New York: Vintage Books, 1992.

––––––. *A Mathematician Reads the Newspaper*. New York: Basic Books, 1995.

Reichmann, W.J. *Use and Abuse of Statistics*. Harmondsworth, UK: Penguin Books, 1983.

Slavin, Steve. *Chances Are: The Only Statistics Book You'll Ever Need*. Lanham, MD: Madison Books, 1998.

Solomon, Robert, and Christopher Winch. *Calculating and Computing for Social Science and Arts Students: An Introductory Guide*. Buckingham, UK: Open University Press, 1994.

Tufte, Edward. *The Visual Display of Quantitative Information*. 2nd ed. Cheshire, CT: Graphics Press, 2001.

A Short Course in Intellectual Self-Defense

Personal Experience

Brunyand, Jan Harold. *Too Good to be True: The Colossal Book of Urban Legends.* New York: W. W. Norton, 1999.

Cialdini, Robert B. *Influence: The Psychology of Persuasion.* New York: William Morrow, 1984.

Festinger, Leon, Henry W. Riecken, and Stanley Schachter. *When Prophecy Fails.* New York: Harper & Row, 1956.

Fulves, Karl. *Self-Working Mental Magic: 67 Foolproof Mind-Reading Tricks.* New York: Dover Publications, 1979.

Hay, Henry, ed. *Cyclopedia of Magic.* New York: Dover Publications, 1975.

Klass, Philip J. *UFO Abductions: A Dangerous Game.* Updated ed. Buffalo, NY: Prometheus Books, 1989.

Loftus, Elizabeth. "Make-Believe Members." *American Psychologist* November 2003: 867–873.

Empirical and Experimental Science, the Paranormal and Pseudoscience

Browne, Neil, and Stuart M. Keeley. *Asking the Right Questions.* Englewood Cliffs, NJ: Prentice Hall, 1981.

Bunge, Mario. *Finding Philosophy in Social Science.* New Haven, CT: Yale University Press, 1996.

Gardner, Martin. "Is Realism a Dirty Word?" *The Night is Large: Collected Essays, 1938–1995.* New York: St. Martin's Griffin, 1997.

Hines, Terence. *Pseudoscience and the Paranormal: A Critical Examination of the Evidence.* Buffalo, NY: Prometheus Books, 1988.

Houdini, Harry. *A Magician Among the Spirits.* New York: Arno Press, 1972.

Katzer, Jeffrey, Kenneth H. Cook, and Wayne Crouch. *Evaluation Information: A Guide for Users of Social Science Research.* Reading, MA: Addison-Wesley, 1978.

Klemke, E.D., et al., eds. *Introductory Readings in the Philosophy of Science.* Amherst, NY: Prometheus Books, 1998.

Marks, David, and Richard Kamman. *The Psychology of the Psychic.* Buffalo, NY: Prometheus Books, 1980.

Plait, Philip C. *Bad Astronomy: Misconceptions and Misuses Revealed, from Astrology to the Moon Landing "Hoax."* New York: John Wiley & Sons, 2002.

Randi, James. *Flim-Flam! Psychics, ESP, Unicorns and other Delusions.* Buffalo, NY: Prometheus Books, 1982.

––––––. *The Faith Healers.* Buffalo, NY: Prometheus Books, 1987.

––––––. *The Mask of Nostradamus: The Prophecies of the World's Most Famous Seer.* Buffalo, NY: Prometheus Books, 1993.

––––––. *An Encyclopedia of Claims, Frauds, and Hoaxes of the Occult and Supernatural: James Randi's Decidedly Skeptical Definitions of Alternative Realities.* New York: St. Martin's Press, 1995.

Suggested Readings

Robert-Houdin, Jean Eugène. *L'Art de gagner à tous les jeux—Les tricheries des Grecs dévoilées*. Genève-Paris: Slatkine, 1981.

Schiffman, Nathaniel. *Abracadabra! Secret Methods Magicians and Others Use to Deceive their Audience*. Amherst, NY: Prometheus Books, 1997.

Searle, John. *The Construction of Social Reality*. New York: Free Press, 1995.

––––––. *Mind, Language, and Society: Philosophy in the Real World*. Toronto: HarperCollins Canada, 1999.

Sebeok, Thomas A., and Robert Rosenthal, eds. *The Clever Hans Phenomenon: Communication with Horses, Whales, Apes, and People*. New York: New York Academy of Sciences, 1981.

The Media

Badgikian, Ben. *The Media Monopoly*. 6th ed. Boston: Beacon Press, 2000.

Barsamian, David, and Noam Chomsky. *Propaganda and the Public Mind: Conversations with Noam Chomsky*. Cambridge, MA: South End Press, 2001.

Carey, Alex. *Taking the Risk out of Democracy: Corporate Propaganda versus Freedom and Liberty*. Urbana, IL: University of Illinois Press, 1997.

Chomsky, Noam. *Necessary Illusions: Thought Control in Democratic Societies*. Concord, ON: Anansi, 1989.

Chomsky, Noam, and E. S. Herman. *Manufacturing Consent: A Propaganda Model*. New York: Pantheon Books, 1988.

Ewen, Stuart. *PR! A Social History of SPIN*. New York: Basic Books, 1996.

Hackett, Robert A., and Richard Gruneau. *The Missing News: Filters and Blind Spots in Canada's Press*. Ottawa: Canadian Center for Policy Alternatives/ Garamond Press, 2000.

Paul, Richard, and Linda Elder. *The Thinker's Guide for Conscientious Citizens on How to Detect Media Bias and Propaganda in National and World News*. Dillon Beach, CA: Foundation for Critical Thinking, 2003.

Rampton, Sheldon, and John Stauber. *Weapons of Mass Deception: The Use of Propaganda in Bush's War on Iraq*. New York: Jeremy P. Tarcher/Penguin, 2003.

Stauber, John C., and Sheldon Rampton. *Toxic Sludge Is Good for You: Lies, Damn Lies and the Public Relations Industry*. Monroe, ME: Common Courage Press, 1995.

Steven, Peter. *The No-Nonsense Guide to Global Media*. Toronto: New Internationalist Publications, 2004.

Tye, Larry. *The Father of Spin: Edward L. Bernays and the Birth of Public Relations*. New York: Owl Books, 2002.

To contact Normand Baillargeon: Baillargeon.normand@uqam.ca

NOTES

Introduction

1. Noam Chomsky, *Necessary Illusions: Thought Control in Democratic Societies* (Concord, ON:Anansi, 1989), viii.
2. S. Larivée's article on this topic, "L'influence socioculturelle sur la vogue des pseudo-sciences," is interesting and available on-line: http://www.sceptiques.qc.ca.

Chapter I (Language)

1. George Kennedy, trans., in Rosamond Kent Sprague, ed., *The Older Sophists: A Complete Translation by Several Hands of the Fragments in Die Fragmente Der Vorsokraticker Edited by Diels-Kranz with a New Edition of Antiphon and of Euthydemus* (Columbia, South Carolina: University of South Carolina Press, 1972), 52.
2. Sheldon Rampton and John Stauber, *Trust Us, We're Experts* (New York: Jeremy P. Tarcher/Putnam, 2001), chap. 3.
3. Adapted from Howard Kahane, *Logic and Contemporary Rhetoric: The Use of Reason in Everyday Life*, 4th ed. (Belmont, CA: Wadsworth, 1984), 137.
4. White House Press Conference, September 15, 2006, http://www.white-house.gov/news/releases/2006/09/20060915-2.html/.
5. These examples were taken from The Writing Center at Rensselaer Polytechnic. See http://www.rpi.edu/dept/llc/writecenter/web/genderfair.html/.
6. Diane Ravitch, *The Language Police: How Pressure Groups Restrict What Students Learn* (New York: Knopf, 2003), 10, 13.
7. Herodotus, *Histories I*, 91.
8. Eduction is an ancient term in philosophy that is seldom used today, referring to the act through which an efficient cause, acting on "matter," gives it a determined form, or removes the surplus, so that a specific form can emerge.
9. É. Tessier, "Situation épistémologique de l'astrologie à travers l'ambivalence fascination rejet dans les sociétés postmodernes" (PhD diss., La Sorbonne, n.d.), summary.
10. Normand Baillargeon and David Barsamian, *Entretiens avec Chomsky* (Montreal: Éditions écosociété, 2002), 45–46.
11. J. Scott Armstrong, "Unintelligible Management Research and Academic Prestige," *Interfaces* 10 no. 2 (1980): 80–86.
12. At this point, there is ample literature concerning the famous Sokal affair. Briefly: Alan Sokal, a physician, succeeded in getting a text advancing the critiques of science and rationality common in certain academic disciplines

published in a cultural studies journal. But his article was riddled with significant stupidities and falsities concerning science, which the editors missed. By doing this, Sokal was trying to suggest that in those milieus, some people had virtually no knowledge of the science they were so blithely critiquing. You can read more on the topic in A. Sokal and A. Bricmont's *Impostures intellectuelles* (Paris: Odile Jacob, 1999).

13. I am following Paul Lazarsfeld's exposition in a classic and frequently republished article: "Des concepts aux indices empiriques" ("From concepts to Empirical Indices"), quoted in R. Bourdon and R. Lazarsfeld, *Le Vocabulaire des sciences sociales* (Paris: Mouton, 1965).

14. The expression is taken from Richard Paul and Linda Elder of the Foundation for Critical Thinking.

15. Howard Kahane, *Logic and Contemporary Rhetoric: The Use of Reason in Everyday Life*, 4th ed. (Belmont, CA: Wadsworth, 1984).

16. *La Presse*, August 1, 2001, A13.

17. I take up the example used by S. Morris Engel, *Fallacies and Pitfalls of Language: The Language Trap* (New York: Dover Publications, 1994), 150.

Chapter 2 (Mathematics)

1. Joel Best, *Damned Lies and Statistics: Untangling Numbers from the Media, Politicians and Activists* (Berkeley, CA: University of California Press, 2001).

2. Stanislav Andreski, *Les Sciences sociales, sorcellerie des temps modernes* (Paris: Presses Universitaires De France, 1975), 143.

3. Note that on November 25, 2006, the cost had hit $345 billion. Source: http://www.costofwar.com.

4. John Allen Paulos, *Innumeracy: Mathematical Illiteracy and Its Consequences* (New York: Hill and Wang, 1990).

5. You can learn much from reading what the magician who unmasked Geller has to say: James Randi, *The Magic of Uri Geller* (New York: Ballantine Books, 1975).

6. Quoted by Robert Todd Carroll, *The Skeptic's Dictionary: A Collection of Strange Beliefs, Amusing Deceptions, and Dangerous Delusions* (Hoboken, NJ: John Wiley & Sons, 2003), 197. The following list is taken from the same source.

7. Darrell Huff, *How to Lie with Statistics* (New York: Norton, 1954).

8. Steve Rubenstein, "Millions suddenly become fat without gaining any weight," *San Francisco Chronicle*, October 16, 1996, A6, quoted in Sherry Diestler, *Becoming a Critical Thinker: A User Friendly Manual*, 2nd ed. (Upper Saddle River, NJ: Prentice Hall, 1998), 73.

9. This example is borrowed from http://www.mathmistakes.com.

10. I follow L. Gonick and W. Smith (1993), among others, in using this particular way to introduce the concept of probability. I strongly recommend their book to those who wish to gently learn about probability and statistics more than I will be able to cover here.

Notes

11. John D. McGervey, *Probabilities in Everyday Life* (Chicago: Nelson-Hall, 1986), 229.
12. Paulos, *Innumeracy*, 7, 97.
13. Eldest son is to be understood as "the first son in the family."
14. Martin Gardner, *Aha! Gotcha: Paradoxes to Puzzle and Delight* (San Francisco: W.H. Freeman, 1982), 114–115.
15. Quoted in J. Rose, *Le hasard du quotidien: Coïncidences, jeux de hasard, sondages* (Paris:Seuil, 1999), 87–88.
16. This illustration is an adaptation taken from the now classic work by Edward Tufte, *The Visual Display of Quantitative Information*, 2nd ed. (Cheshire, CT: Graphics Press, 2001).
17. S.K. Campbell, *Flaws and Fallacies in Statistical Thinking* (Mineola, NY: Dover Publications, 2002), 60–65.
18. Darrell Huff and Irving Geis, *How to Figure the Odds on Everything* (New York:Dreyfus Publications, 1972), 404.
19. Ibid., 405.
20. Ibid.
21. Adapted from Huff, *How to Lie*, 61.
22. Ibid., 62.
23. Ibid., 63.

Chapter 3 (On the Justification of Belief)

1. Bruno Dubuc's Web site about the brain has many examples. See http://www.thebrain.mcgill.ca/.
2. Terence Hines, *Pseudoscience and the Paranormal: A Critical Examination of the Evidence* (Buffalo, NY: Prometheus Books, 1988), 168.
3. See http://www.thebrain.mcgill.ca/.
4. Examples are from the Web site http://www.thebrain.mcgill.ca/. The site also has a very clear explanation of optical illusions and you can take a look at one of the most remarkable ones, Adelson's Chessboard, which cannot be reproduced here because it requires color.
5. Joe Nickell, "Holy Grilled Cheese?" *Skeptical Inquirer* 29 (March–April 2005): 9.
6. Worth reading on this topic: P. Thuillier, "La triste histoire des rayons N," *Le petit savant illustré* (Paris: Seuil, 1980), 58–67.
7. Elizabeth Loftus offers a very interesting and accessible synthesis of her work in "Make-Believe Memories," *American Psychologist* (November 2003): 867–873.
8. Leon Festinger, Henry W. Riecken, and Stanley Schachter, *When Prophecy Fails* (New York: Harper & Row, 1956).
9. B. R. Forer, "The Fallacy of Personal Validation: A Classroom Demonstration of Gullibility," *Journal of Abnormal Psychology* 44: 11–121, quoted in Carroll, The Skeptic's Dictionary, 146–147.

10. C. Snyder et al., "The P.T. Barnum Effect," *Psychology Today*, March 1975, 52–54, quoted in Schick and Vaughn, *How to Think About Weird Things*, 58–59.

11. Researchers in evolutionary psychology believe that it can be explained by the fact that when the problem is posed in the second way, a cheating detection module is activated. The idea is at least plausible. Broadly speaking, it goes as follows: our species evolved for thousands of years in small groups in which it was very useful to know who to trust. Yet the capacity and the usefulness of formalizing this sort of problem in terms of abstract logic developed much later. Thus, our brain is less adapted to the latter kind of operation.

12. Bernard Shaw, *Pygmalion*, Act 5.

13. Robert Rosenthal and Lenore Jacobson, *Pygmalion in the Classroom* (New York: Holt, Rinehart and Winston, 1968).

14. Ibid., 180.

15. Schick and Vaughn, *How to Think About Weird Things*, 61.

16. David Hume, "Of Miracles," *An Enquiry Concerning Human Understanding (1748)*, Part 1.

17. Jean Bricmont in Association Française pour l'information scientifique, "Un argument fondé sur le sens commun," *Science . . . et pseudoo-sciences* 251 (March 2002), http://pseudo-sciences.org/spip.php?article105/.

18. Sagan first put forward this formulation of the maxim in the television series *Cosmos*.

Chapter 4 (Empirical and Experimental Science)

1. Randi describes this experiment in J. Randi, *Flim-Flam! Psychics, ESP, Unicorns, and other Delusions* (Buffalo, NY: Prometheus Books, 1982), chap. 13.

2. P. Cobb et al., "Assessment of a Problem-Centered Second-Grade Mathematics Project," *Journal For Research in Mathematics Education* 22, no. 1 (Jan. 1991): 3–29.

3. You can read more about the phenomenon that this famous case brought to light: Thomas A. Sebeok and Robert Rosenthal, *The Clever Hans Phenomenon: Communication with Horses, Whales, Apes, and People* (New York: New York Academy of Sciences, 1981).

4. For the sake of convenience, I will take up the criteria of classification put forward by Robert Blanché in *L'Épistémologie* (Paris: PUF, 1981).

5. This exposition is inspired by John Searle, *Mind, Language, and Society: Philosophy in the Real World* (Toronto: HarperCollins Canada, 1999), 1–37. A more systematic exposition can be found in John Searle, *The Construction of Social Reality* (New York: Free Press, 1995), *passim*, Chap. 7–9.

6. Martin Gardner, "Is Realism a Dirty Word?" *The Night is Large: Collected Essays, 1938–1995* (New York: St. Martin's Griffin, 1995), 423.

7. Aristotle, Metaphysics, Book IV.

Notes

8. Nathan Newman, "Big Pharma, Bad Science," *The Nation*, posted July 25, 2002, http://www.thenation.com/doc/20020805/newman20020725/.
9. Mario Bunge, *Finding Philosophy in Social Science* (New Haven, CT: Yale University Press, 1995), 207–208.
10. Schick and Vaughn, *How to Think About Weird Things*, 235–243.
11. Ibid.
12. Homeopathy is derived from two Greek words: homeo (like) and pathos (suffering).

Chapter 5 (The Media)

1. They caused 500,000 children to die. Asked a few years later about the effects of these sanctions, Secretary of State Madeleine Albright replied frankly: "We think the price is worth it." Source: *60 Minutes*, December 5, 1996.
2. Quoted by Scott Peterson, "In war, some facts less factual," *The Christian Science Monitor*, September 6, 2002.
3. It was most notably exposed in John R. MacArthur, *Second Front: Censorship and Propaganda in the Gulf War* (Berkeley, CA: University of California Press, 2004).
4. It was in *La Presse*, January 11, 1992, B4.
5. John R. MacArthur, "Remember Nayirah, Witness for Kuwait," *The New York Times*, January 6, 1992. Available on the Web at http://www.mindfully.org/Reform/Nayira-Witness-Incubator-Kuwait6jan92.htm/.
6. The history of public relations firms from the Creel Commission to the 1950s is told admirably in S. Ewen's book, *PR! A Social History of SPIN* (New York: Basic Books, 1996).
7. Quoted by Noam Chomsky in "Media Control," http://www.zmag.org/chomsky/talks/9103-media-control.html/.
8. Born in 1892, Bernays died in 1995 at the age of 103. In his book cited above, Stuart Ewen recounts his meeting with Bernays.
9. You can read more about him: Larry Tye, *The Father of Spin: Edward L. Bernays and the Birth of Public Relations* (New York: Henry Holt, 2002).
10. Edward L. Bernays, *Crystallizing Public Opinion* (Whitefish, MT: Kessinger Publishing, 2004).
11. All these stories are related and examined in Tye's *The Father of Spin* and in Ewen's *PR!*
12. Alex Carey, *Taking the Risk Out of Democracy: Corporate Propaganda versus Freedom and Liberty* (Urbana, IL: University of Illinois Press, 1997), 18.
13. For news about PR firms, you can consult http://www.prwatch.org/.
14. Noam Chomsky and E. S. Herman, *Manufacturing Consent: The Political Economy of the Mass Media* (New York: Pantheon Books, 1988), xi.
15. Ben Badgikian, *Media Monopoly* (Boston: Beacon Press, 1983).
16. *The Simpsons*, television show, episode 2F20, May 17, 1995.

17. M. and J. Boykoff, "Journalistic Balance as Global Warming Bias: Creating Controversy where Science finds Consensus," *Extra* (November–December 2004), http://www.fair.org/index.
18. M. Achbar, ed., *Manufacturing Consent:Noam Chomsky and the Media* (Montreal: Black Rose Books, 1994), 58.
19. Chomsky, *Necessary Illusions*, Appendix 1.
20. Herman and Chomsky, *Manufacturing Consent*, xi.
21. Ibid., xii.
22. M. Achbar, ed., *Manufacturing Consent*, 40.

ABOUT THE AUTHOR

Normand Baillargeon is Professor of Education Funda-
mentals at the University of Québec in Montreal, where
he teaches the history of pedagogy and the philosophy of
education.

ABOUT SEVEN STORIES PRESS

Seven Stories Press is an independent book publisher based in New York City, with distribution throughout the United States, Canada, England, and Australia. We publish works of the imagination by such writers as Nelson Algren, Octavia E. Butler, Assia Djebar, Ariel Dorfman, Barry Gifford, Lee Stringer, and Kurt Vonnegut, to name a few, together with political titles by voices of conscience, including the Boston Women's Health Book Collective, Noam Chomsky, Ralph Nader, Gary Null, Project Censored, Barbara Seaman, Gary Webb, and Howard Zinn, among many others. Our books appear in hardcover, paperback, pamphlet, and e-book formats, in English and in Spanish. We believe publishers have a special responsibility to defend free speech and human rights, and to celebrate the gifts of the human imagination, wherever we can.

For more information about us, visit our Web site at www.sevenstories.com or write for a free catalogue to Seven Stories Press, 140 Watts Street, New York, NY 10013.